Basics of Statistics and Statistical Application with Excel

统计学基础及Excel统计应用

黎 明 编

化学工业出版社

·北京·

The edition of *Basics of Statistics and Statistical Application with Excel* emphasizes concepts of statistics, statistical methods are carefully presented with a focus on understanding both the suitability of the method and the meaning of the result. Statistical methods and measurements are developed in the context of applications. The text also introduces the application of statistical knowledge with Excel, which solving practical problems is intended for anyone looking to learn the basics of applying Excel's powerful statistical tools to their business courses or work activities.

This book clearly and methodically shows and explains how to create and use these statistical tests to solve practical problems in business. Excel is an easily available computer program for students, instructors, and managers. It is also an effective teaching and learning tool for quantitative analyses in business couerse.

图书在版编目（CIP）数据

统计学基础及Excel统计应用＝Basics of Statistics and Statistical Application with Excel：英文/黎明编．—北京：化学工业出版社，2019.12
ISBN 978-7-122-35351-1

Ⅰ.①统⋯　Ⅱ.①黎⋯　Ⅲ.①统计学-英文②表处理软件-应用-统计分析-英文　Ⅳ.①C8

中国版本图书馆CIP数据核字（2019）第223220号

责任编辑：满悦芝　　　　　　　　　　文字编辑：李　曦
责任校对：杜杏然　　　　　　　　　　装帧设计：张　辉

出版发行：化学工业出版社（北京市东城区青年湖南街13号　邮政编码100011）
印　　装：三河市航远印刷有限公司
装　　订：三河市宇新装订厂
787mm×1092mm　1/16　印张14　字数355千字　2019年12月北京第1版第1次印刷

购书咨询：010-64518888　　　售后服务：010-64518899
网　　址：http://www.cip.com.cn
凡购买本书，如有缺损质量问题，本社销售中心负责调换。

定　价：58.00元　　　　　　　　　　　　　　　　　版权所有　违者必究

Preface

Welcome to the exciting world of statistics! We have written this book to make statistics accessible to everyone, including those with a limited mathematics background. Statistics affects all aspects of our lives. Whether we are testing new medical devices of determining what will entertain us, applications of statistics are so numerous that, in a sense, we are limited only by our own imagination in discovering new uses for statistics.

The edition of *Basics of Statistics and Statistical Application with Excel* continues to emphasize concepts of statistics. Statistical methods are carefully presented with a focus on understanding both the suitability of the method and the meaning of the result. Statistical methods and measurements are developed in the context of applications.

We have retained and expanded features that made the teaching materials used in Hubei University of Technology very readable. New procedure displays summarize steps for analyzing data. Examples, exercises, and problems touch on applications appropriate to a broad range of interests. Technology-based components give both students and researchers additional resources.

The book, which helps to solve practical problems, also introduces the application of statistical knowledge of Excel, and is intended for anyone reading it to learn the basics and apply Excel's powerful statistical tools to their business courses or work activities. If understanding statistics isn't your strongest suit, you are not especially mathematically-inclined, or if you are wary of computers, then this is the right book for you.

You will learn how to use key statistical tests using Excel without being overpowered by the underlying statistical theory. This book clearly and methodically shows and explains how to create and use these statistical tests to solve practical problems in business. Excel is an easily available computer program for students, instructors, and managers. It is also an effective teaching and learning tool for quantitative analyses in business courses. The powerful numerical computational ability and the graphical functions available in Excel make learning statistics much easier than in years past.

However, this is the first book to introduce the basics of statistics and the Excel application. We hope the Excel's capabilities will be more effective to teach business statistics; it also focuses exclusively on this topic in an effort to render the subject matter not only applicable and practical, but also easy to comprehend and apply.

Ming Li
2019. 12

Contents

Part I Introduction of Basic Statistics ································· 1
  1.1 The Nature of Statistics ··· 1
    1.1.1 What Is Statistics? ··· 1
    1.1.2 Population and sample ··· 2
    1.1.3 Descriptive and Inferential Statistics ···························· 3
    1.1.4 Parameters and Statistics ·· 4
    1.1.5 Statistical Data Analysis ··· 5
  1.2 Variables and Organization of the Data ································ 5
    1.2.1 Variables ··· 5
    1.2.2 Organization of the Data ·· 7
  1.3 Describe data by Tables and Graphs ···································· 7
    1.3.1 Qualitative Variable ··· 7
    1.3.2 Quantitative Variable ··· 9
    1.3.3 Samples and Population Distributions ······················· 14
  1.4 Measures of Center ··· 15
    1.4.1 The Mode ··· 15
    1.4.2 The Median ·· 17
    1.4.3 The Mean ··· 18
    1.4.4 Which Measure to Choose? ······································ 19
  1.5 Measures of Variation ··· 19
    1.5.1 Range ··· 19
    1.5.2 Interquartile Range ··· 20
    1.5.3 Standard Deviation ·· 22
    1.5.4 Sample Statistics and Population Parameters ············· 24
  1.6 Probability Distributions and Normal Distributions ·············· 25
    1.6.1 Probability Distributions ·· 25
    1.6.2 Mean and Standard Deviation of Random Variables ······ 28
    1.6.3 Normal Distributions ··· 29
  1.7 Sampling Distributions and Sample Means ·························· 31
    1.7.1 Sampling Distributions ·· 31
    1.7.2 Sampling Distributions of Sample Means ················· 32
  1.8 Estimation ··· 35
    1.8.1 Point Estimation ··· 35
    1.8.2 Confidence Interval ··· 36

1.9 Hypothesis Testing 39
  1.9.1 Hypotheses 39
  1.9.2 Significance Test for a Population Mean μ 41
1.10 Summarization of Bivariate Data 44
  1.10.1 Qualitative Variables 44
  1.10.2 Qualitative Variables and Quantitative Variables 48
  1.10.3 Quantitative Variables 52
1.11 Scatterplot and Correlation Coefficient 53
  1.11.1 Scatterplot 53
  1.11.2 Correlation Coefficient 54

Part II Statistical Application with Excel 58

2.1 Sample Size, Mean, Standard Deviation, and Standard Error of the Mean 58
  2.1.1 Mean 58
  2.1.2 Standard Deviation 59
  2.1.3 Standard Error of the Mean 59
  2.1.4 Sample Size, Mean, Standard Deviation, and Standard Error of the Mean 60
  2.1.5 Saving a Spreadsheet 66
  2.1.6 Printing a Spreadsheet 67
  2.1.7 Formatting Numbers in Currency Format (2 Decimal Places) 68
  2.1.8 Formatting Numbers in Number Format (3 Decimal Places) 69
  2.1.9 End-of-chapter Practice Problems 69
2.2 Random Number Generator 71
  2.2.1 Creating Frame Numbers for Generating Random Numbers 71
  2.2.2 Creating Random Numbers in an Excel Worksheet 73
  2.2.3 Sorting Frame Numbers into a Random Sequence 74
  2.2.4 Printing an Excel File So That All of the Information Fits onto One Page 77
  2.2.5 End-of-chapter Practice Problems 79
2.3 Confidence Interval about the Mean by Using the TINV Function and
    Hypothesis Testing 81
  2.3.1 Confidence Interval about the Mean 81
  2.3.2 Hypothesis Testing 90
  2.3.3 Alternative Ways to Summarize the Result of a Hypothesis Test 100
  2.3.4 End-of-chapter Practice Problems 101
2.4 One-group t-test for the Mean 105
  2.4.1 The 7 Steps for Hypothesis-testing by Using the One-group t-test 105
  2.4.2 One-group t-test for the Mean 109
  2.4.3 Can You Use Either the 95 Percent Confidence Interval about the Mean or
        the One-group t-test When Testing Hypothesis? 112
  2.4.4 End-of-chapter Practice Problems 113
2.5 Two-group t-test of the Difference of the Means for Independent Groups 116
  2.5.1 The 9 Steps for Hypothesis-testing by Using the Two-group t-test 117

	2.5.2	Formula #1: Both Groups Have More Than 30 People in Them	123
	2.5.3	Formula #2: One or Both Groups Have Fewer than 30 People in Them	128
	2.5.4	End-of-chapter Practice Problems	132
2.6	Correlation and Simple Linear Regression		135
	2.6.1	What Is a "Correlation"?	135
	2.6.2	Using Excel to Compute a Correlation Between Two Variables	141
	2.6.3	Creating a Chart and Drawing the Regression Line onto the Chart	143
	2.6.4	Printing a Spreadsheet So That the Table and Chart Fit onto One Page	150
	2.6.5	Finding the Regression Equation	151
	2.6.6	Adding the Regression Equation to the Chart	160
	2.6.7	How to Recognize Negative Correlations in the Summary Output Table	161
	2.6.8	Printing Only Part of a Spreadsheet Instead of the Entire Spreadsheet	162
	2.6.9	End-of-chapter Practice Problems	165
2.7	Multiple Correlation and Multiple Regression		169
	2.7.1	Multiple Regression Equation	169
	2.7.2	Finding the Multiple Correlation and the Multiple Regression Equation	171
	2.7.3	Using the Regression Equation to Predict Annual Sales	174
	2.7.4	Using Excel to Create a Correlation Matrix in Multiple Regression	175
	2.7.5	End-of-chapter Practice Problems	178
2.8	One-way Analysis of Variance (ANOVA)		183
	2.8.1	Using Excel to Perform a One-way Analysis of Variance (ANOVA)	185
	2.8.2	How to Interpret the ANOVA Table Correctly?	187
	2.8.3	Using the Decision Rule for the ANOVA F-test	187
	2.8.4	Testing the Difference Between Two Groups by Using the ANOVA t-test	188
	2.8.5	End-of-chapter Practice Problems	193

Appendix ···· **199**

TABLE 1	Table of Random Numbers	199
TABLE 2	The Cumulative Standardized Normal Distribution	202
TABLE 3	Critical Values of t	205
TABLE 4	Critical Values of χ^2	208
TABLE 5	Critical Values of F	209

Reserences ···· **217**

Part I

Introduction of Basic Statistics

1.1 The Nature of Statistics

1.1.1 What Is Statistics?

Statistics is a very broad subject, with applications in a vast number of different fields. In general, one can say that statistics is the methodology of collecting, analyzing, interpreting and drawing conclusions from information.

Putting it in other words, statistics is the methodology which scientists and mathematicians have developed for interpreting and drawing conclusions from collected data. Everything that deals even remotely with the collection, processing, interpretation and presentation of data belongs to the domain of statistics, and so does the detailed planning that precedes all these activities.

Definition 1.1.1 (Statistics). *Statistics consists of a body of methods for collecting and analyzing data.* (Agresti & Finlay, 1997)

From above, it should be clear that statistics is much more than just the tabulation of numbers and the graphical presentation of these tabulated numbers.

Statistics is the science of gaining information from numerical and categorical data. Statistical methods can be used to find answers to the questions like:

- What kind and how much data need to be collected?
- How should we organize and summarize the data?
- How can we analyze the data and draw conclusions from it?
- How can we assess the strength of the conclusions and evaluate their uncertainty?

Categorical data (or qualitative data) results from descriptions, e.g. the blood type of a person, marital status or religious affiliation.

That is, statistics provides methods for:

① Design: Planning and carrying out research studies.

② Description: Summarizing and exploring data.

③ Inference: Making predictions and generalizing about phenomena represented by the data.

Furthermore, statistics is the science of dealing with uncertain phenomena and events. Statistics in practice is applied successfully to studying the effectiveness of medical treatments, the reaction of consumers to television advertising, the attitudes of young people towards sex and marriage, and much more. It's safe to say that nowadays statistics is used in every field of science.

Example 1.1.1 (Statistics in practice). Consider the following problems:

—Agricultural problem: Is the new grain seed or fertilizer more productive?

—Medical problem: What is the right amount of dosage of a drug to treatment?

—Political science: How accurate are the gallup and opinion polls?

—Economics: What will be the unemployment rate next year?

—Technical problem: How to improve quality of products?

1.1.2 Population and sample

Population and sample are two basic concepts of statistics (see Fig. 1.1.1). Population can be characterized as the set of individual persons or objects in which an investigator is primarily interested during his or her research problem. Sometimes wanted measurements for all individuals in the population are obtained, but often only a set of individuals of that population is observed; such a set of individuals constitutes a sample. This gives us the following definitions of population and sample.

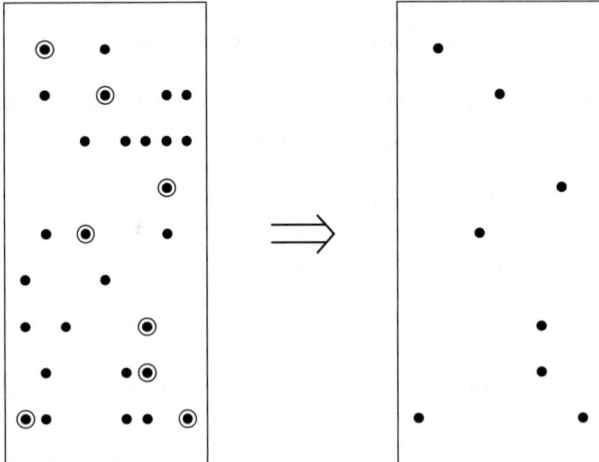

Fig. 1.1.1 Population and sample

Definition 1.1.2 (Population). *Population is the collection of all individuals, items or data under consideration in a statistical study.* (Weiss, 1999)

Definition 1.1.3 (Sample). *Sample is that part of the population from which information is collected.* (Weiss, 1999)

Always only a certain, relatively few, features of an individual person or object are under investigation at the same time. Not all the properties are wanted to be measured from individuals in the population. This observation emphasizes the importance of a set of measurements and thus gives us alternative definitions of population and sample.

Definition 1.1.4 (Population). *A (statistical) population is the set of measurements (or record of some qualitative trait) corresponding to the entire collection of units for which inferences are to be made.* (Johnson & Bhattacharyya, 1992)

Definition 1.1.5 (Sample). *A sample from statistical population is the set of measurements that are actually collected in the course of an investigation.* (Johnson & Bhattacharyya, 1992)

When population and sample is defined in a way of Johnson & Bhattacharyya, then it's useful to define the source of each measurement as sampling unit, or simply, a unit. The population always represents the target of an investigation. We learn about the population by sampling from the collection. There can be many different populations, following examples demonstrating possible discrepancies on populations.

Example 1.1.2 (Finite population). In many cases, the population under consideration is the one which could be physically listed. For example:

—The students of the Hubei University of Technology.

—The books in a library.

Example 1.1.3 (Hypothetical population). Also in many cases, the population is much more abstract and may arise from the phenomenon under consideration.

Consider e.g. a factory producing light bulbs. If the factory keeps using the same equipment, raw materials and methods of production also in future then the bulbs that will be produced in this factory constitute a hypothetical population. That is, sample of light bulbs taken from the current production line can be used to make inference about qualities of light bulbs produced in future.

1.1.3 Descriptive and Inferential Statistics

There are two major types of statistics. The branch of statistics devoted to the summarization and description of data is called descriptive statistics and the branch of statistics concerned with using sample data to make an inference about a population of data is called inferential statistics.

Definition 1.1.6 (Descriptive Statistics). *Descriptive statistics consists of methods for organizing and summarizing information.* (Weiss, 1999)

Definition 1.1.7 (Inferential Statistics). *Inferential statistics consists of methods for draw-*

ing and measuring the reliability of conclusions about population based on information obtained from a sample of the population. (Weiss, 1999)

Descriptive statistics includes the construction of graphs, charts, and tables, and the calculation of various descriptive measures such as averages, measures of variation, and percentiles. In fact, the most part of this course deals with descriptive statistics.

Inferential statistics includes methods like point estimation, interval estimation and hypothesis testing which are all based on probability theory.

Example 1.1.4 (Descriptive and Inferential Statistics). Consider the event of tossing a dice. The dice is rolled 100 times and the results are forming the sample data. Descriptive statistics is used to group the sample data in the following table. (see table 1.1.1).

Table 1.1.1 Description of the Sample Data

Outcome of the roll	Frequencies in the sample data
1	10
2	20
3	18
4	16
5	11
6	25

Inferential statistics can now be used to verify whether the dice is fair or not. Descriptive statistics and inferential statistics are interrelated. It is almost always necessary to use methods of descriptive statistics to organize and summarize the information obtained from a sample before methods of inferential statistics can be used to make more thorough analysis of the subject under investigation. Furthermore, the preliminary descriptive analysis of a sample often reveals features that lead to the choice of the appropriate inferential method to be later used.

Sometimes it is possible to collect the data from the whole population. In that case, it is possible to perform a descriptive study on the population as well as usually on the sample. Only when an inference is made about the population based on information obtained from the sample does the study become inferential.

1.1.4 Parameters and Statistics

Usually the features of the population under investigation can be summarized by numerical parameters. Hence the research problem usually becomes an investigation of the values of parameters. These population parameters are unknown and sample statistics is used to make inference about them. That is, statistic describes a characteristic of the sample which can then be used to make inference about unknown parameters.

Definition 1.1.8 (Parameters and Statistics). *A parameter is an unknown numerical summary of the population. A statistic is a known numerical summary of the sample which can be used to make inference about parameters*. (Agresti & Finlay, 1997)

So the inference about some specific unknown parameter is based on a statistic. We use known sample statistics in making inferences about unknown population parameters. The primary focus of most research studies is the parameters of the population, not statistics calculated for the particular sample selected. The sample and statistics describing are important only in so far as the information they provide about the unknown parameters.

Example 1.1.5 (Parameters and Statistics). Consider the research problem and find out what percentage of 18~30 year-olds are going to the movies at least once a month.

- Parameter: The proportion of 18~30 year-olds going to the movies at least once a month.

- Statistic: The proportion of 18~30 year-olds going to the movies at least once a month calculated from the sample of 18~30 year-olds.

1.1.5 Statistical Data Analysis

The goal of statistics is to gain understanding from data. Any data analysis should contain the following steps:

◆ Beginning

◆ Formulating the research problem

◆ Defining population and sample

◆ Collecting the data

◆ Doing descriptive data analysis

◆ Using appropriate statistical methods to solve the research problem

◆ Reporting the results

◆ Ending

To conclude this section, we can note that the major objective of statistics is to make inferences about population from an analysis of information contained in sample data. This includes assessments of the extent of uncertainty involved in these inferences.

1.2 Variables and Organization of the Data

1.2.1 Variables

A characteristic that varies from one person or thing to another is called a variable, i.e, a variable is any characteristic that varies from one individual member of the population to another. Examples of variables for humans are height, weight, number of siblings, sex, marital status, and eye color. The first three of these variables yield numerical information (yield numerical measurements) and are examples of quantitative (or numerical) variables; the last three yield non-numerical information (yield non-numerical measurements) and are examples of qualitative (or categorical) variables.

Quantitative variables can be classified as either discrete or continuous.

Discrete variables. Some variables, such as the numbers of children in family, the numbers of car accidents on the certain road on different days, or the numbers of students taking basics of the statistics course are the results of counting and thus these are discrete variables. Typically, a discrete variable is a variable whose possible values are some or all of the ordinary counting numbers like 0,1,2,3, …As a definition, we can say that a variable is discrete if it has only a countable number of distinct possible values. That is, a variable is discrete if it can assume only a finite number of values or as many values as there are integers.

Continuous variables. Quantities such as length, weight, or temperature can in principle be measured arbitrarily and accurately. There is no indivisible unit. Weight may be measured to the nearest gram, but it could be measured more accurately, say to the tenth of a gram. Such a variable, called to be continuous, is intrinsically different from a discrete one.

Scales

Scales for qualitative variables. Besides being classified as either qualitative or quantitative, variables can be described according to the scale on which they are defined. The scale of the variable gives a certain structure to the variable and also defines the meaning of it.

The categories into which a qualitative variable falls may or may not have a natural ordering. For example, occupational categories have no natural ordering. If the categories of a qualitative variable are unordered, then the qualitative variable is said to be defined on a nominal scale, the word nominal referring to the fact that the categories are merely names. If the categories can be put in order, the scale is called an ordinal scale. Based on what scale a qualitative variable is defined, the variable can be called as a nominal variable or an ordinal variable. Examples of ordinal variables are education (classified e. g. as low, high) and "strength of opinion" on some proposal (classified according to whether the individual favors the proposal, is indifferent towards it, or opposites it) and position at the end of the race (first, second, etc.).

Scales for quantitative variables. Quantitative variables, whether discrete or continuous, are defined either on an interval scale or on a ratio scale. If one can compare the differences between measurements of the variable meaningfully, but not the ratio of the measurements, then the quantitative variable is defined on an interval scale. If, on the other hand, one can compare both the differences between measurements of the variable and the ratio of the measurements meaningfully, then the quantitative variable is defined on a ratio scale. In order that the ratio of the measurements can be meaningful, the variable must have natural, meaningful and absolute zero point, i. e, a ratio scale is an interval scale with a meaningful and absolute zero point. For example, temperature measured on the centigrade system is an interval variable and the height of a person is a ratio variable.

1.2.2 Organization of the Data

Observing the values of the variables for one person or more people or things yield data. Each individual datum is called an observation and the collection of all observations for particular variables is called a datum set or datum matrix. Data sets are the values of variables recorded for a set of sampling units.

In order to make it easy to manipulate (record and sort) their values, the qualitative variables are often coded by assigning numbers to the different categories, and thus converting the categorical data to numerical data in a trivial sense. For example, marital status might be coded by letting 1,2,3 and 4, denoting a person's being single, married, widowed, or divorced, but coded data still continue to be nominal data. Coded numerical data do not share any of the properties of the numbers we deal with in the ordinary arithmetic field. With regards to the codes for marital status, we cannot write $3>1$ or $2<4$, and we cannot write $2-1=4-3$ or $1+3=4$. This illustrates how important it is always to check whether the mathematical treatment of statistical data is really legitimate.

Data is presented in a matrix form (data matrix). All the values of particular variables is organized to the same column; the values of variables form the column in a data matrix. Observation, i. e. measurements collected from a sampling unit, forms a row in a data matrix. Consider the situation where there are k numbers of variables and n numbers of observations (sample size is n). Then the data set should look like variables:

$$\text{Sampling units} \begin{bmatrix} x_{11} & x_{12} & x_{13} & x_{1k} \\ x_{21} & x_{22} & x_{23} & x_{2k} \\ x_{31} & x_{32} & x_{33} & x_{3k} \\ x_{n1} & x_{n2} & x_{n3} & x_{nk} \end{bmatrix}$$

where xij is a value of the jth variable collected from i: th observation, $i=1,2,\ldots, n$ and $j=1,2,\ldots, k$.

1.3 Describe data by Tables and Graphs

1.3.1 Qualitative Variable

The number of observations that fall into particular class (or category) of the qualitative variable is called the frequency (or count) of that class. A table listing all classes and their frequencies is called a frequency distribution.

In addition to the frequencies, we are often interested in the percentage of a class. We find the percentage by dividing the frequency of the class by the total number of observations and multiplying the result by 100. The percentage of the class, expressed as a decimal, is usually referred to as the relative frequency of the class.

Relative frequency of the class=Frequency in the class

Total number of observation

A table listing all classes and their relative frequencies is called a relative frequency distribution. The relative frequencies provide the most relevant information as to the pattern of the data. One should also state the sample size, which serves as an indicator of the creditability of the relative frequencies. Relative frequencies sum to 1 (100%).

A cumulative frequency (cumulative relative frequency) is obtained by summing the frequencies (relative frequencies) of all classes up to the specific class. In a case of qualitative variables, cumulative frequencies make sense only for ordinal variables, not for nominal variables.

The qualitative data are presented graphically either as a pie chart or as a horizontal or vertical bar graph. A pie chart is a disk divided into pie-shaped pieces proportional to the relative frequencies of the classes. To obtain angles for any class, we multiply the relative frequencies by 360 degrees, which corresponds to the complete circle.

A horizontal bar graph displays the classes on the horizontal axis and the frequencies (or relative frequencies) of the classes on the vertical axis. The frequency (or relative frequency) of each class is represented by a vertical bar whose height is equal to the frequency (or relative frequency) of the class.

In a bar graph, its bars do not touch each other. At a vertical bar graph, the classes are displayed on the vertical axis and the frequencies of the classes on the horizontal axis.

Nominal data are best displayed by a pie chart and ordinal data by a horizontal or vertical bar graph.

Example 1.3.1 The blood types of 40 persons are as follows:

O O A B A O A A A O B O B O O A O O A A A A AB A B A A O O A O O A A A O A O O A B

Summarizing data in a frequency table by using Excel (see table 1.3.1):

Table 1.3.1 **Frequency Distribution of Blood Types**

Blood	Frequency	Percent/%
O	16	40.0
A	18	45.0
B	4	10.0
AB	2	5.0
Total	40	100.0

Graphical presentation of data in Excel (see Fig. 1.3.1):

Graphs→Interactive→Pie→Simple (see Fig. 1.3.1),

Graphs→Interactive→Bar (see Fig. 1.3.2)

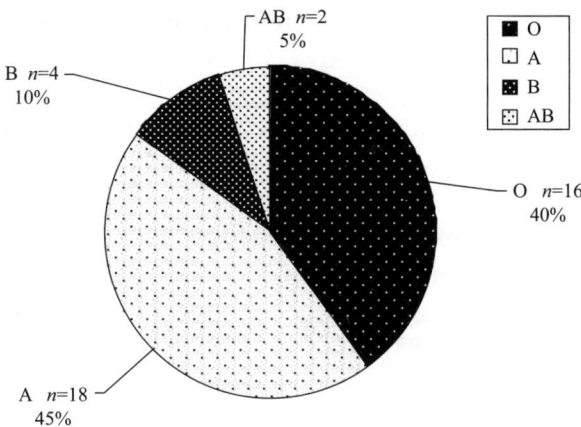

Fig. 1.3.1　Pie Chart for Blood Types

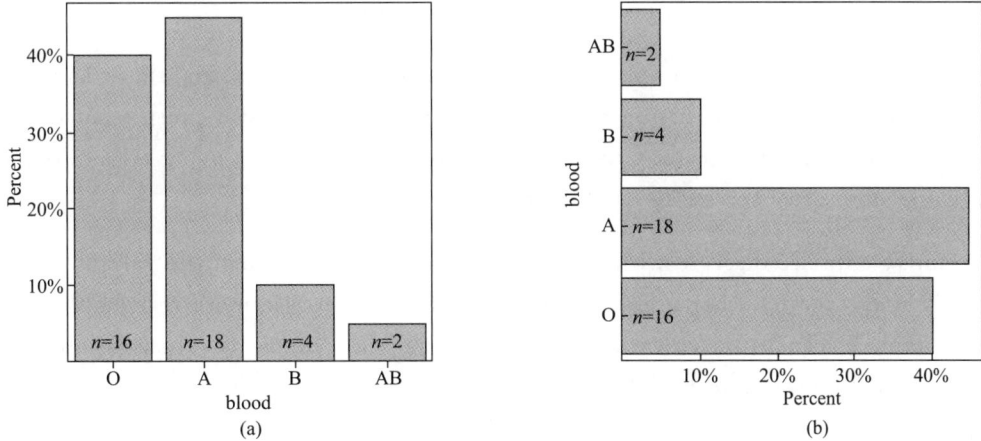

Fig. 1.3.2　Bar Charts for Blood Types

1.3.2　Quantitative Variable

The data of the quantitative variable can be also presented by a frequency distribution. If the discrete variable can obtain only a few different values, then the data of the discrete variable can be summarized in the same way as qualitative variables in a frequency table. In a place of the qualitative categories, we now list in a frequency table the distinct numerical measurements that appear in the discrete data set and then count their frequencies.

If the discrete variable can have a lot of different values or the quantitative variable is the continuous variable, then the data must be grouped into classes (categories) before the table of frequencies can be formed. The main steps in a process of grouping quantitative variable into classes are:

(a) Find the minimum and the maximum value variables in the data set.

(b) Choose intervals of equal length that cover the range between the minimum and the maximum without overlapping. These are called class intervals, and their end points are called class limits.

(c) Count the number of observations in the data that belongs to each class interval. The count in each class is the class frequency.

(d) Calculate the relative frequencies of each class by dividing the class frequency by the total number of observations in the data.

The number in the middle of the class is called class mark of the class. The number in the middle of the upper class limit of one class and the lower class limit of the other class is called the real class limit. As a rule of thumb, it is generally satisfactory to group observed values of numerical variable in the data into 5 to 15 class intervals. A smaller number of intervals is used if the number of observations is relatively small; if the number of observations is large, the number on intervals may be greater than 15.

The quantitative data are usually presented graphically either as a histogram or as a horizontal or vertical bar graph. The histogram is like a horizontal bar graph except that its bars do touch each other. The histogram is formed from grouped data, displaying either frequencies or relative frequencies (percentages) of each class interval.

If quantitative data are discrete with only a few possible values, then the variable should be graphically presented by a bar graph. Also if for some reason it is more reasonable to obtain frequency table for quantitative variables with unequal class intervals, then variables should be also graphically presented by a bar graph!

Example 1.3.2   Age (in years) of 102 people:

34, 67, 40, 72, 37, 33, 42, 62, 49, 32, 52, 40, 31, 19, 68, 55, 57, 54, 37, 32, 54, 38, 20, 50, 56, 48, 35, 52, 29, 56, 68, 65, 45, 44, 54, 39, 29, 56, 43, 42, 22, 30, 26, 20, 48, 29, 34, 27, 40, 28, 45, 21, 42, 38, 29, 26, 62, 35, 28, 24, 44, 46, 39, 29, 27, 40, 22, 38, 42, 39, 26, 48, 39, 25, 34, 56, 31, 60, 32, 24, 51, 69, 28, 27, 38, 56, 36, 25, 46, 50, 36, 58, 39, 57, 55, 42, 49, 38, 49, 36, 48, 44

Summarizing data in a frequency table by using Excel (see table 1.3.2):

Analyze→Descriptive Statistics→Frequencies,

Analyze→Custom Tables→Tables of Frequencies

Table 1.3.2 Frequency Distribution of People's Age

Interval	Frequency	Percent/%	Cumulative Percent/%
18~22	6	5.9	5.9
23~27	10	9.8	15.7
28~32	14	13.7	29.4
33~37	11	10.8	40.2
38~42	19	18.6	58.8
43~47	8	7.8	66.7
48~52	12	11.8	78.4
53~57	12	11.8	90.2
58~62	4	3.9	94.1
63~67	2	2.0	96.1
68~72	4	3.9	100.0
Total	102	100.0	

Graphical presentation of data in Excel:

Graphs→Interactive→Histogram (see Fig. 1.3.3),

Graphs→Histogram

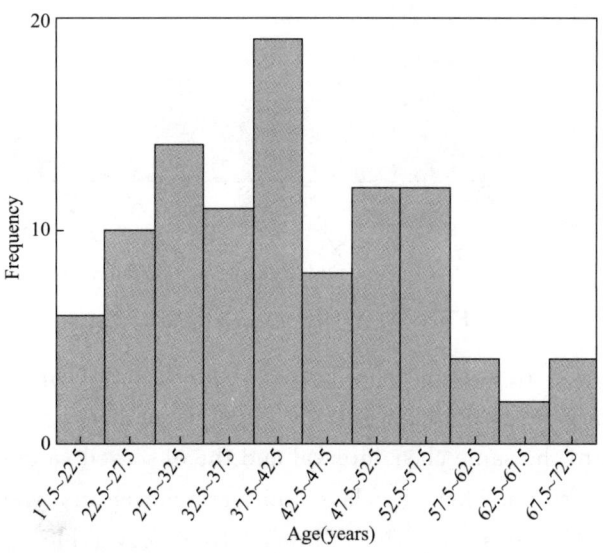

Fig. 1.3.3 Histogram for People's Age

Example 1.3.3. Prices of hotdogs ($/oz.):

0.11, 0.17, 0.11, 0.15, 0.10, 0.11, 0.21, 0.20, 0.14, 0.14, 0.23, 0.25, 0.07, 0.09, 0.10, 0.10, 0.19, 0.11, 0.19, 0.17, 0.12, 0.12, 0.12, 0.10, 0.11, 0.13, 0.10, 0.09, 0.11, 0.15, 0.13, 0.10, 0.18, 0.09, 0.07, 0.08, 0.06, 0.08, 0.05, 0.07, 0.08, 0.08, 0.07, 0.09, 0.06, 0.07, 0.08, 0.07, 0.07, 0.07, 0.08, 0.06, 0.07, 0.06

Frequency table (see table 1.3.3):

Table 1.3.3 Frequency Distribution of Prices of Hotdogs

Interval	Frequency	Percent/%	Cumulative Percent/%
0.030~0.060	5	9.3	9.3
0.060~0.090	19	35.2	44.4
0.090~0.120	15	27.8	72.2
0.120~0.150	6	11.1	83.3
0.150~0.180	3	5.6	88.9
0.180~0.210	4	7.4	96.3
0.210~0.240	1	1.9	98.1
0.240~0.270	1	1.9	100.0
Total	54	100.0	

Graphical presentation of the data (see Fig. 1.3.4):

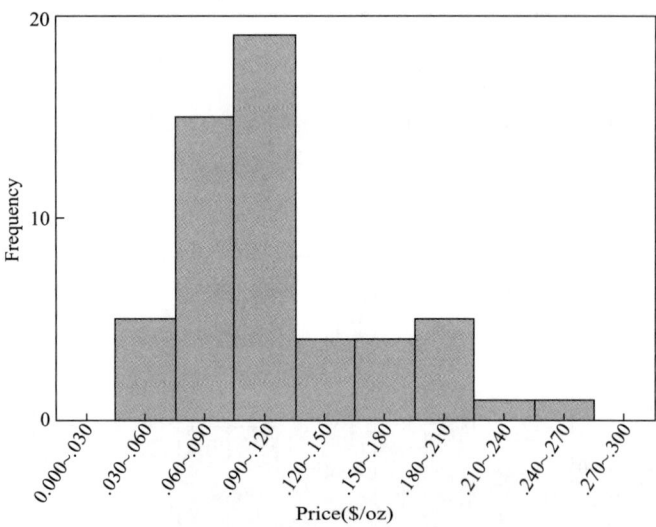

Fig. 1.3.4 Histogram for Prices

Let's look at another way of summarizing hotdogs' prices in a frequency table. First we notice that the minimum price of hotdogs is 0.05. Then we make a decision to put the observed values 0.05 and 0.06 to the same class interval and the observed values 0.07 and 0.08 to the same class interval and so on. Then the class limits are chosen in a way that they are middle values of 0.06 and 0.07 and so on. The following frequency table and histogram are then formed (see table 1.3.4; see Fig. 1.3.5):

Table 1.3.4 Frequency Distribution of Prices of Hotdogs

Interval	Frequency	Percent/%	Cumulative Percent/%
0.045~0.065	5	9.3	9.3
0.065~0.085	15	27.5	37.0
0.085~0.105	10	18.5	55.6
0.105~0.125	9	16.7	72.2

Continued

Interval	Frequency	Percent/%	Cumulative Percent/%
0.125~0.145	4	7.4	79.6
0.145~0.165	2	3.7	83.3
0.165~0.185	3	5.6	88.9
0.185~0.205	3	5.6	94.4
0.205~0.225	1	1.9	96.3
0.225~0.245	1	1.9	98.1
0.245~0.265	1	1.9	100.0
Total	54	100.0	

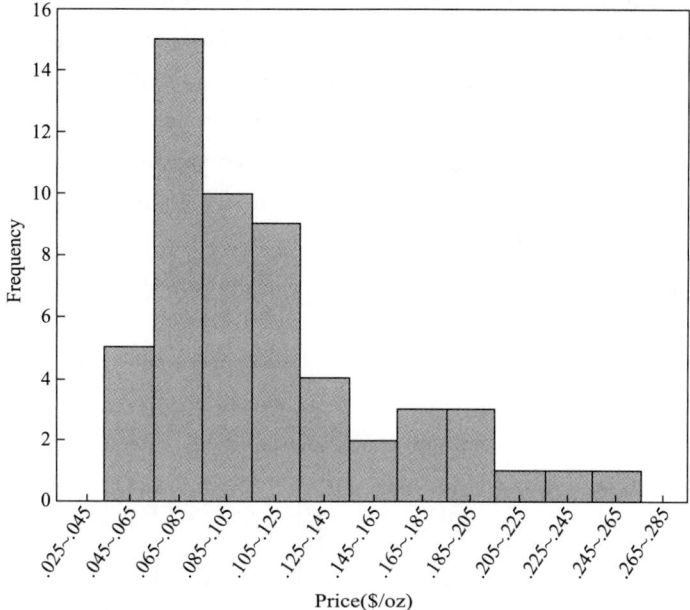

Fig. 1.3.5 Histogram for Prices

Other types of graphical displays for quantitative data are:

(a) dotplot

Graphs→Interactive→Dot

(b) stem-and-leaf diagram of just stem-plot

Analyze→Descriptive Statistics→Explore

(c) frequency and relative-frequency polygon for frequencies and relative frequencies (Graphs→Interactive→Line)

(d) gives for cumulative frequencies and cumulative relative frequencies

(Graphs→Interactive→Line)

1.3.3 Samples and Population Distributions

Frequency distributions for a variable apply both to a population and to samples from that population. The first type is called the population distribution of the variable, and the second type is called a sample distribution.

In a sense, the sample distribution is a blurry photograph of the population distribution. As the sample size increases, the sample relative frequency in any class interval gets closer to the true population relative frequency. Thus, the photograph gets clearer, and the sample distribution looks more like the population distribution.

When a variable is continuous, one can choose class intervals in the frequency distribution and for the histogram as narrow as desired. Now, as the sample size increases indefinitely and the number of class intervals simultaneously increases, with their width narrowing, the shape of the sample histogram gradually approaches a smooth curve. We use such curves to represent population distributions. Fig. 1.3.6. shows two sample histograms, one based on a sample of size 100 and the second based on a sample of size 2000, and also a smooth curve representing the population distribution.

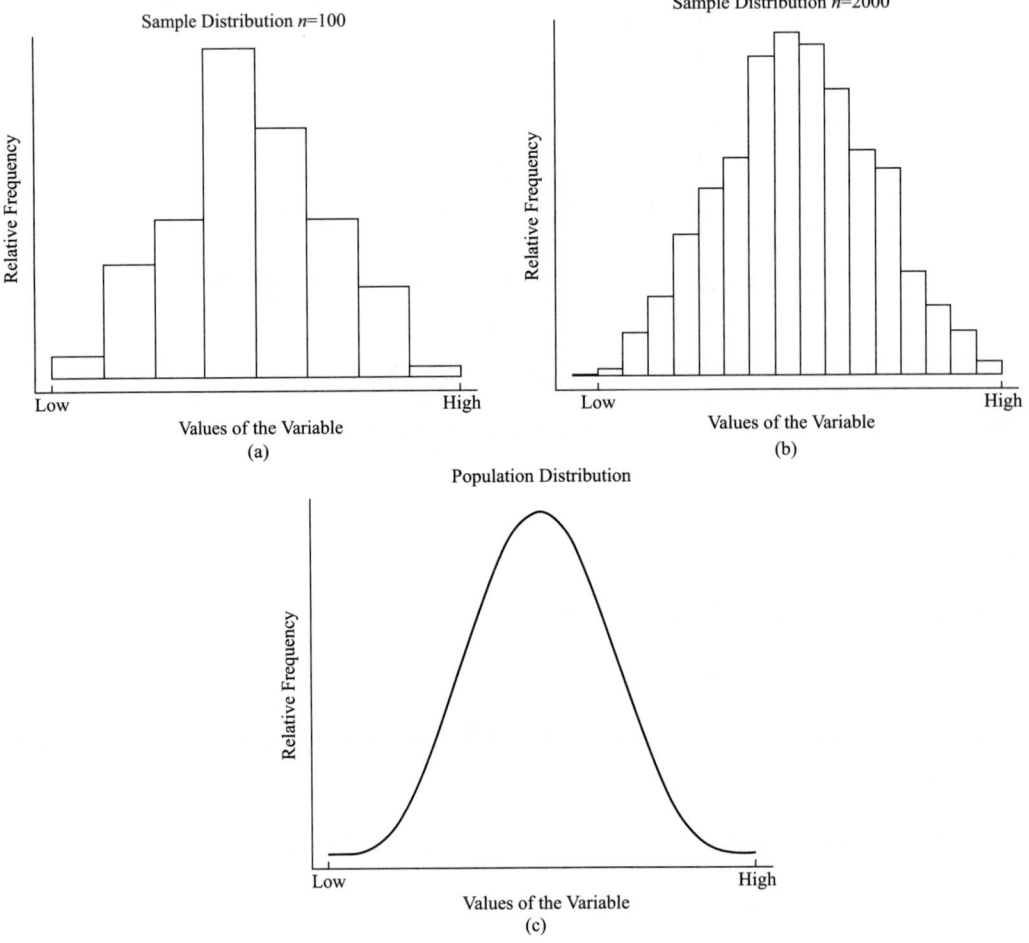

Fig. 1.3.6　Sample and Population Distributions

One way to summarize a sample of population distribution is to describe its shape. A group for which the distribution is bell-shaped is fundamentally different from the one for which the distribution is U-shaped, for example. The bell-shaped and U-shaped distributions in Fig. 1. 3. 7. are symmetric. On the other hand, a nonsymmetric distribution is said to be the right or skewed to the left, according to whose tail is longer (see Fig. 1. 3. 8).

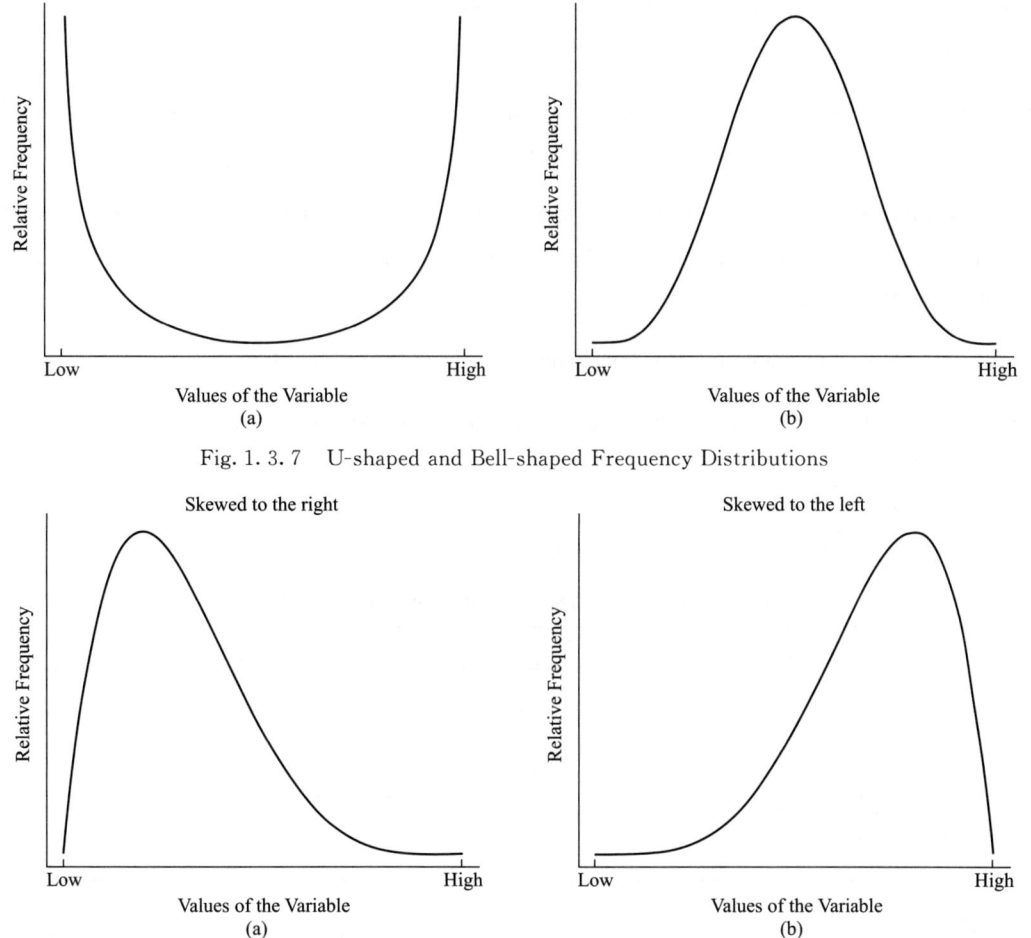

Fig. 1. 3. 7   U-shaped and Bell-shaped Frequency Distributions

Fig. 1. 3. 8   Skewed Frequency Distributions

1. 4 Measures of Center

Descriptive measures that indicate where the center or the most typical value of the variable lies in a collected set of measurements are called measures of center. Measures of center are often referred to as averages. The median and the mean apply only to quantitative data, whereas the mode can be used with either quantitative or qualitative data.

1. 4. 1 The Mode

Definition 1. 4. 1 (Mode). *The sample mode of a qualitative or a discrete quantitative vari-*

able is that value of the variable which occurs with the greatest frequency in a data set. A more exact definition of the mode is given below.

Obtain the frequency of each observed value of the variable in a data and note the greatest frequency.

(1) If the greatest frequency is 1 (i.e. no value occurs more than once), then the variable has no mode.

(2) If the greatest frequency is 2 or greater, then any value that occurs with the greatest frequency is called a sample mode of the variable.

To obtain the mode (s) of a variable, we first construct a frequency distribution for the data using classes based on the single value. The mode (s) can then be determined easily from the frequency distribution.

Example 1.4.1 Let us consider the frequency table for blood types of 40 persons.

We can see from the frequency table that the mode of blood types is A.

The mode in Excel:

Analyze→Descriptive Statistics→Frequencies (see table 1.4.1)

Table 1.4.1 **Frequency Distribution of Blood Types**

Blood	Frequency	Percent/%
O	16	40.0
A	18	45.0
B	4	10.0
AB	2	5.0
Total	40	100.0

When we measure a continuous variable (or a discrete variable having a lot of different values) such as height or weight of a person, all the measurements may be different. In such a case there is no mode because every observed value has frequency 1. However, the data can be grouped into class intervals and the mode can then be defined in terms of class frequencies. With grouped quantitative variable, the mode class is the class interval with the highest frequency.

Example 1.4.2 Let's consider the frequency table for prices of hotdogs ($/oz.): the mode class is 0.065~0.085 (see table 1.4.2).

Table 1.4.2 **Frequency Distribution of Prices of Hotdogs**

Intervals	Frequency	Percent/%	Cumulative Percent/%
0.045~0.065	5	9.3	9.3
0.065~0.085	15	27.8	37.0

Continued

Intervals	Frequency	Percent/%	Cumulative Percent/%
0.085~0.105	10	18.2	55.6
0.105~0.125	9	16.7	72.2
0.125~0.145	4	7.4	79.6
0.145~0.165	2	3.7	83.3
0.165~0.185	3	5.6	88.9
0.185~0.205	3	5.6	94.4
0.205~0.225	1	1.9	96.3
0.225~0.245	1	1.9	98.1
0.245~0.265	1	1.9	100.0
Total	54	100.0	

1.4.2 The Median

Definition 1.4.2 (Median). *The sample median of a quantitative variable is that value of the variable in a data set that divides the set of observed values in half, so that the observed values in one half are less than or equal to the median value and the observed values in the other half are greater or equal to the median value. To obtain the median of the variable, we arrange observed values in a data set in an increasing order and then determine the middle value in the ordered list.*

Arrange the observed values of variable in a data in increasing order.

(1) If the number of the observation is odd, then the sample median is exactly the observed value in the middle of the ordered list.

(2) If the number of the observation is even, then the sample median is the number halfway between the two middle observed values in the ordered list.

In both cases, if we let n denote the number of observations in a data set, then the sample median is at position $(n+1)/2$ in the ordered list.

Example 1.4.3 Seven participants in a bike race had the following finishing time in minutes: 28, 22, 26, 29, 21, 23, 24. What is the median?

Example 1.4.4 Eight participants in a bike race had the following finishing time in minutes: 28, 22, 26, 29, 21, 23, 24, 50. What is the median?

The median in Excel:

Analyze→Descriptive Statistics→Frequencies

The median is a "central" value—there are as many values greater than it as there are less than it.

1.4.3 The Mean

The most commonly used measure of center for quantitative variables is the (arithmetic) sample mean. When people speak of taking an average, it means that they are most often referred to.

Definition 1.4.3 (Mean). *The sample mean of the variable is the sum of observed values in data divided by the number of observations.*

Example 1.4.5 Seven participants in a bike race had the following finishing time in minutes: 28, 22, 26, 29, 21, 23, 24. What is the mean?

Example 1.4.6 Eight participants in a bike race had the following finishing time in minutes: 28, 22, 26, 29, 21, 23, 24, 50. What is the mean?

The mean in Excel:

Analyze→Descriptive Statistics→Frequencies,

Analyze→Descriptive Statistics→Descriptive

To effectively present the ideas and associated calculations, it is convenient to represent variables and observed values of variables by symbols to prevent the discussion from becoming anchored to a specific set of numbers. So let's use x to denote the variable in question, and then the symbol x_i denotes *ith* observation of that variable in the data set.

If the sample size is n, then the mean of the variable x is

$$\frac{x_1+x_2+x_3+\cdots x_n}{n}.$$

To further simplify the writing of a sum, the Greek letter P (sigma) is used as a shorthand. The sum $x_1 + x_2 + x_3 + \cdots + x_n$ is denoted as

$$\sum_{i=1}^{n} x_i,$$

and read as "the sum of all x_i with i ranging from 1 to n". Thus we can now formally define the mean as follows.

Definition 1.4.4. *The sample mean of the variable is the sum of observed values x_1, x_2, x_3, ..., x_n in a data divided by the number of observations n.*

The sample mean is denoted by $\bar{x}$, and expressed operationally,

$$\bar{x} = \frac{\sum_{i=1}^{n} x_i}{n} \text{ or } \frac{\sum x_i}{n}$$

1.4.4 Which Measure to Choose?

The mode should be used when we calculate measures of the center for the qualitative variable. When the variable is quantitative with symmetric distribution, then the mean is the proper measure of the center. In a case of quantitative variables with skewed distribution, the median is a good choice for the measure of the center. This is related to the fact that the mean can be highly influenced by an observation that falls far from the rest of the data, called an outlier. It should be noted that the sample mode, the sample median and the sample mean of the variable in question have corresponding population measures of center, i. e. , we can assume that the variable in question has also the population mode, the population median and the population mean, which are all unknown. Then the sample mode, the sample median and the sample mean can be used to estimate the values of these corresponding unknown population values.

1.5 Measures of Variation

In addition to locating the center of the observed values of the variable in the data, another important aspect of a descriptive study of the variable is numerically measuring the extent of variation around the center. Two data sets of the same variable may exhibit similar positions of the center but may be remarkably different with respect to variability.

Just as there are several different measures of the center, there are also several different measures of variation. In this section, we will examine three of the most frequently used measures of variation: the sample range, the sample interquartile range and the sample standard deviation. Measures of variation are used mostly and only for quantitative variables.

1.5.1 Range

The sample range is obtained by computing the difference between the largest observed value of the variable in a data set and the smallest one.

Definition 1.5.1 (Range). *The sample range of the variable is the difference between its maximum and minimum values in a data set*:

$$\text{Range} = \text{Max} - \text{Min}$$

The sample range of the variable is quite easy to compute. However, in using the range, a great deal of information is ignored, that is, only the largest and smallest values of the variable are considered; the other observed values are disregarded. It should be also remarked that the range cannot ever decrease, but can increase, when additional observations are included in the data set and that in sense the range is overly sensitive to the sample size.

Example 1.5.1. Seven participants in a bike race had the following finishing time in minutes: 28, 22, 26, 29, 21, 23, 24. What is the range?

Example 1.5.2. Eight participants in a bike race had the following finishing time in minutes:
28, 22, 26, 29, 21, 23, 24, 50. What is the range?

Example 1.5.3 Prices of hotdogs ($/oz.):

0.11, 0.17, 0.11, 0.15, 0.10, 0.11, 0.21, 0.20, 0.14, 0.14, 0.23, 0.25, 0.07, 0.09, 0.10, 0.10, 0.19, 0.11, 0.19, 0.17, 0.12, 0.12, 0.12, 0.10, 0.11, 0.13, 0.10, 0.09, 0.11, 0.15, 0.13, 0.10, 0.18, 0.09, 0.07, 0.08, 0.06, 0.08, 0.05, 0.07, 0.08, 0.08, 0.07, 0.09, 0.06, 0.07, 0.08, 0.07, 0.07, 0.07, 0.08, 0.06, 0.07, 0.06

The range in Excel:

Analyze→Descriptive Statistics→Frequencies,

Analyze→Descriptive Statistics→Descriptive

1.5.2 Interquartile Range

Before we can define the sample interquartile range, we have to first define the percentiles, the deciles and the quartiles of the variable in a data set. As was shown in section 1.4.2, the median of the variable divides the observed values into two equal parts—the bottom 50% and the top 50%.

The percentiles of the variable divide observed values into hundredths, or 100 equal parts. Roughly speaking, the first percentile, $P1$, is the number that divides the bottom 1% of the observed values from the top 99%; the second percentile, $P2$, is the number that divides the bottom 2% of the observed values from the top 98%; and so forth. The median is the 50th percentile.

The deciles of the variable divide the observed values into tenths, or 10 equal parts. The variable has nine deciles, denoted by $D1, D2, \ldots, D9$. The first decile $D1$ is the 10th percentile, the second decile $D2$ is the 20th percentile, and so forth.

The most commonly used percentiles are quartiles. The quartiles of the variable divide the observed values into quarters, or 4 equal parts. The 31 variable has three quartiles, denoted by $Q1$, $Q2$ and $Q3$. Roughly speaking, the first quartile, $Q1$, is the number that divides the bottom 25% of the observed values from the top 75%; the second quartile, $Q2$, is the median, which is the number that divides the bottom 50% of the observed values from the top 50%; and the third quartile, $Q3$, is the number that divides the bottom 75% of the observed values from the top 25%.

At this point our intuitive definitions of percentiles and deciles will suffice. However, quartiles need to be defined more precisely, which is done below.

Definition 1.5.2 (Quartiles). *Let n denote the number of observations in a data set. Arrange the observed values of variable in a data in an increasing order.*

(1) *The first quartile $Q1$ is at position $(n+1)/4$;*

(2) *The second quartile $Q2$ (the median) is at position $(n+1)/2$;*

(3) *The third quartile $Q3$ is at position $3(n+1)/4$, in the ordered list.*

If a position is not a whole number, linear interpolation is used. Next we define the sample interquartile range. Since the interquartile range is defined using quartiles, it is preferred measure of variation when the median is used as the measure of center (i. e. in case of skewed distribution).

Definition 1.5.3 (Interquartile range). *The sample interquartile range of the variable, denoted IQR, is the difference between the first and the third quartiles of the variable.* That is,

$$IQR = Q3 - Q1$$

Roughly speaking, the IQR gives the range of the middle 50% of the observed values.

The sample interquartile range represents the length of the interval covered by the center half of the observed values of the variable. This measure of variation is not disturbed if a small fraction of the observed values are very large or very small.

Example 1.5.4 Seven participants in a bike race had the following finishing time in minutes: 28, 22, 26, 29, 21, 23, 24. What is the interquartile range?

Example 1.5.5 Eight participants in a bike race had the following finishing time in minutes: 28, 22, 26, 29, 21, 23, 24, 50. What is the interquartile range?

Example 1.5.6 The interquartile range for prices of hotdogs ($/oz.) in Excel:

Analyze→Descriptive Statistics→Explore

Interquartile range of the prices of hotdogs

Price ($/oz) Interquartile Range 0.0625

Statistic

Five-number Summary and Boxplots

Minimum, maximum and quartiles together provide information on center and variation of the variable in a nice compact way. Written in an increasing order, they comprise what is called the five-number summary of the variable.

Definition 1.5.4 (Five-number summary). *The five-number summary of the variable consists of minimum, maximum and quartiles written in an increasing order:*

Min, $Q1$, $Q2$, $Q3$, Max.

Actually, two types of boxplots are in common use: boxplot and modified boxplot. The main difference between the two types of boxplots is that potential outliers (i. e. observed value, which do not appear to follow the characteristic distribution of the rest of the data) are plotted individually in a modified boxplot, but not in a boxplot. Below is given the procedure how to construct a boxplot.

Definition 1.5.5 (Boxplot). *To construct a boxplot*

(1) *Determine the five-number summary;*

(2) *Draw a horizontal (or vertical) axis on which the numbers obtained in step 1 can be located. Above this axis, mark the quartiles and the minimum and maximum with vertical (horizontal) lines;*

(3) *Connect the quartiles to each other to make a box, and then connect the box to the minimum and maximum with lines.*

The modified boxplot can be constructed in a similar way, except that the potential outliers are first identified and plotted individually and the minimum and maximum values in boxplot are replaced with the adjacent values, which are the most extreme observations that are not potential outliers.

Example 1.5.7 Seven participants in a bike race had the following finishing time in minutes: 28, 22, 26, 29, 21, 23, 24. Construct the boxplot.

Example 1.5.8 The five-number summary and boxplot for prices of hotdogs ($/oz.) in Excel (see table 1.5.1):

Analyze→Descriptive Statistics→Descriptives

Table 1.5.1 The Five-number Summary of the Prices of Hotdogs

N	Valid		54
	Missing		0
Median			0.1000
Minimum			0.05
Maximum			0.25
Percentiles/%		25	0.0700
		50	0.1000
		75	0.1325

Graphs→Interactive→Boxplot (see Fig. 1.5.1),

Graphs→Boxplot

1.5.3 Standard Deviation

The sample standard deviation is the most frequently used measure of variability, although it is not as easily understood as ranges. It can be considered as a kind of average of the absolute

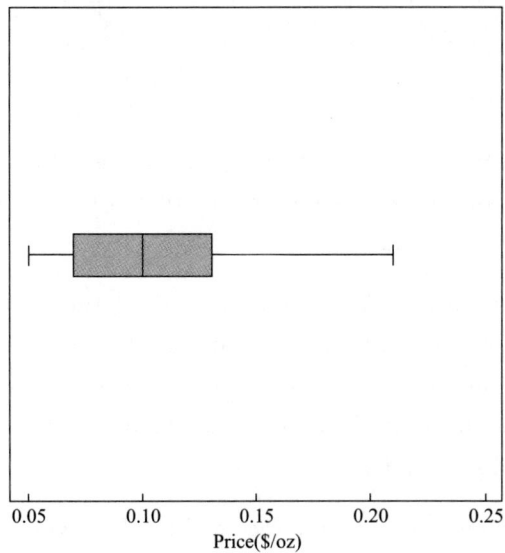

Fig. 1.5.1 Boxplot for the Prices of Hotdogs

deviations of observed values from the mean of the variable in question.

Definition 1.5.6 (Standard deviation). *For a variable x, the standard deviation of the sample, denoted by s_x (or when no confusion arises, simply by s), is*

$$s_x = \sqrt{\frac{\sum_{i=1}^{n}(x_i - \bar{x})^2}{n-1}}.$$

Since the standard deviation is defined using the sample mean $\bar{x}$ of the variable x, it is a preferred measure of variation when the mean is used as the measure of center (i.e. in case of symmetric distribution). Note that the standard deviation is always positive numbers, i.e., $s_x \geq 0$.

In a formula of the standard deviation, the sum of the squared deviations 35 from the mean,

$$\sum_{i=1}^{n}(x_i - \bar{x})^2 = (x_1 - \bar{x})^2 + (x_2 - \bar{x})^2 + \cdots + (x_n - \bar{x})^2,$$

is called a sum of squared deviations and provides a measure of total deviations from the mean for all the observed values of the variable. Once the sum of squared deviations is divided by $n-1$, we get

$$s_x^2 = \frac{\sum_{i=1}^{n}(x_i - \bar{x})^2}{n-1},$$

which is called the sample variance. The standard deviation of the sample has the following alternative formulas:

$$s_x = \sqrt{\frac{\sum_{i=1}^{n}(x_i - \bar{x})^2}{n-1}} = \sqrt{\frac{\sum_{i=1}^{n} x_i^2 - n\bar{x}^2}{n-1}} = \sqrt{\frac{\sum_{i=1}^{n} x_i^2 - (\sum_{i=1}^{n} x_i)^2/n}{n-1}}$$

The formulas are useful from the computational point of view. In hand calculation, the use of these alternative formulas often reduces the arithmetic work, especially when $\bar{x}$ turns out to be a number with many decimal places.

The more variation there is in the observed values, the larger is the standard deviation for the variable in question. Thus the standard deviation satisfies the basic criterion for a measure of variation and like said, it is the most commonly used measure of variation. However, the standard deviation does have its drawbacks. For instance, its values can be strongly affected by a few extreme observations.

Example 1.5.9 Seven participants in a bike race had the following finishing time in minutes: 28, 22, 26, 29, 21, 23, 24. What is the sample standard deviation?

Example 1.5.10 The standard deviation for prices of hotdogs ($/oz.) in Excel (see table 1.5.2):

Analyze→Descriptive Statistics→Frequencies,

Analyze→Descriptive Statistics→Descriptive

Table 1.5.2 The Standard Deviation of the Prices of Hotdogs

Item	N	Mean	Std.	Deviation
Price ($/oz)	54	0.1113	0.04731	0.002
Valid N (listwise)	54			

Empirical rule for symmetric distributions.

For bell-shaped symmetric distributions (like the normal distribution), empirical rule relates to the standard deviation to the proportion of the observed values of the variable in a datum set that lies in an interval around the mean $\bar{x}$.

Empirical guideline for symmetric bell-shaped distributions, approximately

68% of the values lie within $\bar{x} \pm sx$,

95% of the values lie within $\bar{x} \pm 2sx$,

99.7% of the values lie within $\bar{x} \pm 3sx$.

1.5.4 Sample Statistics and Population Parameters

Of the measures of center and variation, the sample mean $\bar{x}$ and the sample standard deviation s are the most commonly reported. Since their values depend on the sample selected, they vary in value from sample to sample. In this sense, they are called random variables to emphasize that their values vary according to the sample selected. Their values are unknown before the sample is chosen. Once the samples are selected and computed, they become known sample statistics.

We shall regularly distinguish between sample statistics and the corresponding measures for the population. Section 1.1.4 introduced the parameter for a summary measure of the population. A statistic describes a sample, while a parameter describes the population from which the sample was taken.

Let μ and σ denote the mean and standard deviation of a variable for the population. We call μ and σ the population mean and population standard deviation. The population mean is the average of the population measurements.

The standard deviation of the population describes the variation of the population measurements about the population mean.

Whereas the statistics $\bar{x}$ are variables, with values depending on the sample chosen, the parameters μ and σ are constants. This is because μ and σ refer to just one particular group of measurements, namely, measurements for the entire population. Of course, parameter values are usually unknown, which is the reason for sampling and calculating sample statistics as estimates of their values. That is, we make inferences about unknown parameters (such as μ and σ) using sample statistics (such as $\bar{x}$ and s).

1.6 Probability Distributions and Normal Distributions

Inferential statistical methods use sample data to make predictions about the values of useful summary descriptions, called parameters, of the population of interest. This chapter treats parameters as known numbers. This is artificial, since parameter values are normally unknown or we would not need inferential methods. However, many inferential methods involve comparing observed sample statistics to the values expected if the parameter values equaled particular numbers. If the data are inconsistent with the particular parameter values, then we infer that the actual parameter values are somewhat different.

1.6.1 Probability Distributions

We first define the term probability, using a relative frequency approach. Imagine a hypothetical experiment consisting of a very long sequence of repeated observations on some random phenomena. Each observation may or may not result in some particular outcome. The probability of that outcome is defined to be the relative frequency of its occurrence, in the long run.

Definition 1.6.1 (Probability). *The probability of a particular outcome is the proportion of times that outcome would occur in a long run of repeated observations.*

A simplified representation of such an experiment is a very long sequence of flips of a coin, the outcome of interest being that a head faces upwards. Any flip may or may not result in a head. If the coin is balanced, then a basic result in probability, called law of large numbers, implies that the proportion of flips resulting in a head tends toward 1/2 as the number of flips increases. Thus, the probability of a head in any single flip of the coin equals 1/2.

Most of the time we are dealing with variables which have numerical outcomes. A variable which can take at least two different numerical values in a long run of repeated observations is called random variable.

Definition 1.6.2 (Random variable). *A random variable is a variable whose value is a numerical outcome of a random phenomenon.*

We usually denote random variables by capital letters near the end of the alphabet, such as X or Y. Some values of the random variable X may be more likely than others. The probability distribution of the random variable X lists the possible outcomes together with the probabilities the variable X can have. The probability distribution of a discrete random variable X assigns a probability to each possible value of the variable. Each probability is a number between 0 and 1, and the sum of the probabilities of all possible values equals.

Let $x_i, i=1,2,\ldots,k$ denote a possible outcome for the random variable X, and let $P(X=x_i)=P(x_i)=p_i$ denote the probability of that outcome. Then

$$0 \leqslant P(x_i) \leqslant 1 \text{ and } \sum_{i=1}^{k} P(x_i) = 1$$

since each probability falls between 0 and 1, and since the total probability equals 1.

A discrete random variable X has a countable number of possible values. The probability distribution of X lists the values and their probabilities (see table 1.6.1):

Table 1.6.1 The Probability Distribution of X Lists

Value of X	x_1	x_2	x_3	...	x_k
Probability	$P(x_1)$	$P(x_2)$	$P(x_3)$	...	$P(x_k)$

The probabilities $P(x_i)$ must possess two requirements:

(1) Every probability $P(x_i)$ is a number between 0 and 1.

(2) $P(x_1) + P(x_2) + \cdots + P(x_k) = 1$.

We can use a probability histogram to picture the probability distribution of a discrete random variable. Furthermore, we can find the probability of any event [such as $P(X \leqslant x_i)$ or $P(x_i \leqslant X \leqslant x_j), i \leqslant j$] by adding the probabilities $P(x_i)$ of the particular values x_i that make up the event.

Example 1.6.1 The instructor of a large class gives 15% each of 5=excellent, 20% each of

4 = very good, 30% each of 3 = good, 20% each of 2 = satisfactory, 10% each of 1 = sufficient, and 5% each of 0 = fail. Choose a student at random from this class. The student's grade is a random variable X. The value of X changes when we repeatedly choose students at random, but it is always one of 0, 1, 2, 3, 4 or 5. What is the probability distribution of X?

Draw a probability histogram for X.

What is the probability that the student got 4 = very good or better, i. e, $P(X \geqslant 4)$?

Continuous random variable X, on the other hand, takes all values in some interval of numbers between a and b. That is, continuous random variable has a continuum of possible values it can have. Let x_1 and x_2, $x_1 \leqslant x_2$ denote possible outcomes for the random variable X which may have values in the interval of numbers between a and b. Then clearly both x_1 and x_2 belong to the interval of a and b, i. e. ,

$$x_1 \in [a,b] \text{ and } x_2 \in [a,b]$$

and x_1 and x_2 themselves are forming the interval of numbers $[x_1, x_2]$. The probability distribution of a continuous random variable X then assigns a probability to each of these possible interval of numbers $[x_1, x_2]$. The probability that random variable X falls in any particular interval $[x_1, x_2]$ is a number between 0 and 1, and the probability of the interval $[a,b]$, containing all possible values, equals 1. That is, it is required that

$$0 \leqslant P(x_1 \leqslant X \leqslant x_2) \leqslant 1 \text{ and } P(a \leqslant X \leqslant b) = 1.$$

Definition 1. 6. 3 (Probability distribution of a continuous random variable). *A continuous random variable X takes all values in an interval of numbers $[a,b]$. The probability distribution of X describes the probabilities $P(x_1 \leqslant X \leqslant x_2)$ of all possible intervals of numbers $[x_1, x_2]$.*

The probabilities $P(x_1 \leqslant X \leqslant x_2)$ must possess two requirements:

(1) For every interval $[x_1, x_2]$, the probability $P(x_1 \leqslant X \leqslant x_2)$ is a number between 0 and 1.

(2) $P(a \leqslant X \leqslant b) = 1$.

The probability model for a continuous random variable assigns probabilities to intervals of outcomes rather than to individual outcomes. In fact, all continuous probability distributions assign probability 0 to every individual outcome.

The probability distribution of a continuous random variable is pictured by a density curve. A density curve is a smooth and continuous one having an area exactly 1 underneath which such curves representing the population distribution in section 1. 3. 3. In fact, the population distribution of a variable is, equivalently, the probability distribution for the value of that variable for a subject selected randomly from the population (see Fig. 1. 6. 1).

Example 1.6.2

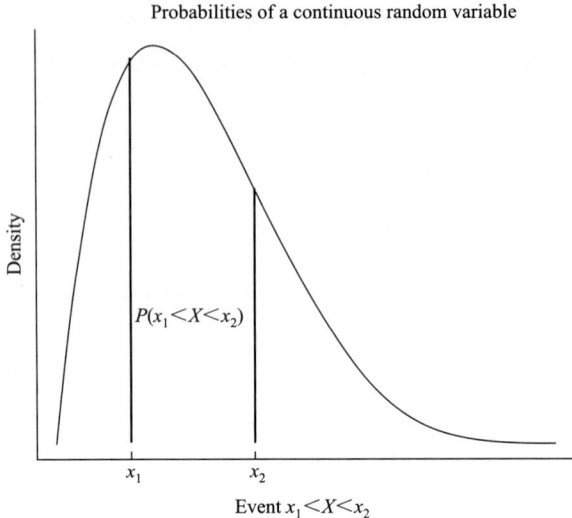

Fig. 1.6.1 The Probability Distribution of a Continuous Random Variable Assign Probabilities as Areas Under a Density Curve.

1.6.2 Mean and Standard Deviation of Random Variables

Like a population distribution, a probability distribution of a random variable has parameters describing its central tendency and variability. The mean describes central tendency and the standard deviation describes variability of the random variable X. The parameter values are the ones these measures would assume, in the long run, if we repeatedly observe the values the random variable X is having.

The mean and the standard deviation of the discrete random variable are defined in the following ways.

Definition 1.6.4 (Mean of a discrete random variable). Suppose that X is a discrete random variable whose probability distribution is as follows (see table 1.6.2).

Table 1.6.2 Probablity Distribution of the Discrete Radom Variable

Value of X	x_1	x_2	x_3	...	x_k
Probability	$P(x_1)$	$P(x_2)$	$P(x_3)$	...	$P(x_k)$

The mean of the discrete random variable X is

$$\mu = x_1 P(x_1) + x_2 P(x_2) + x_3 P(x_3) + \cdots + x_k P(x_k) = \sum_{i=1}^{k} x_i P(x_i).$$

The mean μ is also called the expected value of X and is denoted by $E(X)$.

Definition 1.6.5 (Standard deviation of a discrete random variable). Suppose that X is a discrete random variable whose probability distribution is as follows (see table 1.6.3).

Table 1.6.3 Probablity Distribution of the Discrete Radom Variable

Value of X	x_1	x_2	x_3	...	x_k
Probability	$P(x_1)$	$P(x_2)$	$P(x_3)$	...	$P(x_k)$

and that μ is the mean of X. The variance of the discrete random variable X is

$$\sigma^2 = (x_1-\mu)^2 P(x_1) + (x_2-\mu)^2 P(x_2) + \cdots + (x_k-\mu)^2 P(x_k) = \sum_{i=1}^{k}(x_i-\mu)^2 P(x_i).$$

The standard deviation σ of X is the square root of the variance.

Example 1.6.3 In an experiment on the behavior of young children, each subject is placed in an area with five toys. The response of interest is the number of toys that the child plays with. Past experiments with many subjects have shown that the probability distribution of the number X of toys played with is as follows (see table 1.6.4).

Table 1.6.4 Probablity Distribution of the Toys

Number of toys x_i	0	1	2	3	4	5
Probability $P(x_i)$	0.03	0.16	0.30	0.23	0.17	0.11

Calculate the mean μ and the standard deviation σ. The mean and standard deviation of a continuous random variable can be calculated, but to do so requires more advanced mathematics, and hence we do not consider them in this course.

1.6.3 Normal Distributions

A continuous random variable graphically described by a certain bell-shaped density curve is said to have the normal distribution. This distribution is the most important one in statistics. It is important partly because it approximates well the distributions of many variables. Histograms of sample data often tend to be approximately bell-shaped. In such cases, we say that the variable is approximately normally distributed. The main reason for its prominence, however, is that most inferential statistical methods make use of properties of the normal distribution even when the sample data are not bell-shaped.

A continuous random variable X following the normal distribution has two parameters: the mean μ and the standard deviation σ.

Definition 1.6.6 (Normal distribution). *A continuous random variable X is said to be normally distributed or to have a normal distribution if its density curve is a symmetric, bell-shaped curve, characterized by its mean μ and standard deviation σ. For each fixed number z, the probability concentrated within interval $[\mu-z\sigma, \mu+z\sigma]$ is the same for all normal distributions.* Particularly, the probabilities

$$P(\mu-\sigma < X < \mu+\sigma) = 0.683$$
$$P(\mu-2\sigma < X < \mu+2\sigma) = 0.954$$
$$P(\mu-3\sigma < X < \mu+3\sigma) = 0.997$$

A random variable X following normal distribution with a mean of μ and a standard deviation of σ is denoted by $X \sim N(\mu, \sigma)$.

There are other symmetric bell-shaped density curves that are not normal. The normal density curves are specified by a particular equation. The height of the density curve at any point x is given by the density function

$$f(x) = \frac{1}{\sigma \sqrt{2\pi}} e^{-\frac{1}{2}\left(\frac{x-\mu}{\sigma}\right)^2}.$$

We will not make direct use of this fact, although it is the basis of mathematical work with normal distribution. Note that the density function is completely determined by μ and σ (see Fig. 1.6.2).

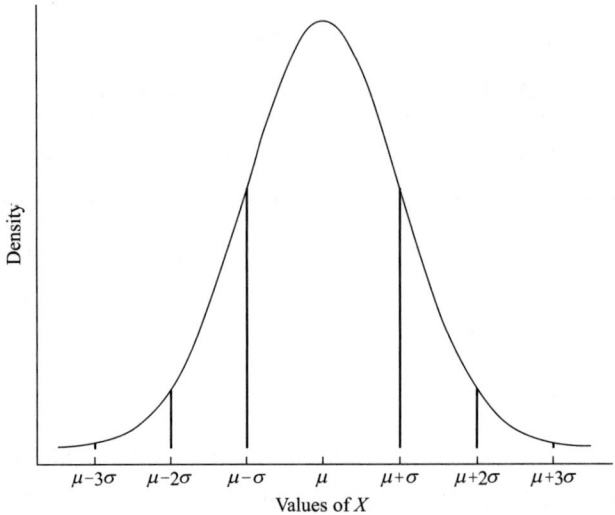

Fig. 1.6.2 Normal Distribution

Definition 1.6.7 (Standard normal distribution). *A continuous random variable Z is said to have a standard normal distribution if Z is normally distributed with mean $\mu = 0$ and standard deviation $\sigma = 1$, i.e., $Z \sim N(0,1)$.*

The standard normal table can be used to calculate probabilities concerning the random variable Z. The standard normal table gives area to the left of a specified value of z under density curve:

$P(Z \leqslant z) =$ Area under curve to the left of z.

For the probability of an interval $[a, b]$:

$P(a \leqslant Z \leqslant b) = [\text{Area to left of } b] - [\text{Area to left of } a]$.

The following properties can be observed from the symmetry of the standard normal distribution about 0:

(a) $P(Z \leqslant 0) = 0.5$

(b) $P(Z \leqslant -z) = 1 - P(Z \leqslant z) = P(Z \geqslant z)$

Example 1.6.4

(a) Calculate $P(-0.155 < Z < 1.60)$.

(b) Locate the value z that satisfies $P(Z > z) = 0.25$.

If the random variable X is distributed as $X \sim N(\mu, \sigma)$, then the standardized variable

$$Z = \frac{X - \mu}{\sigma}$$

has the standard normal distribution. That is, if X is distributed as $X \sim N(\mu, \sigma)$, then

$$P(a \leqslant X \leqslant b) = P\left(\frac{a - \mu}{\sigma} \leqslant Z \leqslant \frac{b - \mu}{\sigma}\right),$$

where Z has the standard normal distribution. This property of the normal distribution allows us to cast a probability problem concerning X into one concerning Z.

Example 1.6.5 The number of calories in a salad on the lunch menu is normally distributed with mean $\mu = 200$ and standard deviation $\sigma = 5$. Find the probability that the salad you select will contain:

(a) More than 208 calories.

(b) Between 190 and 200 calories.

1.7 Sampling Distributions and Sample Means

1.7.1 Sampling Distributions

Statistical inference draws conclusions about population on the basis of data. The data are summarized by statistics such as the sample mean and the sample standard deviation. When the data are produced by random sampling or randomized experimentation, a statistic is a random variable that obeys the laws of probability theory. The link between probability and data is formed by the sampling distributions of statistics. A sampling distribution shows how a statistic would vary in repeated data production.

Definition 1.7.1 (Sampling distribution). *A sampling distribution is a probability distribution that determines probabilities of the possible values of a sample statistic.*

Each statistic has a sampling distribution. A sampling distribution is simply a type of probability distribution. Unlike the distributions studied so far, a sampling distribution refers not to individual observations but to the values of statistics computed from those observations, in sample after sample.

Sampling distributions reflect the sampling variability that occurs in collecting data and using sample statistics to estimate parameters. A sampling distribution of statistics based on n observations is the probability distribution for that statistic resulting from repeatedly taking samples of size n, each time calculating the statistic value. The form of sampling distributions is often known theoretically. We can then make probabilistic statements about the value of statistics for one sample of some fixed size n.

1.7.2 Sampling Distributions of Sample Means

Because the sample mean is used so much, its sampling distribution merits special attention. First we consider the mean and standard deviation of the sample mean. Select a simple random sample of size n from population, and measure a variable X on each individual in the sample. The data consist of observations on n random variables $X_1, X_2, \ldots, X_n$. A single X_i is a measurement on one individual selected at random from the population and therefore X_i is a random variable with probability distribution equalling the population distribution of variable X. If the population is large relatively to the sample, we can consider $X_1, X_2, \ldots, X_n$ to be independent random variables each having the same probability distribution. This is our probability model for measurements on each individual in a simple random sample. The sample mean of a simple random sample of size n is

$$\overline{X} = \frac{X_1 + X_2 + \cdots + X_n}{n}.$$

Note that we now use notation $\overline{X}$ for the sample mean to emphasize that $\overline{X}$ is a random variable. Once the values of random variables $X_1, X_2, \ldots, X_n$ are observed, i.e., we have values $x_1, x_2, \ldots, x_n$ in our use, then we can actually compute the sample mean $\overline{X}$ in a usual way.

If the population variable X has a population mean μ, the μ is also mean of each observation X. Therefore, by the addition rule for means of random variables,

$$\mu_{\overline{X}} = E(\overline{X}) = E\left(\frac{X_1 + X_2 + \cdots + X_n}{n}\right)$$
$$= \frac{E(X_1 + X_2 + \cdots + X_n)}{n}$$
$$= \frac{E(X_1) + E(X_2) + \cdots + E(X_n)}{n}$$
$$= \frac{\mu_{X_1} + \mu_{X_2} + \cdots + \mu_{X_n}}{n}$$
$$= \frac{\mu + \mu + \cdots + \mu}{n}$$
$$= \mu$$

That is, the mean of $\overline{X}$ is the same as the population mean μ of the variable X. Furthermore, based on the addition rule for variances of independent random variables, $\overline{X}$ has the variance

$$\sigma_{\overline{X}}^2 = \frac{\sigma_{X_1}^2 + \sigma_{X_2}^2 + \cdots + \sigma_{X_n}^2}{n^2}$$

$$= \frac{\sigma^2 + \sigma^2 + \cdots + \sigma^2}{n^2}$$

$$= \frac{\sigma^2}{n}$$

and hence the standard deviation of $\overline{X}$ is

$$\sigma_{\overline{X}} = \frac{\sigma}{\sqrt{n}}.$$

The standard deviation of $\overline{X}$ is also called the standard error of $\overline{X}$.

Key Fact 1.7.1 (Mean and standard error of $\overline{X}$). For a random sample of size n from a population having mean μ and standard deviation σ, the sampling distribution of the sample mean $\overline{X}$ has mean μ, $\overline{X} = \mu$ and standard deviation, i.e., standard error $\sigma_{\overline{X}} = \frac{\sigma}{\sqrt{n}}$. (Moore & McCabe, 1998)

The mean and standard error of $\overline{X}$ shows that the sample mean $\overline{X}$ tends to be closer to the population mean μ for larger values of n, since the sampling distribution becomes less spread about μ. This agrees with our intuition that larger samples provide more precise estimates of population characteristics.

Example 1.7.1 Consider the Following Population Distribution of the Variable X (see table 1.7.1):

Table 1.7.1 Population Distribution of the Variable

Values of X	2	3	4
Relative frequencies of X	1/3	1/3	1/3

and let X_1 and X_2 be random variables following the probability distribution of population distribution of X.

(a) Verify that the population mean and population variance are $\mu = 3$, $\sigma^2 = 2/3$.

(b) Construct the probability distribution of the sample mean $\overline{X}$.

(c) Calculate the mean and standard deviation of the sample mean $\overline{X}$.

We have above described the center and spread of the probability distribution of a sample mean $\overline{X}$, but not its shape. The shape of the distribution $\overline{X}$ depends on the shape of the population distribution. The special case is when population distribution is normal.

Key Fact 1.7.2 (Distribution of sample mean). Suppose a variable X of a population is normally distributed with mean μ and standard deviation σ. Then, for samples of size n, the sample mean $\overline{X}$ is also normally distributed and has mean μ and standard deviation $\frac{\sigma}{\sqrt{n}}$. That is, if $X \sim N(\mu, \sigma)$, then $\overline{X} \sim N(\mu, \frac{\sigma}{\sqrt{n}})$. (Weiss, 1999)

Example 1.7.2 Consider a normal population with mean $\mu = 82$ and standard deviation $\sigma = 12$.

(a) If a random sample of size 64 is selected, what is the probability that the sample mean $\overline{X}$ will lie between 80.8 and 83.2?

(b) With a random sample of size 100, what is the probability that the sample mean $\overline{X}$ will lie between 80.8 and 83.2? (Johnson & Bhattacharyya, 1992)

When sampling from non-normal population, the distribution of $\overline{X}$ depends on what is the population distribution of the variable X. A surprising result, known as the central limit theorem states that when the sample size n is large, the probability distribution of the sample mean $\overline{X}$ is approximately normal, regardless of the shape of the population distribution.

Key Fact 1.7.3 (Central limit theorem). Whatever is the population distribution of the variable X, the probability distribution of the sample mean $\overline{X}$ is approximately normal when n is large. That is, when n is large, then $\overline{X}$ approximately $N\left(\mu, \frac{\sigma}{\sqrt{n}}\right)$ (Johnson & Bhattacharyya, 1992).

In practice, the normal approximation for $\overline{X}$ is usually adequate when n is greater than 30. The central limit theorem allows us to use normal probability calculations to answer questions about sample means from many observations even when the population distribution is not normal (see Fig. 1.7.1).

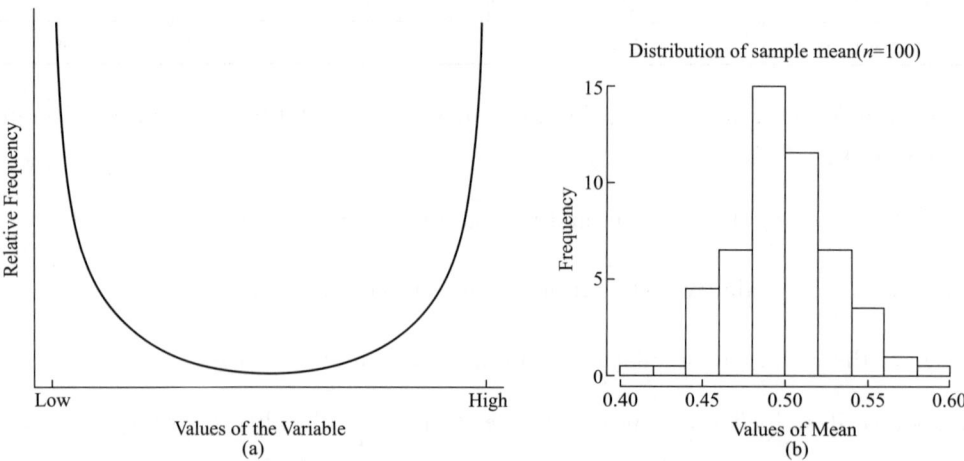

Fig. 1.7.1 U-shaped and Sample Mean Frequency Distributions with $n = 100$

1.8 Estimation

In this section we consider how to use sample data to estimate unknown population parameters. Statistical inference uses sample data to form two types of estimators of parameters. A point estimate consists of a single number, calculated from the data, which is the best single guess for the unknown parameter. An interval estimate consists of a range of numbers around the point estimate, within which the parameter is believed to fall.

1.8.1 Point Estimation

The object of point estimation is to calculate, from the sample data, a single number that is likely to be close to the unknown value of the population parameter. The available information is assumed to be in the form of a random sample $X_1, X_2, \ldots, X_n$ of size n taken from the population. The object is to formulate a statistic so that its value computed from the sample data would reflect the value of the population parameter as closely as possible.

Definition 1.8.1 (Point estimation). *A point estimator of an unknown population parameter is a statistic that estimates the value of that parameter. A point estimate of a parameter is the value of the statistic that is used to estimate the parameter.* (Agresti & Finlay, 1997 and Weiss, 1999)

For instance, to estimate a population mean μ, perhaps the most intuitive point estimator is the sample mean:

$$\overline{X} = \frac{X_1 + X_2 + \cdots + X_n}{n}$$

Once the observed values $x_1, x_2, \ldots, x_n$ of the random variables X_n are available, we can actually calculate the observed value of the sample mean $\overline{x}$, which is called a point estimate of μ.

A good point estimator of a parameter is the one with sampling distribution that is centered around parameters, and has a small standard error as possible. A point estimator is called unbiased if its sampling distribution centers around the parameter in the sense that the parameter is the mean of the distribution.

For example, the mean of the sampling distribution of the sample mean $\overline{x}$ equals μ. Thus, $\overline{x}$ is an unbiased estimator of the population mean μ.

A second preferable property for an estimator is a small standard error. An estimator whose standard error is smaller than those of other potential estimators is said to be efficient. An efficient estimator is desirable because, on the average, it falls closer than other estimators to the parameter. For example, it can be shown that under normal distributions, the sample mean is an efficient estimator, and hence has smaller standard error compared, e.g, to the sample median.

1.8.1.1 Point Estimators of the Population Mean and Standard Deviation

The sample mean $\overline{X}$ is the obvious point estimator of a population mean μ. In fact, $\overline{X}$ is unbiased, and it is relatively efficient for most population distributions. It is the point estimator, denoted by $\hat{\mu}$, used in this text:

$$\hat{\mu} = \overline{X} = \frac{X_1 + X_2 + \cdots + X_n}{n}$$

Moreover, the sample standard deviation s is the most popular point estimator of the population standard deviation s. That is,

$$\hat{\sigma} = s = \sqrt{\frac{\sum_{i=1}^{n}(x_i - \overline{x})^2}{n-1}}$$

1.8.2 Confidence Interval

For point estimation, a single number lies in the forefront even though a standard error is attached. Instead, it is often more desirable to produce an interval of values that is likely to contain the true value of the unknown parameter.

A confidence interval estimator of a parameter consists of an interval of numbers obtained from a point estimator of the parameter together with a percentage that specifies how confident we are that the parameter lies in the interval. The confidence percentage is called the confidence level.

Definition 1.8.2 (Confidence interval). *A confidence interval for a parameter is a range of numbers within which the parameter is believed to fall. The probability that the confidence interval contains the parameter is called the confidence coefficient. This is a chosen number close to 1, such as 0.95 or 0.99.* (Agresti & Finlay, 1997)

1.8.2.1 Confidence Interval for μ When σ Known

We first confine our attention to the construction of a confidence interval for a population mean μ assuming that the population variable X is normally distributed and its standard deviation is known.

Recall the Key Fact 1.7.1 that when the population is normally distributed, the distribution of $\overline{X}$ is also normal, i.e., $\overline{X} \sim N\left(\mu, \frac{\sigma}{\sqrt{n}}\right)$. The normal table shows that the probability is 0.95 that a normal random variable will lie within 1.96 standard deviations from its mean. For $\overline{X}$, we then have

$$P(\mu - 1.96 \frac{\sigma}{\sqrt{n}} < \overline{X} < \mu + 1.96 \frac{\sigma}{\sqrt{n}}) = 0.95.$$

Now the relation

$$\mu - 1.96 \frac{\sigma}{\sqrt{n}} < \overline{X} \text{ equals } \mu < \overline{X} + 1.96 \frac{\sigma}{\sqrt{n}}$$

and

$$\overline{X} < \mu + 1.96 \frac{\sigma}{\sqrt{n}} \text{ equals } \overline{X} - 1.96 \frac{\sigma}{\sqrt{n}} < \mu.$$

Hence the probability statement

$$P\left(\mu - 1.96 \frac{\sigma}{\sqrt{n}} < \overline{X} < \mu + 1.96 \frac{\sigma}{\sqrt{n}}\right) = 0.95$$

can be also expressed as

$$P\left(\overline{X} - 1.96 \frac{\sigma}{\sqrt{n}} < \mu < \overline{X} + 1.96 \frac{\sigma}{\sqrt{n}}\right) = 0.95.$$

The second form tells us that the random interval

$$\left(\overline{X} - 1.96 \frac{\sigma}{\sqrt{n}}, \overline{X} + 1.96 \frac{\sigma}{\sqrt{n}}\right)$$

will include the unknown parameter with a probability 0.95. Because σ is assumed to be known, both the upper and lower end points can be computed as soon as the sample data are available. Thus, we say that the interval

$$\left(\overline{X} - 1.96 \frac{\sigma}{\sqrt{n}}, \overline{X} + 1.96 \frac{\sigma}{\sqrt{n}}\right)$$

is a 95% confidence interval for μ when population variable X is normally distributed and σ is known.

We do not always need consider confidence intervals to the choice of a 95% level of confidence. We may wish to specify a different level of probability. We denote this probability by $1-\alpha$ and speak of a $100(1-\alpha)\%$ confidence level. The only change is to replace 1.96 with $z_{\alpha/2}$, where $z_{\alpha/2}$ is a number that $P(-z_{\alpha/2} < Z < z_{\alpha/2}) = 1-\alpha$ when $Z \sim N(0,1)$.

Key Fact 1.8.1 When population variable X is normally distributed and σ is known, a $100(1-\alpha)\%$ confidence interval for μ is given by

$$\left(\overline{X} - z_{\alpha/2} \frac{\sigma}{\sqrt{n}}, \overline{X} + z_{\alpha/2} \frac{\sigma}{\sqrt{n}}\right).$$

Example 1.8.1 Given a random sample of 25 observations from a normal population for which μ is unknown and $\sigma = 8$, the sample mean is calculated to be $\overline{X} = 42.7$. Construct 95% and 99% confidence intervals for μ. (Johnson & Bhattacharyya, 1992)

1.8.2.2 Large Sample Confidence Interval for μ

We consider now more realistic situation for which the population standard deviation is unknown. We require the sample size n to be large, and hence the central limit theorem tells us that probability statement

$$P\left(\overline{X} - z_{\alpha/2}\frac{\sigma}{\sqrt{n}} < \mu < \overline{X} + z_{\alpha/2}\frac{\sigma}{\sqrt{n}}\right) = 1 - \alpha$$

approximately holds, whatever is the underlying population distribution. Also, because n is large, replacing $\frac{\sigma}{\sqrt{n}}$ with its estimator $\frac{s}{\sqrt{n}}$ does not appreciably affect the above probability statement. Hence we have the following Key Fact.

Key Fact 1.8.2 When n is large and σ is unknown, a $100(1-\alpha)\%$ confidence interval for μ is given by

$$\left(\overline{X} - z_{\alpha/2}\frac{s}{\sqrt{n}}, \overline{X} + z_{\alpha/2}\frac{s}{\sqrt{n}}\right),$$

where s is the sample standard deviation.

1.8.2.3 Small Sample Confidence Interval for μ

When population variable X is normally distributed with mean μ and standard deviation σ, then the standardized variable

$$Z = \frac{\overline{X} - \mu_0}{\sigma/\sqrt{n}}$$

has the standard normal distribution $Z \sim N(0,1)$. However, if we consider the ratio

$$t = \frac{\overline{X} - \mu_0}{s/\sqrt{n}},$$

then the random variable t has the student's t distribution with $n-1$ degrees of freedom.

Let $t_{\alpha/2}$ be a such number that $P(-t_{\alpha/2} < t < t_{\alpha/2}) = 1 - \alpha$ when t has the student's t distribution with $n-1$ degrees of freedom. Hence we have the following equivalent probability statements:

$$P\left(\overline{X} - t_{\alpha/2}\frac{s}{\sqrt{n}} < \mu < \overline{X} + t_{\alpha/2}\frac{s}{\sqrt{n}}\right) = 1 - \alpha$$

The last expression gives us the following small sample confidence interval for μ.

Key Fact 1.8.3 When population variable X is normally distributed and standard deviation is unknown, a $100(1-\alpha)\%$ confidence interval for μ is given by

$$\left(\overline{X}-t_{\alpha/2}\frac{s}{\sqrt{n}}, \overline{X}+t_{\alpha/2}\frac{s}{\sqrt{n}}\right)$$

where $t_{\alpha/2}$ is the upper $\alpha/2$ point of the student's t distribution with $n-1$ degrees of freedom.

Example 1.8.2. Consider a random sample from a normal population for which μ and σ are unknown:

$$10, \quad 7, \quad 15, \quad 9, \quad 10, \quad 14, \quad 9, \quad 9, \quad 12, \quad 7.$$

Construct the 95% and 99% confidence intervals for μ.

Example 1.8.3. Suppose the finishing time in a bike race follows the normal distribution with μ and σ unknown. Consider that seven participants in the bike race had the following finishing time in minutes:

$$28, \quad 22, \quad 26, \quad 29, \quad 21, \quad 23, \quad 24.$$

Construct a 90% confidence interval for μ.

Analyze→Descriptive Statistics→Explore (see table 1.8.1)

Table 1.8.1   The 90% Confidence Interval for μ of the Finishing Time in the Bike Race

	Mean	Bound	Statistic	Std. Error
Bike 7			24.7143	1.14879
	90% Confidence Interval for Mean	Lower Bound	22.4820	—
		Upper Bound	26.9466	—

1.9 Hypothesis Testing

1.9.1 Hypotheses

A common aim in many studies is to check whether the data agree with certain predictions. These predictions are hypotheses about variables measured in the study.

Definition 1.9.1 (Hypothesis). *A hypothesis is a statement about some characteristic of a variable or a collection of variables.* (Agresti & Finlay, 1997)

Hypotheses arise from the theory that drives the research. When a hypothesis relates to characteristics of a population, such as population parameters, one can use statistical methods with sample data to test its validity.

A significance test is a way of statistically testing a hypothesis by comparing the data to values predicted by the hypothesis. Data that fall far from the predicted values provide evidence against the hypothesis. All significance tests have five elements: assumptions, hypotheses, test statistic, p-value, and conclusion.

All significance tests require certain assumptions for the tests to be valid. These assumptions refer, e. g., to the type of data, the form of the population distribution, method of sampling, and sample size.

A significance test considers two hypotheses about the value of a population parameter: the null hypothesis and the alternative hypothesis.

Definition 1.9.2 (Null and alternative hypotheses). *The null hypothesis H_0 is the hypothesis that is directly tested. This is usually a statement that the parameter has value corresponding to, in some sense, no effect. The alternative hypothesis H_1 (or Ha) is a hypothesis that contradicts the null hypothesis. This hypothesis states that the parameter falls in some alternative set of values to what null hypothesis specifies* (Agresti & Finlay, 1997).

A significance test analyzes the strength of sample evidence against the null hypothesis. The test is conducted to investigate whether the data contradict the null hypothesis, hence suggesting that the alternative hypothesis is true. The alternative hypothesis is judged acceptable if the sample data are inconsistent with the null hypothesis. That is, the alternative hypothesis is supported if the null hypothesis appears to be incorrect. The hypotheses are formulated before collecting or analyzing the data.

The test statistics is a statistic calculated from the sample data to test the null hypothesis. This statistic typically involves a point estimate of the parameter to which the hypotheses refer.

Using the sampling distribution of the test statistic, we calculate the probability that values of the statistic like one observed would occur if the null hypothesis were true. This provides a measure of how unusual the observed test statistic value is compared to what H_0 predicts. That is, we consider the set of possible test statistic values that provide at least as much evidence against the null hypothesis as the observed test statistic. This set is formed with reference to the alternative hypothesis: the values providing stronger evidence against the null hypothesis are those providing stronger evidence in favor of the alternative hypothesis. The p-value is the probability, if H_0 were true, that the test statistic would fall in this collection of values.

Definition 1.9.3 (p-value). *The p-value is the probability, when H_0 is true, of a test statistic value at least as contradictory to H_0 as the value actually observed. The smaller the p-value, the more strongly the data contradict H_0* (Agresti & Finlay, 1997).

The p-value summarizes the evidence in the data about the null hypothesis. A moderate to large p-value means that the data are consistent with H_0. For example, a p-value such as 0.3 or 0.8 indicates that the observed data would not be unusual if H_0 were true. But a p-value such as 0.001 means that such data would be very unlikely, if H_0 were true. This provides strong evidence against H_0.

The p-value is the primary reported result of a significance test. An observer of the test results can then judge the extent of the evidence against H_0. Sometimes it is necessary to make a formal decision about validity of H_0. If p-value is sufficiently small, one rejects H_0 and accepts H_1. However, the conclusion should always include an interpretation of what the p-value or decision about H_0 tells us about the original question motivating the test. Most studies require very small p-value, such as $p \leqslant 0.05$, before concluding that the data sufficiently contradict H_0 to reject it. In such cases, results are said to be significant at the 0.05 level. This means that if the null hypothesis were true, the chance of getting such extreme results in the sample data would be no greater than 5%.

1.9.2 Significance Test for a Population Mean μ

Correspondingly to the confidence intervals for μ, we now present three different significance tests about the population mean μ. Hypotheses are all equal in these tests, but the used test statistic varies depend on the assumptions we made.

1.9.2.1 Significance Test for μ When σ Is Known

◆ Assumptions

Let the population variable X be normally distributed with the mean μ unknown and standard deviation σ known.

◆ Hypotheses

The null hypothesis is considered to have form

$$H_0 : \mu = \mu_0$$

where μ_0 is some particular number. In other words, the hypothesized value of μ in H_0 is a single value. The alternative hypothesis refers to alternative parameter values from the one in the null hypothesis. The most common form of alternative hypothesis is

$$H_1 : \mu \neq \mu_0.$$

This alternative hypothesis is two-sided, since it includes values falling both below and above the value μ_0 listed in H_0.

◆ Test statistic

The sample mean $\overline{X}$ estimates the population mean μ. If $H_0 : \mu = \mu_0$ is true, then the center of the sampling distribution of $\overline{X}$ should be the number μ_0. The evidence about H_0 is the distance of the sample value $\overline{X}$ from the null hypothesis value μ_0, relative to the standard error. An observed value $\overline{X}$ of $\overline{X}$ falling far out in the tail of this sampling distribution of $\overline{X}$ casts doubt on the validity of H_0, because it would be unlikely to observe value $\overline{X}$ of $\overline{X}$ very far from μ_0 if truly $\mu = \mu_0$.

The test statistic is the Z-statistic

$$Z = \frac{\overline{X} - \mu_0}{\sigma/\sqrt{n}}.$$

When H_0 is true, the sampling distribution of Z-statistic is σ standard normal distribution, $Z \sim N(0,1)$. The farther the observed value $\overline{x}$ of $\overline{X}$ far from μ_0, the larger is the absolute value of the observed value z of Z-statistic. Hence, the larger the value of $|z|$, the stronger the evidence against H_0.

◆ p-value

We calculate the p-value under assumption that H_0 is true. That is, we give the benefit of the doubt to the null hypothesis, analyzing how likely the observed data would be if that hypothesis were true. The p-value is the probability that the Z-statistic is at least as large in absolute value as the observed value z of Z-statistic. This means that p is the probability of $\overline{X}$ having value at least far from μ_0 in either direction as the observed value $\overline{x}$ of $\overline{X}$. That is, let z be observed value of Z-statistic:

$$z = \frac{\overline{x} - \mu_0}{\sigma/\sqrt{n}}.$$

Then p-value is the probability

$$2 \cdot P(Z \geqslant |z|) = p,$$

where $Z \sim N(0,1)$.

◆ Conclusion

The study should report the p-value, so others can view the strength of evidence. The smaller p is, the stronger the evidence against H_0 and in favor of H_1. If p-value is small like 0.01 or smaller, we may conclude that the null hypothesis H_0 is strongly rejected in favor of H_1. If p-value is between $0.05 \leqslant p \leqslant 0.01$, we may conclude that the null hypothesis H_0 is rejected in favor of H_1. In other cases, i.e., $p > 0.05$, we may conclude that the null hypothesis H_0 is accepted.

Example 1.9.1 Given a random sample of 25 observations from a normal population for which μ is unknown and $\sigma = 8$, the sample mean is calculated to be $\overline{x} = 42.7$. Test the hypothesis $H_0 : \mu = \mu_0 = 35$ for μ against alternative two sided hypothesis $H_1 : \mu \neq \mu_0$.

1.9.2.2 Large Sample Significance Test for μ

Assumptions now are that the sample size n is large ($n \geqslant 50$), and σ is unknown. The hypotheses are similar as above:

$$H_0 : \mu = \mu_0 \text{ and } H_1 : \mu \neq \mu_0.$$

Test statistic in a large sample case is the following Z-statistic

$$Z = \frac{\overline{X} - \mu_0}{s/\sqrt{n}},$$

where s is the sample standard deviation. Because of the central limit theorem, the above Z-statistic is now following approximately the standard normal distribution if H_0 is true, see correspondence to the large sample confidence interval for μ. Hence the p-value is again the probability

$$2 \cdot P(Z \geqslant |z|) = p,$$

where Z approximately $N(0,1)$, and conclusions can be made similarly as previously.

1.9.2.3 Small Sample Significance Test for μ

In a small sample situation, we assume that population is normally distributed with mean μ and standard deviation σ is unknown. Again hypotheses are formulated as:

$$H_0 : \mu = \mu_0 \text{ and } H_1 : \mu \neq \mu_0.$$

Test statistic is now based on student's t distribution. The t-statistic

$$t = \frac{\overline{X} - \mu_0}{s/\sqrt{n}}$$

has the student's t distribution with $n-1$ degrees of freedom if H_0 is true. Let t^* be observed value of t-statistic. Then the p-value is the probability

$$2 \cdot P(t \geqslant |t^*|) = p,$$

Conclusions are again formed similarly as in previous cases.

Example 1.9.2 Consider a random sample from the normal population in which μ and σ are unknown:

$$10 \quad 7 \quad 15 \quad 9 \quad 10 \quad 14 \quad 9 \quad 9 \quad 12 \quad 7$$

Test the hypotheses $H_0 : \mu = \mu_0 = 7$ and $H_0 : \mu = \mu_0 = 10$ for μ against the alternative two-sided hypothesis $H_1 : \mu \neq \mu_0$.

Example 1.9.3 Suppose the finishing time in a bike race follows the normal distribution with μ and σ unknown. Consider that seven participants in the bike race had the following finishing time in minutes:

$$28 \quad 22 \quad 26 \quad 29 \quad 21 \quad 23 \quad 24$$

Test the hypothesis $H_0 : \mu = \mu_0 = 28$ for μ against the alternative two-sided hypothesis $H_1 : \mu = \mu_0$.

Analyze→Compare Means→One-Sample T-test (see table 1.9.1)

Table 1.9.1 The T-test for $H_0 : \mu = \mu_0 = 28$ against $H_1 : \mu \neq \mu_0$

Bike 7	Test Value=28					
	t	df	Sig. (2-tailed)	Mean Difference	95% Confidence Interval of the Difference	
					Lower	Upper
	2.860	6	0.029	−3.28571	6.0967	0.4747

1.10 Summarization of Bivariate Data

So far we have discussed summary description and statistical inference of a single variable. But most statistical studies involve more than one variable. In this section we examine the relationship between two variables. The observed values of the two variables in question, bivariate data, may be qualitative or quantitative in nature. That is, both variables may be either qualitative or quantitative. Obviously it is also possible that one of the variables under study is qualitative and the other is quantitative. We examine all the possibilities.

1.10.1 Qualitative Variables

Bivariate qualitative data result from the observed values of the two qualitative variables. At section 1.3.1, in a case a single qualitative variable, the frequency distribution of the variable was presented by a frequency table. In a case two qualitative variables, the joint distribution of the variables can be summarized in the form of a two-way frequency table.

In a two-way frequency table, the classes (or categories) for one variable (called row variable) are marked along the left margin, those for the other (called column variable) along the upper margin, and the frequency counts were recorded in the cells. Summary of bivariate data by two-way frequency tables is called a cross-tabulation or cross-classification of observed values. In statistical terminology two-way frequency tables are also called as contingency tables.

The simplest frequency table is a 2×2 frequency table, where each variable has only two classes. Similarly, there may be 2×3 tables, 3×3 tables, etc., where the first number tells the amount of rows the table has and the second number the amount of columns.

Example 1.10.1 The blood types and genders of 40 persons are as follows.

(O,Male), (O,Female), (A,Female), (B,Male), (A,Female), (O,Female), (A,Male), (A,Male), (A,Female), (O,Male), (B,Male), (O,Male), (B,Female), (O,Male), (O,Male), (A,Female), (O,Male), (O,Male), (A,Female), (A,Female), (A,Male), (A,Male), (AB,Female), (A,Female), (B,Female), (A,Male), (A,Female), (O,Male), (O,Male), (A,Female), (O,Male), (O,Female), (A,Female), (A,Male), (A,Male), (O,Male), (A,Male), (O,Female), (O,Female), (AB,Male).

The summarizing data in a two-way frequency table by using Excel:

Analyze→Descriptive Statistics→Crosstabs,

Analyze→Custom Tables→Tables of Frequencies (see table 1.10.1)

Table 1.10.1 Frequency Distribution of Blood Types and Genders

Blood type	Male	Female
O	11	5
A	8	10
B	2	2
AB	1	1

Let one qualitative variable have i classes and the other j classes. Then the joint distribution of the two variables can be summarized by $i \times j$ frequency table. If the sample size is n and the ijth cell has a frequency f_{ij}, then the relative frequency of the ijth cell is

$$\frac{\text{Frequency in the } ij \text{th cell}}{\text{total number of observation}} = \frac{f_{ij}}{n}.$$

Percentages are again just relative frequencies multiplied by 100.

From a two-way frequency table, we can calculate row and column (marginal) totals. For the ith row, the row total f_i is

$$f_i = f_{i1} + f_{i2} + f_{i3} + \ldots + f_{ij},$$

and similarly for the jth column, the column total f_j is

$$f_j = f_{1j} + f_{2j} + f_{3j} + \ldots + f_{ij}.$$

Both row and column totals have the obvious property:

$$n = \sum_{k=1}^{i} f_k = \sum_{k=1}^{j} f_k.$$

Based on row and column totals, we can calculate the relative frequencies by rows and relative frequencies by columns. For the ijth cell, the relative frequency by row i is relative frequency by row of an ijth cell $= \dfrac{f_{ij}}{f_i}$, and the relative frequency by column j is relative frequency by column of an ijth cell $= \dfrac{f_{ij}}{f_j}$.

The relative frequencies by row i give us the conditional distribution of the column variable for the value i of the row variable. That is, the relative frequencies by row i give us the answer to the question, which is the distribution of the column variable once the observed value of row variable is i. Similarly, the relative frequency by column j gives us the conditional distribution of the row variable for the value j of the column variable.

Also we can define the relative row totals by total and relative column totals, which are for the ith row total and the jth column total $\frac{f_i}{n}$, $\frac{f_j}{n}$ respectively.

Example 1.10.2 Let's continue the blood type and gender example (see table 1.10.2):

Table 1.10.2 Column Percentages of Blood Types and Genders

Blood Type		Gender		Total
		Male	Female	
O	Count	11	5	16
	% within Gender	50.0%	27.8%	40.0%
A	Count	8	10	18
	% within Gender	36.4%	55.6%	45.0%
B	Count	2	2	4
	% within Gender	9.1%	11.1%	10.0%
AB	Count	1	1	2
	% within Gender	4.5%	5.6%	5.0%
Total	Count	22	18	40
	% within Gender	100.0%	100.0%	100.0%

In the above example, we calculated the row and column percentages, i.e., conditional distributions of the column variable for one specific value of the row variable and conditional distributions of the row variable for one specific value of the column variable, respectively. The question is now, why did we calculate all those conditional distributions and which conditional distributions should we use?

The conditional distributions are the ways of finding out whether there is association between the row and column variables or not. If the row percentages are clearly different in each row, then the conditional distributions of the column variable are varying in each row and we can interpret that there is association between variables, i.e., value of the row variable affects the value of the column variable. Again completely similarly, if the column percentages are clearly different in each column, then the conditional distributions of the row variable are varying in each column and we can interpret that there is association between variables, i.e., value of the column variable affects the value of the row variable.

The direction of association depends on the shapes of conditional distributions. If row percentages (or the column percentages) are pretty similar from row to row (or from column to column), then there is no association between variables and we say that the variables are independent.

Whether to use the row and column percentages for the inference of possible association depends on which the variable is the response variable and which is the explanatory variable.

Let's first give more general definition for the response variable and explanatory variable.

Definition 1.10.1 (Response and explanatory variable). *A response variable measures an outcome of a study. An explanatory variable attempts to explain the observed outcomes.*

In many cases it is not even possible to identify which a variable is the response variable and which is the explanatory variable. In that case we can use either row or column percentage to find out whether there is association between variables or not. If we now find out that there is association between variables, we cannot say that one variable is causing changes in other variables, i.e., association does not imply causation.

On the other hand, if we can identify that the row variable is the response variable and the column variable is the explanatory variable, then conditional distributions of the row variable for the different categories of the column variable should be compared in order to find out whether there is association and causation between the variables. Similarly, if we can identify that the column variable is the response variable and the row variable is the explanatory variable, then conditional distributions of the column variable should be compared. But especially in case of two qualitative variables, we have to be very careful about whether the association does really mean that there is also causation between variables.

The qualitative bivariate data are best presented graphically either by the clustered or stacked bar graphs. Also a pie chart divided for different categories of one variable (called plotted pie chart) can be informative.

Example 1.10.3 Continue the blood type and the gender example (see Fig. 1.10.1, Fig. 1.10.2):

Graphs→Interactive→Bar,

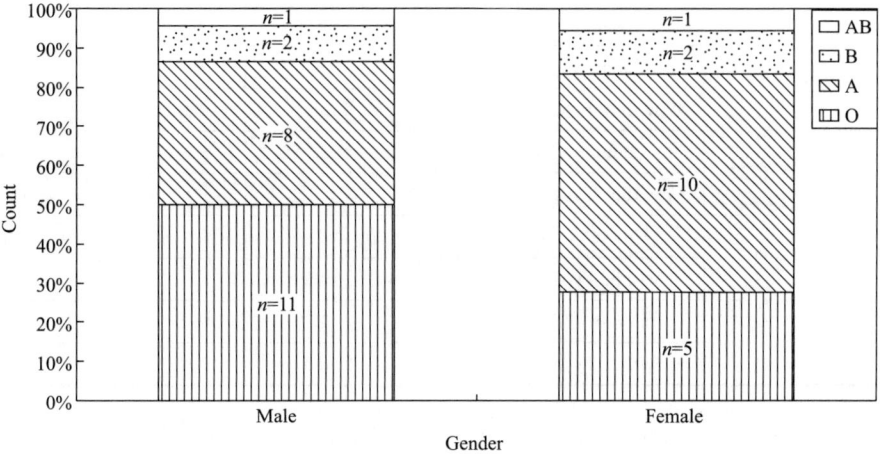

Fig. 1.10.1 Stacked Bar Graph for the Blood Type and Gender

Graphs→Interactive→Pie→Plotted

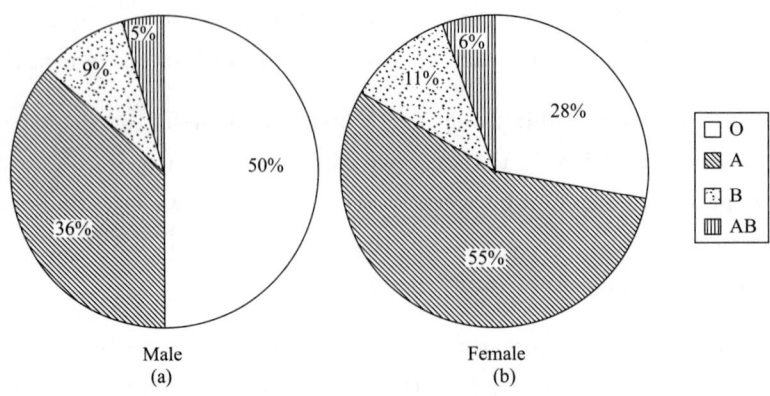

Fig. 1.10.2 Plotted Pie Chart for the Blood Type and Gender

1.10.2 Qualitative Variables and Quantitative Variables

In a case of one variable being qualitative and the other quantitative, we can still use a two-way frequency table to find out whether there is association between the variables or not. This time, though, the quantitative variable needs to be first grouped into classes in a way it was shown in section 2.3.2 and then the joint distribution of the variables can be presented in a two-way frequency table. Inference is then based on the conditional distributions calculated from the two-way frequency table. Especially if it is clear that the response variable is the qualitative one and the explanatory variable is the quantitative one, then the two-way frequency table is a tool to find out whether there is association between the variables.

Example 1.10.4 Prices and types of hotdogs (see Table 1.10.3 and Fig. 1.10.3):

Table 1.10.3 Column Percentages of Prices and Types of Hotdogs

Title			Type			Total
			beef	meat	poultry	
Prices	≤0.08	Count	1	3	16	20
		% within Type	5.0%	17.6%	94.1%	37.0%
	0.081~0.14	Count	10	12	1	23
		% within Type	50.0%	70.6%	5.9%	42.6%
	≥0.141	Count	9	2		11
		% within Type	45.0%	11.8%		20.4%
Total		Count	20	17	17	54
		% within Type	100.0%	100.0%	100.0%	100.0%

Usually, in case of one variable being qualitative and the other quantitative, we are interested in how the quantitative variable is distributed in different classes of the qualitative variable, i.e., what is the conditional distribution of the quantitative variable for one specific value of the qualitative variable and whether are these conditional distributions varying in each

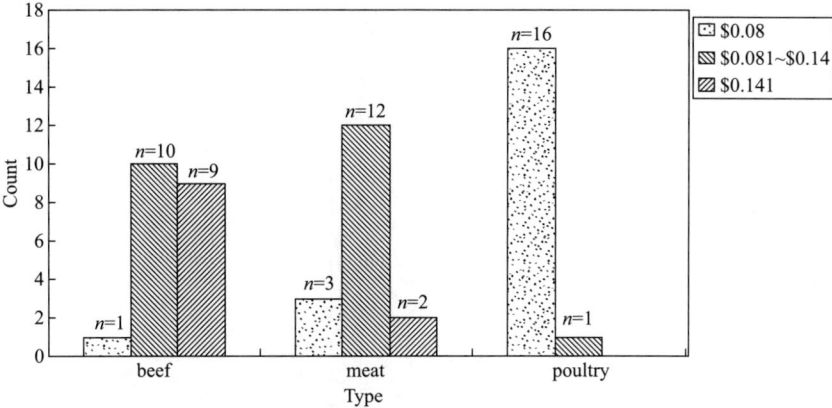

Fig. 1.10.3 Clustered Bar Graph for Prices and Types of Hotdogs

class of the qualitative variable? By analyzing conditional distributions in this way, we assume that the quantitative variable is the response variable and qualitative the explanatory variable.

Example 1.10.5 198 Newborns were weighted and the information about their genders and weights were collected (see table 1.10.4):

Table 1.10.4 Weight Data Distrbution

Gender	Weight/g
boy	4870
girl	3650
girl	3650
girl	3650
girl	2650
girl	3100
boy	3480
boy	4870
boy	4870
...	...

Histograms are showing the conditional distributions of the weight (see Fig. 1.10.4, Fig. 1.10.5):

Data→Split File→ (Compare groups) and then Graphs→Histogram

When the response variable is quantitative and the explanatory variable is qualitative, the comparison of the conditional distributions of the quantitative variable must be based on some specific measures that characterize the conditional distributions. We know from previous sections that measures of center and measures of variation can be used to characterize the distribution of the variable in question. Similarly, we can characterize the conditional distributions by calculating conditional measures of center and conditional measures of variation from the observed values of the response variable in case that the explanatory variable has a

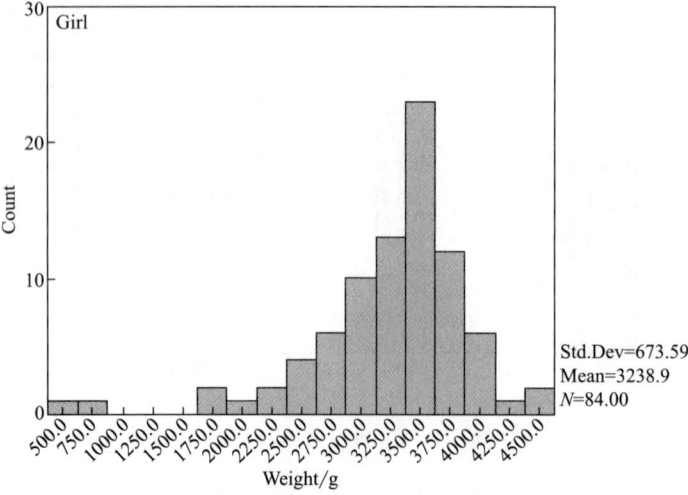

Fig. 1.10.4 Distributions of Birthweights in Girls

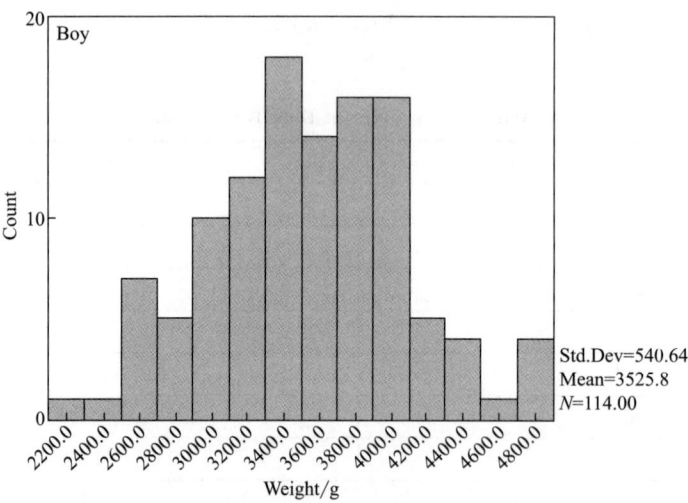

Fig. 1.10.5 Distributions of Birthweights in Boys

specific value. More specifically, these conditional measures of center are called as conditional sample means and conditional sample medians and similarly, conditional measures of variation can be called as conditional sample range, conditional sample interquartile range and conditional sample deviation.

These conditional measures of center and variation can be now used to find out whether there is association (and causation) between variables or not. For example, if the values of conditional means of the quantitative variable differ clearly in each class of the qualitative variable, then we can interpret that there is association between the variables. When the conditional distributions are symmetric, then conditional means and conditional deviations should be calculated and compared, and when the conditional distributions are skewed, conditional medians and conditional interquartiles should be used.

Example 1.10.6. Calculating conditional means and conditional standard deviations for the weight of 198 newborns on condition of genders in Excel (see table 1.10.5):

Analyze→Compare Means→Means

Table 1.10.5 Conditional Means and Standard Deviations for the Weight of Newborns   g

The gender of a child	Mean	N	Std.
girl	3238.93	84	673.591
boy	3525.78	114	540.638
Total	3404.09	198	615.648

Calculating other measures of center and variation for the weight of 198 newborns on condition of genders in Excel (see table 1.10.6):

Analyze→Descriptive Statistics→Explore

Table 1.10.6 Other Measures of Center and Variation for the Weight of Newborns   g

Title	Girl		Boy	
	Statistic	Std.	Statistic	Std.
Mean	3238.93	73.495	3525.78	50.635
95% Confidence Interval for Mean Lower Bound	3092.75		3425.46	
95% Confidence Interval for Mean Upper Bound	3385.11		3626.10	
5% Trimmed Mean	3289.74		3517.86	
Median	3400.00		3500.00	
Variance	453725.3		292289.1	
Std. Deviation	673.591		540.638	
Minimum	510		2270	
Maximum	4550		4870	
Range	4040		2600	
Interquartile Range	572.50		735.00	
Skewness	−1.565	0.263	0.134	0.226
Kurtosis	4.155	0.520	−0.064	0.449

Graphically, the best way to illustrate the conditional distributions of the quantitative variable is to draw boxplots from each conditional distribution. Also the error bars are the nice way to describe graphically whether the conditional means actually differ from each other.

Example 1.10.7 Constructing boxplots for the weight of 198 newborns on condition of genders in Excel:

Graphs→Interactive→Boxplot

Constructing error bars for the weight of 198 newborns on condition of genders in Excel:

Graphs→Interactive→Error Bar (see Fig. 1.10.6, Fig. 1.10.7)

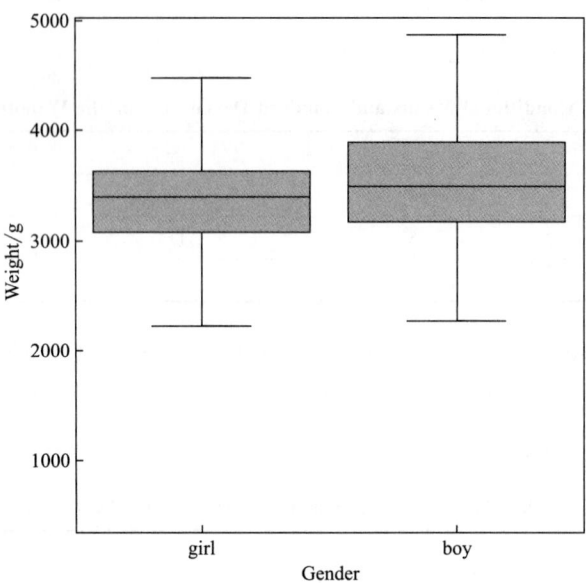

Fig. 1.10.6 Boxplots for the Weight of Newborns

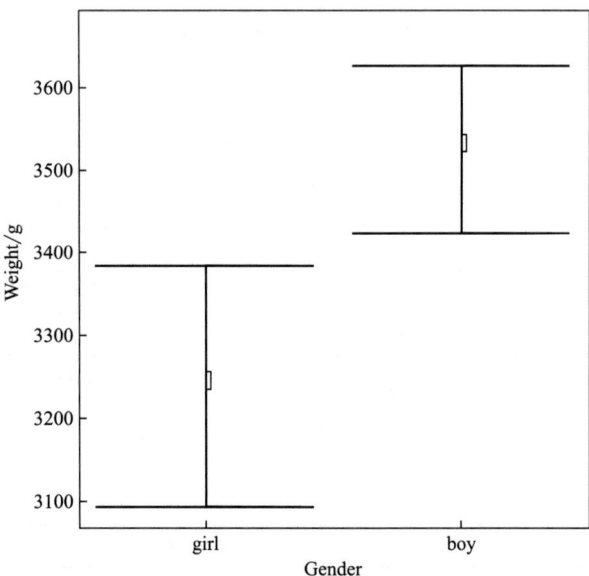

Fig. 1.10.7 Error Bars for the Weight of Newborns

1.10.3 Quantitative Variables

When both variables are quantitative, the methods presented above can obviously be applied for detection of possible association of the variables. Both variables can be first grouped and then joint distribution can be presented by a two-way frequency table. Also it is possible to group just one of the variables and then compare conditional measures of center and variation of the other variable in order to find out possible association.

But when both variables are quantitative, the best way, graphically, to see the relationship of the variables is to construct a scatterplot. The scatterplot gives visual information of the amount and direction of association, or correlation, as it is termed for quantitative variables. Construction of scatterplots and calculation of correlation coefficients are studied more carefully in the next section.

1.11 Scatterplot and Correlation Coefficient

1.11.1 Scatterplot

The most effective way to display the relation between two quantitative variables is a scatterplot. A scatterplot shows the relationship between two quantitative variables measured on the same individuals. The values of one variable appear on the horizontal axis, and the values of the other variable appear on the vertical axis. Each individual in the data appears as the point in the plot fixed by the values of both variables for that individual. Always plot the explanatory variable, if there is one, on the horizontal axis (the x-axis) of a scatterplot. As a reminder, we usually call the explanatory variable x and the response variable y. If there is no explanatory-response distinction, either variable can go on the horizontal axis.

Example 1.11.1 The height and weight of 10 persons are as follows (see table 1.11.1).

Table 1.11.1 The height and Weight of 10 Persons

Height/cm	Weight/kg
158	48
162	57
163	57
170	60
154	45
167	55
177	62
170	65
179	70
179	68

Scatterplot in Excel:

Graphs→Interactive→Scatterplot (see Fig. 1.11.1)

To interpret a scatterplot, first look for an overall pattern. This pattern should reveal the direction, form and strength of the relationship between the two variables.

Two variables are positively associated when above-average values of one tend to accompany

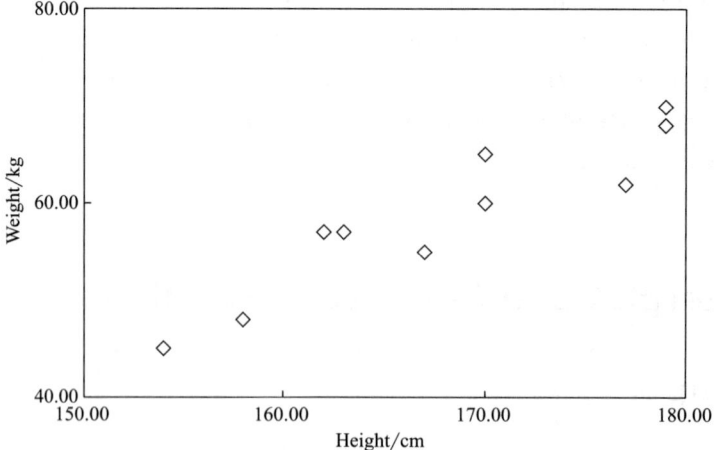

Fig. 1.11.1 Scatterplot of the Height and Weight

above-average values of the other and below-average values tend to occur together. Two variables are negatively associated when above-average values of one accompany below-average values of the other, and vice versa.

The important form of the relationships between variables are linear relationships, where the points in the plot show a straight-line pattern. Curved relationships and clusters are other forms to watch for.

The strength of the relationship is determined by how close the points in the scatterplot lie to a simple form such a line.

1.11.2 Correlation Coefficient

The scatterplot provides a visual impression of the nature of the relation between the x and y values in a bivariate data set. In a great many cases the points appear to band around the straight line. Our visual impression of the closeness of the scatter to a linear relation can be quantified by calculating a numerical measure, called the sample correlation coefficient.

Definition 1.11.1 (Correlation coefficient). *The sample correlation coefficient, denoted by r (or in some cases rxy), is a measure of the strength of the linear relation between the x and y variables.*

$$r = \frac{\sum_{i=1}^{n}(x_i - \overline{x})(y_i - \overline{y})}{\sqrt{\sum_{i=1}^{n}(x_i - \overline{x})^2}\sqrt{\sum_{i=1}^{n}(y_i - \overline{y})^2}}$$

$$= \frac{\sum_{i=1}^{n}x_i y_i - \overline{xy}}{\sqrt{\sum_{i=1}^{n}x_i^2 - n\overline{x}^2}\sqrt{\sum_{i=1}^{n}y_i^2 - n\overline{y}^2}}$$

$$= \frac{\frac{1}{n-1}\sum_{i=1}^{n}(x_i - \bar{x})(y_i - \bar{y})}{s_x s_y}$$

$$= \frac{S_{xy}}{\sqrt{S_{xx}}\sqrt{S_{yy}}}$$

The quantities S_{xx} and S_{yy} are the sums of squared deviations of the x observed values and the y observed values, respectively. S_{xy} is the sum of cross products of the x deviations with the y deviations.

Example 1.11.2 to be continued (see table 1.11.2).

Table 1.11.2 Component of the Correlation Coefficient Calculation

Height/cm	Weight/kg	$(x_i - \bar{x})$/kg	$(x_i - \bar{x})^2$/kg²	$(y_i - \bar{y})$/kg	$(y_i - \bar{y})^2$/kg²	$(x_i - \bar{x})(y_i - \bar{y})$/kg²
158	48	−9.9	98.01	−10.7	114.49	105.93
162	57	−5.9	34.81	−1.7	2.89	10.03
163	57	−4.9	24.01	−1.7	2.89	8.33
170	60	2.1	4.41	1.3	1.69	2.73
154	45	−13.9	193.21	−13.7	187.69	190.43
167	55	−0.9	0.81	−3.7	13.69	3.33
177	62	9.1	82.81	3.3	10.89	30.03
170	65	2.1	4.41	6.3	39.69	13.23
179	70	11.1	123.21	11.3	127.69	125.43
179	68	11.1	123.21	9.3	86.49	103.23
Total			688.9	—	588.1	592.7

This gives us the correlation coefficient as

$$r = \frac{592.7}{\sqrt{688.9}\sqrt{588.1}} = 0.9311749$$

Correlation coefficient in Excel (see Table 1.11.3, Fig. 1.11.2):

Analyze→Correlate→Bivariate

Table 1.11.3 Correlation Coefficient Between Height and Weight

Title		Height	Weight
Height/cm	Pearson Correlation	1	0.931
	N	10	10
Weight/kg	Pearson Correlation	0.931	1
	N	10	10

Let us outline some important features of the correlation coefficient.

(1) Positive r indicates positive association between the variables, and negative r indicates

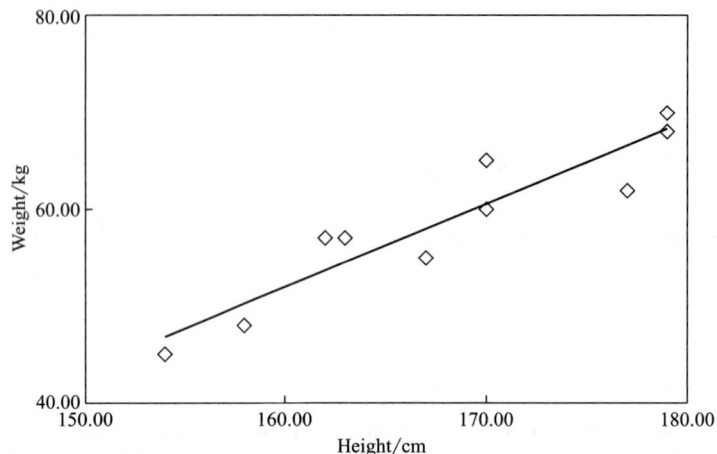

Fig. 1. 11. 2 Scatterplot with Linear Line

negative association.

(2) The correlation r always falls between -1 and 1. Values of r near 0 indicate a very weak linear relationship. The strength of the linear relationship increases as r moves away from 0 toward either -1 or 1.

Values of r close to -1 or 1 indicate that the points lie close to a straight line. The extreme values $r=-1$ and $r=1$ occur only in the case of a perfect linear relationship, when the points in a scatterplot lie exactly along a straight line.

(3) Because r uses the standardized values of the observations (i. e. values $x_i - \bar{x}$ and $y_i - \bar{y}$), r does not change when we change the units of measurement of x, y or both. Changing from centimeters to inches and from kilograms to pounds does not change the correlation between variables height and weight. The correlation r itself has no unit of measurement; it is just a number between -1 and 1.

(4) Correlation measures the strength of only a linear relationship between two variables. Correlation does not describe curved relationships between variables, no matter how strong they are.

(5) Like the mean and standard deviation, the correlation is strongly affected by few outlying observations. Use r with caution when outliers appear in the scatterplot.

Example 1. 11. 3 What are the correlation coefficients in below cases (see Fig. 1. 11. 3)?
Example 1. 11. 4 How to interpret these scatterplots (see Fig. 1. 11. 4)?
Two variables may have a high correlation without being causally related. Correlation ignores the distinction between explanatory and response variables and just measures the strength of a linear association between two variables. Two variables may be also strongly correlated because they are both associated with other variables, called lurking variables, and that cause changes in the two variables under consideration.

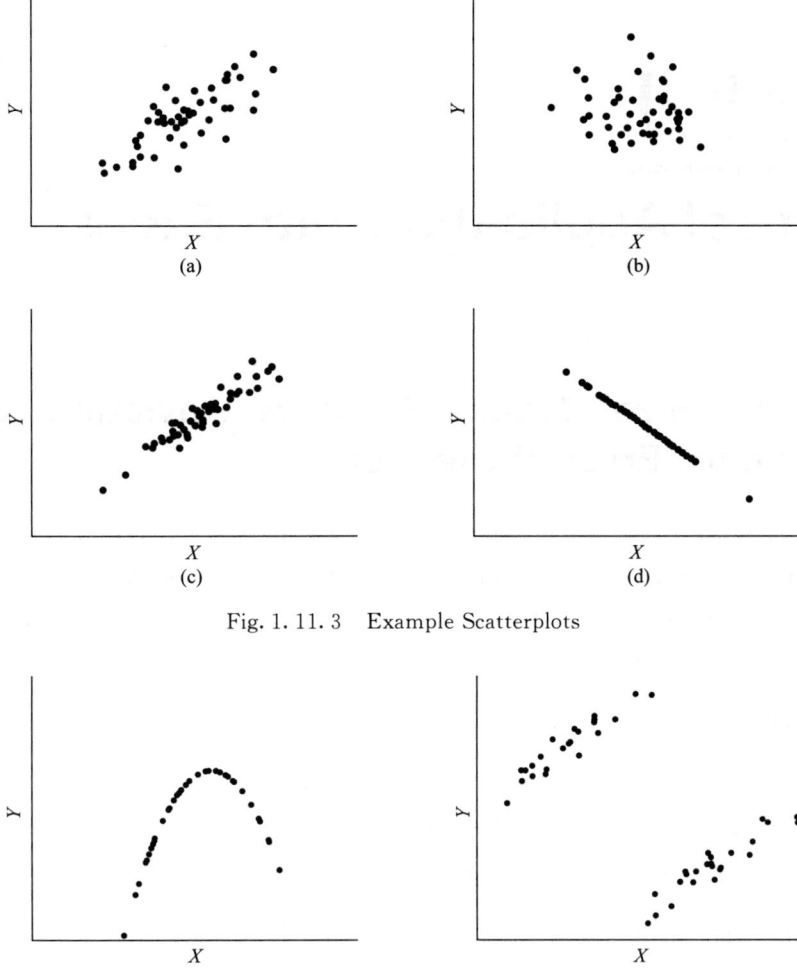

Fig. 1.11.3 Example Scatterplots

Fig. 1.11.4 Example Scatterplots

The sample correlation coefficient is also called as Pearson correlation coefficient. As it is clear now that Pearson correlation coefficient can be calculated only when both variables are quantitative, i. e, defined at least on an interval scale. When variables are qualitative ordinal scale variables, then Spearman correlation coefficient can be used as a measure of association between two ordinal scale variables. Spearman correlation coefficient is based on ranking of subjects, but the more accurate description of the properties of Spearman correlation coefficient is not within the scope of this course.

Part II

Statistical Application with Excel

2.1 Sample Size, Mean, Standard Deviation, and Standard Error of the Mean

This chapter deals with how you can use Excel to find the average (i. e., "mean") of a set of scores, the standard deviation of these scores (STDEV), and the standard error of the mean (s. e.) of these scores. All three of these statistics are used frequently and form the basis for additional statistical tests in business.

2.1.1 Mean

The mean is the "arithmetic average" of a set of scores. It will be much easier for you because Excel will do all of the steps for you. We will call this average of the scores the "mean" which we will symbolize as $\overline{X}$, and we will pronounce it as "X bar."

The formula for finding the mean with your calculator looks like this:

$$\overline{X} = \frac{\Sigma X}{n}$$

The symbol Σ is the Greek letter sigma, which stands for "sum". It tells you to add up all the scores that are indicated by the letter X, and then to divide your answer by n (the number of numbers that you have).

Let's give a simple example.

Suppose that you had these six scores:

6
4
5
3
2
5

To find the mean of these scores, you add them up, and then divide by the number of scores. So, the mean is 25/6=4.17.

2.1.2 Standard Deviation

The standard deviation tells you "how close the scores are to the mean." If the standard deviation is a small number, this tells you that the scores are "bunched together" close to the mean. If the standard deviation is a large number, this tells you that the scores are "spread out" a greater distance from the mean. The formula for the standard deviation (which we will call STDEV) and use the letter, s, to symbolize is:

$$\text{STDEV} = s = \sqrt{\frac{\sum_{i=1}^{n}(x_i - \overline{x})^2}{n-1}}$$

The formula looks complicated, but what it asks you to do is this:

(1) Subtract the mean from each score $(x_i - \overline{x})$.

(2) Then, square the resulting number to make it a positive number.

(3) Then, add up these squared numbers to get a total score.

(4) Then, take this total score and divide it by $n-1$ (where n stands for the number of numbers that you have).

(5) The final step is to take the square root of the number you found in step (4).

You will not be asked to compute the standard deviation using your calculator in this book, but you could see examples of how it is computed in any basic statistics book. Instead, we will use Excel to find the standard deviation of a set of scores. When we use Excel on the six numbers we gave in the description of the mean above, you will find that the STDEV of these numbers, s, is 1.47.

2.1.3 Standard Error of the Mean

The formula for the standard error of the mean (s.e., which we will use se to symbolize) is:

$$se = \frac{s}{\sqrt{n}}$$

To find se, all you need to do is to take the standard deviation, STDEV, and divide it by the square root of n, where n stands for the number of numbers that you have in your data set. In the example under the standard deviation description above, the se=0.60. (You can check this on your calculator.)

If you want to learn more about the standard deviation and the standard error of the mean, see Weiers (2011).

Year	First-year sales/$1000
1	10
2	10
3	12
4	16
5	22
6	29
7	39
8	47

Fig. 2. 1. 1 Worksheet Data for First-year Sales (Practical Example)

Now, let's learn how to use Excel to find the sample size, the mean, the standard deviation, and the standard error or the mean using a problem from sales.

Suppose that you wanted to estimate the first-year sales of a new product that your company was about to launch into the marketplace. You have decided to look at the first-year sales of similar products that your company has launched to get an idea of what sales are typical for your new product launches.

You decide to use the first-year sales of a similar product over the past eight years, and you have created the table in Fig. 2. 1. 1.

Note that the first-year sales are in thousands of dollars ($1000), so that 10 means that the first-year sales of that product were really $10,000.

2.1.4 Sample Size, Mean, Standard Deviation, and Standard Error of the Mean

Objective: To find the sample size (n), mean, standard deviation (STDEV), and standard error of the mean (se) for these data.

Start your computer, and click on the Excel 2013 icon to open a blank Excel spreadsheet.

Enter the data in this way:

A3: Year

B3: First-year sales/$1000

A4: 1

2.1.4.1 Using the Fill/Series/Columns Commands

Objective: To add the years 2—8 in a column underneath year 1

Put pointer in A4

Home (top left of screen)

Fill (top right of screen; click on the down arrow; see Fig. 2. 1. 2)

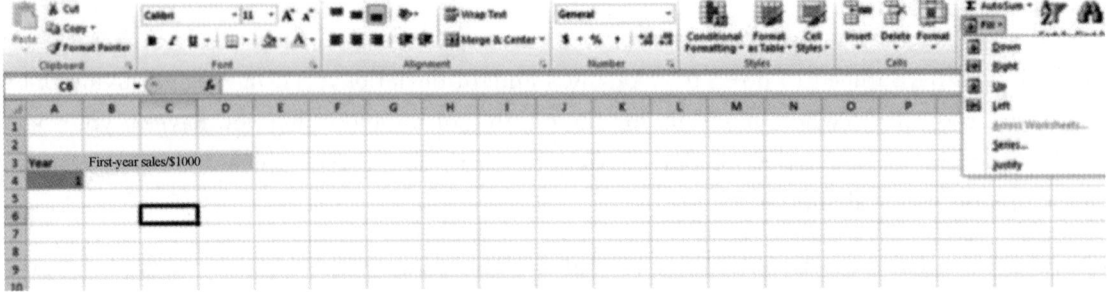

Fig. 2. 1. 2 Home/Fill/Series Commands

Series

Columns

Step value: 1

Stop value: 8 (see Fig. 2.1.3)

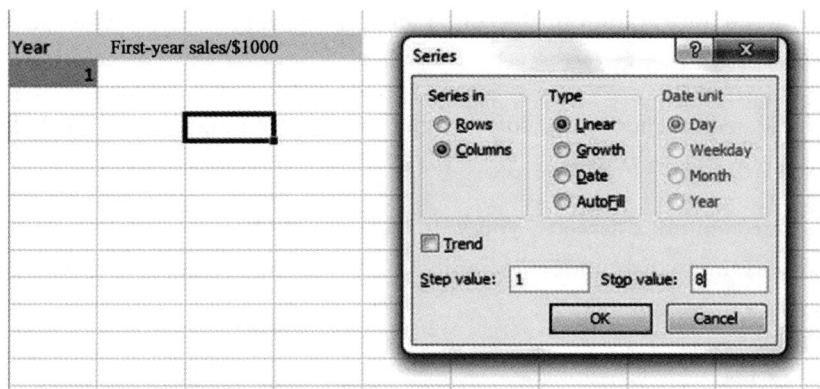

Fig. 2.1.3 Example of Dialogue Box for Fill/Series/Columns/Step Value/Stop Value commands

OK

The years should be identified as 1~8, with 8 in cell A11.

Now, enter the first-year sales figures in cells B4: B11 using the above table. Since your computer screen shows the information in a format that does not look professional, you need to learn how to "widen the column width" and how to "center the information" in a group of cells. Here is how you can do those two steps.

2.1.4.2 Changing the Width of a Column

Objective: To make a column width wider so that all of the information fits inside that column. If you look at your computer screen, you can see that Column B is not wide enough for all of the information to fit inside this column. To make Column B wider:

Click on the letter, B, at the top of your computer screen

Place your mouse pointer at the far right corner of B until you create a "cross sign" on that corner.

Left-click on your mouse, hold it down, and move this corner to the right until it is "wide enough to fit all of the data". Take your finger off the mouse to set the new column width (see Fig. 2.1.4).

Then, click on any empty cell (i.e., any blank cell) to "deselect" column B so that it is no longer a darker color on your screen.

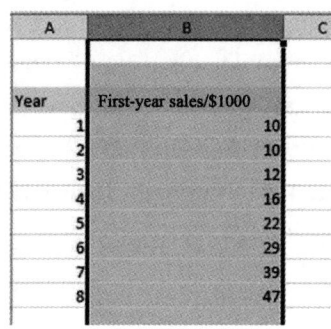

Fig. 2.1.4 Example of How to Widen the Column Width

When you widen a column, you will make all the cells in all of the rows in this column with the same width.

Now, let's go through the steps to center the information in both Column A and Column B.

2.1.4.3 Centering Information in a Range of Cells

Objective: To center the information in a group of cells.

In order to make the information in the cells look "more professional", you can center the information using the following steps:

Left-click your mouse on and drag it to the right and down to highlight cells A3: B11 so that these cells appear in a darker color.

At the top of your computer screen, you will see a set of "lines" in which all of the lines are "centered" to the same width under "Alignment" (It is the second icon at the bottom left of the Alignment box; see Fig. 2.1.5).

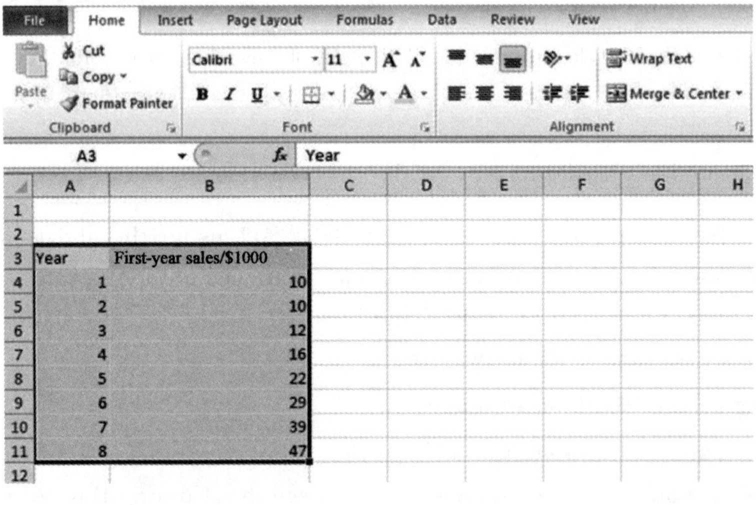

Fig. 2.1.5 Example of How to Center Information Within Cells

Click on this icon to center the information in the selected cells (see Fig. 2.1.6).

Since you will need to refer to the first-year sales figures in your formulas, it will be much easier to do this if you "name the range of data" with a name instead of having to remember the exact cells B4: B11 in which these figures are located. Let's call that group of cells product, but we could give them any name that you want to use.

2.1.4.4 Naming a Range of Cells

Objective: To name the range of data for the first-year sales figures with the name: Product

Highlight cells B4: B11 by left-clicking your mouse on B4 and dragging it down to B11

Formulas (top left of your screen).

Part Ⅱ   Statistical Application with Excel   **63**

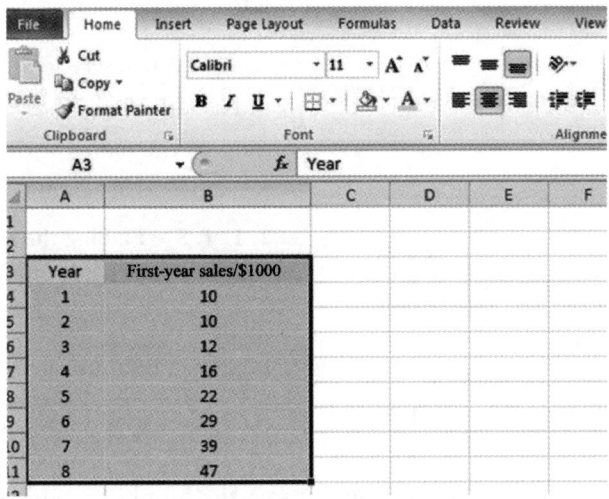

Fig. 2.1.6   Final Result of Centering Information in the Cells

Define Name (top center of your screen)

Product (type this name in the top box; see Fig. 2.1.7)

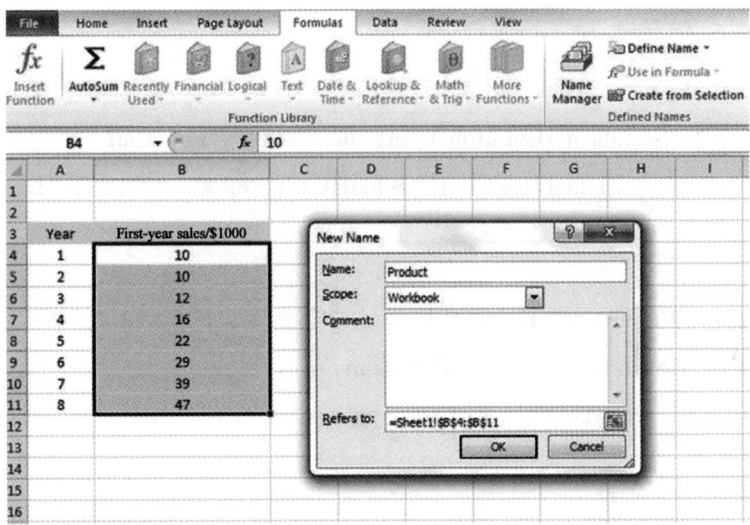

Fig. 2.1.7   Dialogue Box for "Naming a Range of Cells" with the Name: Product

OK

Then, click on any cell of your spreadsheet that does not have any information in it (i.e., it is an "empty cell") to deselect cells B4：B11

Now, add the following terms to your spreadsheet:

E6: n

E9: Mean

E12: STDEV

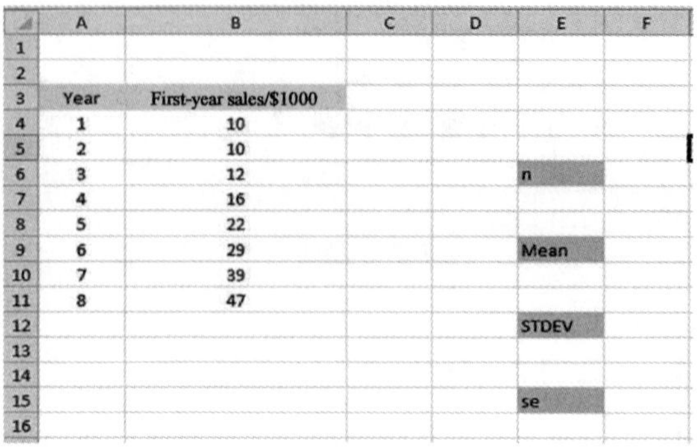

64 Basics of Statistics and Statistical Application with Excel

Fig. 2.1.8 Example of Entering the Sample Size, Mean, STDEV, and se Labels

E15: se (see Fig. 2.1.8)

Note: Whenever you use a formula, you must add an equal sign (=) at the beginning of the name of the function so that Excel knows that you intend to use a formula.

2.1.4.5 Finding the Sample Size Using the=COUNT Function

Objective: To find the sample size (n) for these data using the=COUNT function

F6: =COUNT (Product)

Hit the Enter key, and this command should insert the number 8 into cell F6 since there are eight first-year sales figures.

2.1.4.6 Finding the Mean Score Using the=AVERAGE Function

Objective: To find the mean sales figure using the=AVERAGE function.

F9: =AVERAGE (Product)

This command should insert the number 23.125 into cell F9.

2.1.4.7 Finding the Standard Deviation Using the=STDEV Function

Objective: To find the standard deviation (STDEV) using the=STDEV function.

F12: =STDEV (Product)

This command should insert the number 14.02485 into cell F12.

2.1.4.8 Finding the Standard Error of the Mean

Objective: To find the standard error of the mean using a formula for these eight data points.

F15: =F12/SQRT (8)

This command should insert the number 4.958533 into cell F15 (see Fig. 2.1.9).

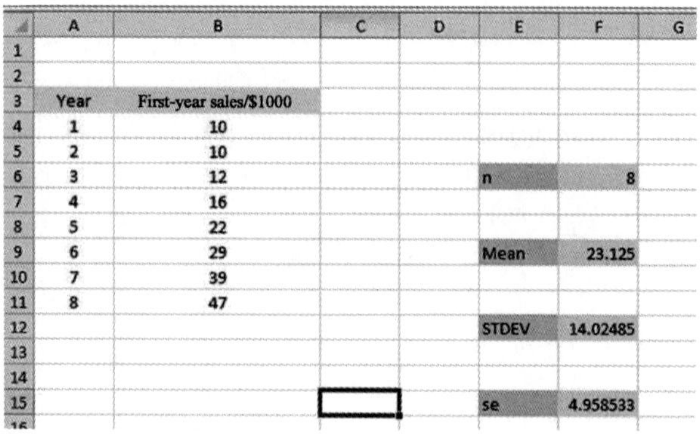

Fig. 2.1.9 Example of Using Excel Formulas for Sample Size, Mean, STDEV, and se

Important note: Throughout this book, be sure to double-check all of the figures in your spreadsheet to make sure that they are in the correct cells, or the formulas will not work correctly!

Formatting Numbers in Number Format (2 Decimal Places)

Objective: To convert the mean, STDEV, and se to two decimal places

Highlight cells F9:F15

Home (top left of screen)

Look under "Number" at the top center of your screen. In the bottom right corner, gently place your mouse pointer on you screen at the bottom of the .00.0 until it says: "Decrease Decimal" (see Fig. 2.1.10).

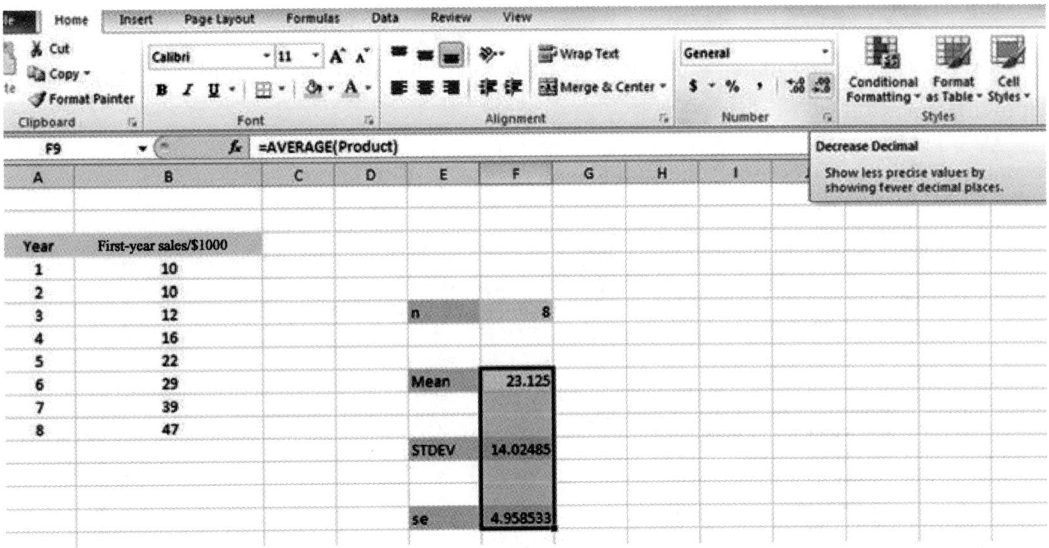

Fig. 2.1.10 Using the "Decrease Decimal Icon" to Convert Numbers to Fewer Decimal Places

Click on this icon once and notice that the cells F9:F15 are now all in just two decimal places (see Fig. 2.1.11).

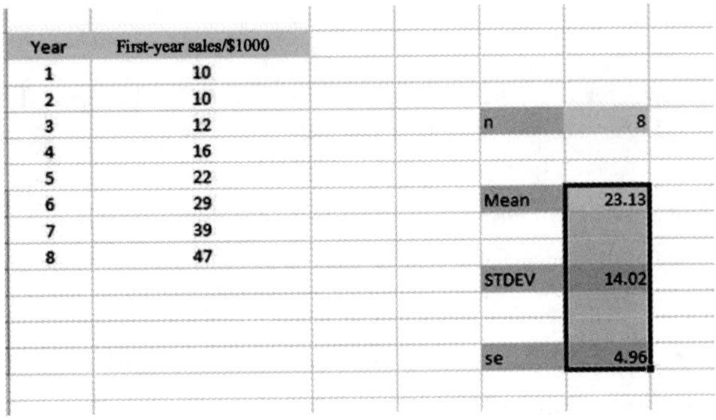

Fig. 2.1.11 Example of Converting Numbers to Two Decimal Places

Important note: The sales figures are in thousands of dollars ($1000), so that the mean is $23,130, the standard deviation is $14,020, and the standard error of the mean is $4,960.

Now, click on any "empty cell" on your spreadsheet to deselect cells F9: F15.

2.1.5 Saving a Spreadsheet

Objective: To save this spreadsheet with the name: Product 6

In order to save your spreadsheet so that you can retrieve it sometime in the future, your first decision is to decide "where" you want to save it. That is your decision and you have several choices. If it is your own computer, you can save it onto your hard drive (you need to ask someone how to do that on your computer). Or, you can save it onto a "CD" or onto a "flash drive". You then need to complete these steps:

File (top of screen, far left icon)

Save as type (select the place where you want to save the file: for example: Computer: My Documents location)

File name: Product 6 (enter this name to the right of File name; see Fig. 2.1.12)

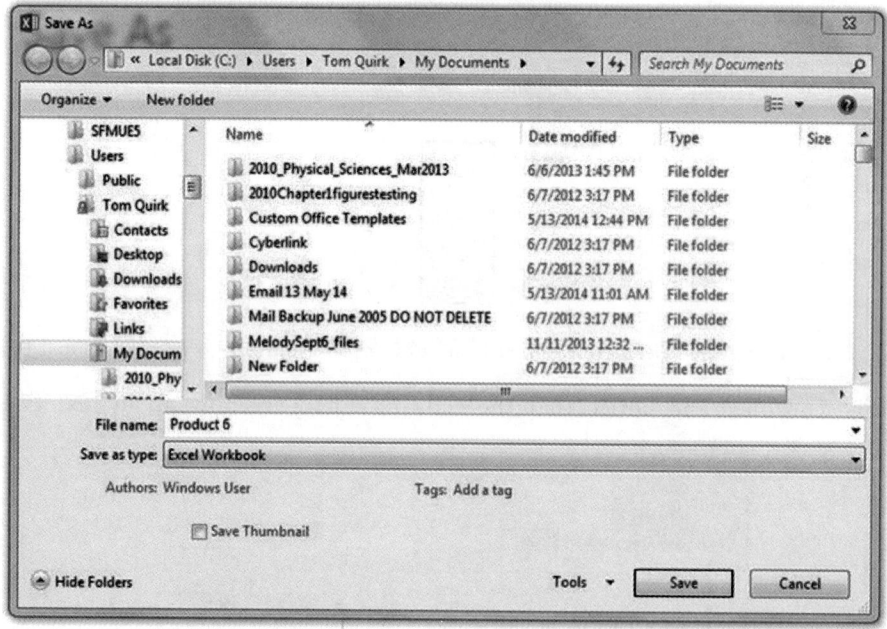

Fig. 2.1.12 Dialogue Box of Saving an Excel Workbook File as "Product 6" in My Documents

Save (bottom right of dialog box)

Important note: Be very careful to save your Excel file spreadsheet every few minutes so that you do not lose your information!

2.1.6 Printing a Spreadsheet

Objective: To print the spreadsheet

Use the following procedure when printing any spreadsheet. File (top of screen, far left icon)

Print (see Fig. 2.1.13)

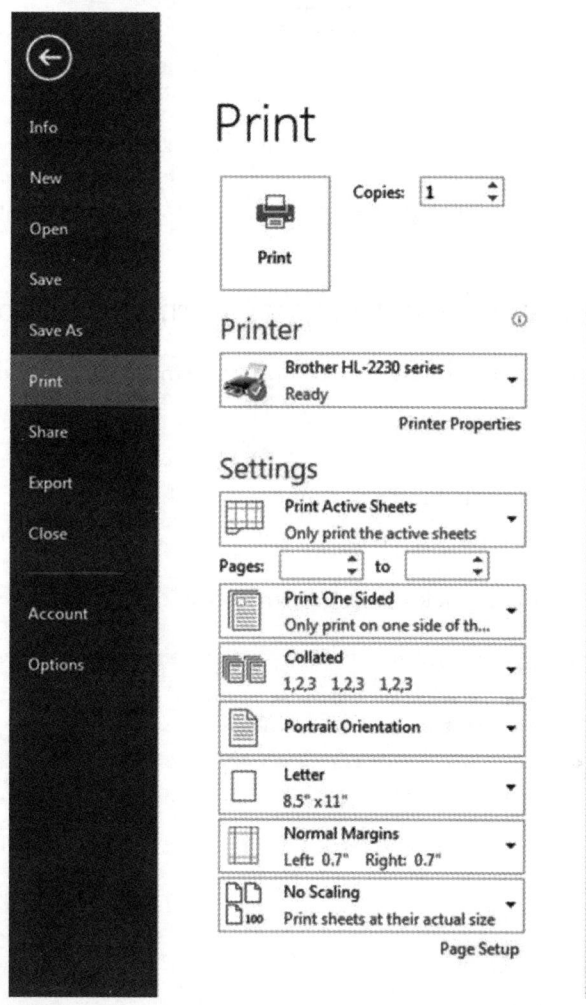

Fig. 2.1.13 Example of How to Print an Excel Worksheet by Using the File/Print Commands

Print (at Top Left of Screen)

The final spreadsheet is given in Fig. 2.1.14.

Before you leave this chapter, let's practice changing the format of the figures on a spreadsheet with two examples: (1) using two decimal places for figures that are dollar amounts, and (2) using three decimal places for figures.

Save the final spreadsheet by: File/Save, then close your spreadsheet by: File/Close, and

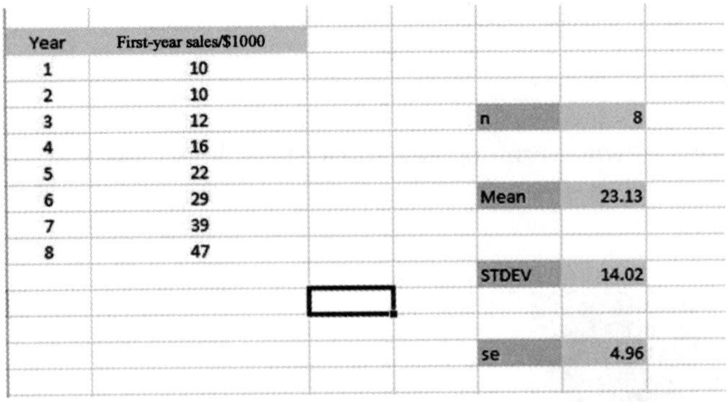

68 Basics of Statistics and Statistical Application with Excel

Year	First-year sales/$1000
1	10
2	10
3	12
4	16
5	22
6	29
7	39
8	47

n	8
Mean	23.13
STDEV	14.02
se	4.96

Fig. 2.1.14 Final Result of Printing an Excel Spreadsheet

then open a blank Excel spreadsheet by using: File/New/Blank Worksheet icon (on the top left of your screen).

2.1.7 Formatting Numbers in Currency Format (2 Decimal Places)

Objective: To change the format of figures to dollar format with two decimal places

Home

Highlight cells A4: A6 by left-clicking your mouse on A4 and dragging it down so that these three cells are highlighted in a darker color

Number (top center of screen: click on the down arrow on the right; see Fig. 2.1.15)

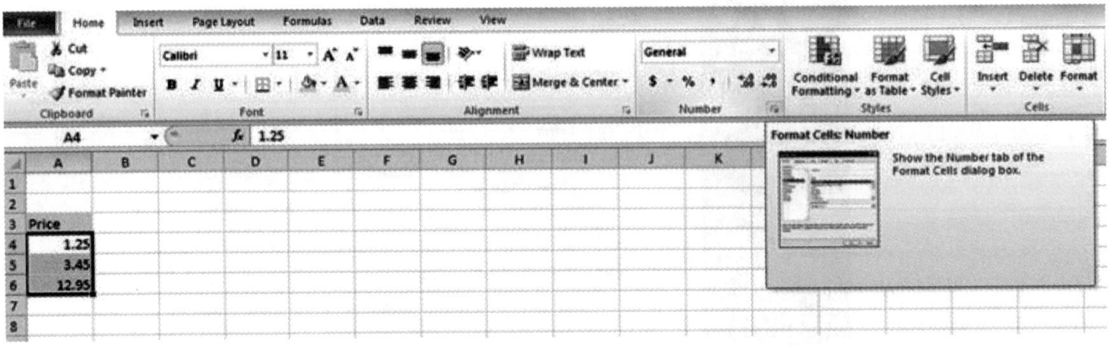

Fig. 2.1.15 Dialogue Box for Number Format Choices

Category: Currency

Decimal places: 2 (then see Fig. 2.1.16)

OK

The three cells should have a dollar sign in them and be in two decimal places. Next, let's practice formatting figures in number format, three decimal places.

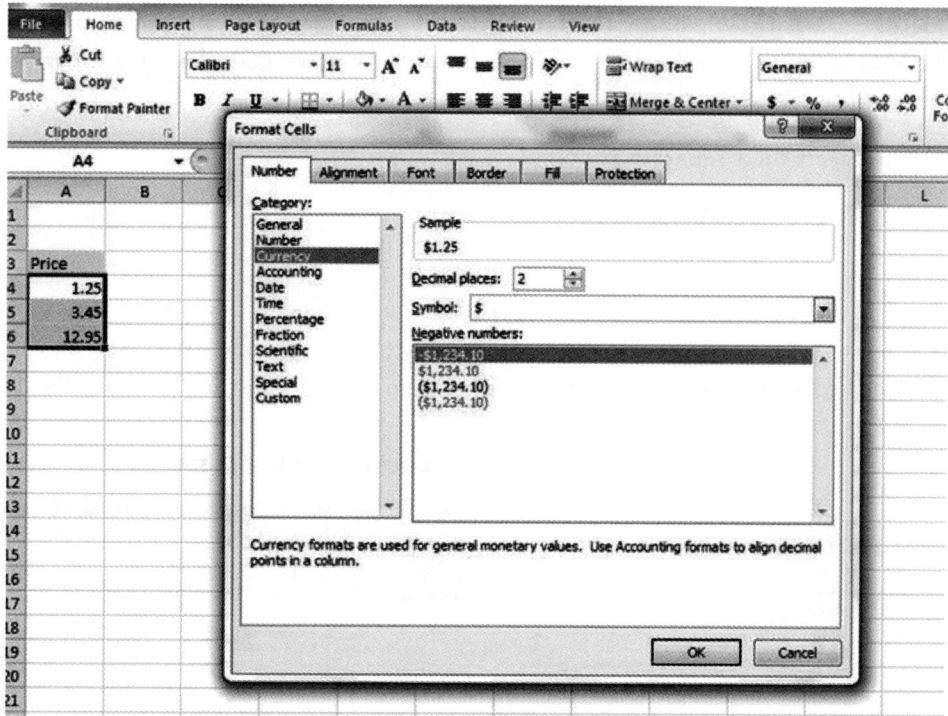

Fig. 2.1.16 Dialogue Box for Currency (2 Decimal Places) Format for Numbers

2.1.8 Formatting Numbers in Number Format (3 Decimal Places)

Objective: To format figures in number format, three decimal places

Home

Highlight cells A4: A6 on your computer screen Number (click on the down arrow on the right)

Category: number

At the right of the box, change 2 decimal places to 3 decimal places by clicking on the "up arrow" once

OK

The three figures should now be in number format, each with three decimals.

Now, click on any blank cell to deselect cells A4: A6. Then, close this file by File/Close/Don't Save (since there is no need to save this practice problem).

You can use these same commands to format a range of cells in percentage format (and many other formats) to whatever number of decimal places you want to specify.

2.1.9 End-of-chapter Practice Problems

(1) Suppose that you have selected a random sample from last week's customers at Wal-Mart. You then created Fig. 2.1.17.

(a) Use Excel to the right of the table to find the sample size, mean, standard deviation, and standard error of the mean for these data. Label your answers, and round off the mean, standard deviation, and standard error of the mean to two decimal places; use currency format for these three figures.

(b) Print the result on a separate page.

(c) Save the file as: WAL6.

(2) Suppose that the human resources department of your company has administered a "Morale Survey" to all middle-level managers and that you have been asked to summarize the results of the survey. You have decided to test your Excel skills on one item to see if you can do this assignment correctly, and you have selected item #21 to test out your skills. The data are given in Fig. 2.1.18.

DOLLAR SALES PER CUSTOMER LAST WEEK
127.12
140.45
104.64
80.06
114.07
109.35
117.28
72.84
67.67
79.85
109.96
117.13
85.25
149.36
147.57
153.54
118.76
69.86
154.47
154.88
109.44
97.36
87.55
154.85
143.82
145.55
142.33
122.57
128.75

Fig. 2.1.17 Worksheet Data for Chapter 2.1: Practice Problem #1

HUMAN RESOURCES MORALE SURVEY

Item #21: "Management is doing a good job of keeping employee morale at a high level."

1 Disagree	2	3	4	5	6	7 Agree

Rating
3
6
5
7
2
3
6
5
4
7
6
1
3
2
4
5
6
4
5
3
6
4
7

Fig. 2.1.18 Worksheet Data for Chapter 2.1: Practice Problem #2

(a) Use Excel to create a table of these ratings, and at the right of the table use Excel to find the sample size, mean, standard deviation, and standard error of the mean for these data. Label your answers, and round off the mean, standard deviation, and standard error of the mean to two decimal places using number format.

(b) Print the result on a separate page.

(c) Save the file as: MORALE4.

(3) Suppose that you have been hired to do analysis of data from the previous 18 days at a Ford assembly plant that produces Ford Focus automobiles. The plant manager wants you to summarize the number of defects per day of this car produced during this three-week peri-

od. A "defect" is defined as any irregularity of the car at the end of the production line that requires the car to be brought off the line and repaired before it is shipped to a dealer. The data from the previous three weeks are given in Fig. 2. 1. 19.

(a) Use Excel to create a table for these data, and at the right of the table, use Excel to find the sample size, mean, standard deviation, and standard error of the mean for these data. Label your answers, and round off the mean, standard deviation, and standard error of the mean to three decimal places using number format.

(b) Print the result on a separate page.

(c) Save the file as: DEFECTS4.

Ford Motor Co.

Number of defects per day for the Ford Focus

Day	No. of defects
1	6
2	8
3	14
4	12
5	6
6	8
7	23
8	17
9	14
10	16
11	18
12	12
13	13
14	15
15	8
16	6
17	9
18	10

Fig. 2. 1. 19　Worksheet Data for Chapter 2. 1: Practice Problem #3

2. 2　Random Number Generator

Suppose that you wanted to take a random sample of 5 of your company's 32 salespeople using Excel so that you could interview these five salespeople about their job satisfaction at your company.

To do that, you need to define a "sampling frame". A sampling frame is a list of people from which you want to select a random sample. This frame starts with the identification ID (code) of the number 1 that is assigned to the name of the first salesperson in your list of 32 salespeople in your company. The second salesperson has a code number of 2, the third a code number of 3, and so forth until the last salesperson has a code number of 32. Since your company has 32 salespeople, your sampling frame would go from 1 to 32 with each salesperson having a unique ID number.

We will first create the frame numbers as follows in a new Excel worksheet.

2. 2. 1　Creating Frame Numbers for Generating Random Numbers

Objective: To create the frame numbers for generating random numbers

A3: FRAME NO.

A4: 1

Now, create the frame numbers in column A with the Home/Fill commands that were explained in the chapter 2. 1 of this book (see Section 2. 1. 4. 1) so that the frame numbers go from 1 to 32, with the number 32 in cell A35. If you need to be reminded about how to do that, here are the steps:

Click on cell A4 to select this cell

Home

Fill (then click on the "down arrow" next to this command and select) Series (see Fig. 2.2.1)

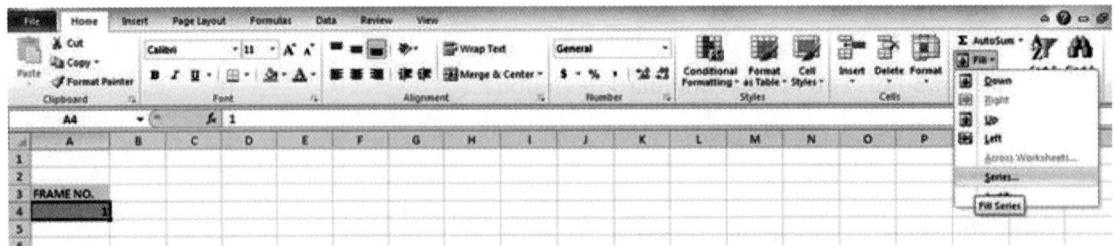

Fig. 2.2.1　Dialogue Box for Fill/Series Commands

Columns

Step value: 1

Stop value: 32 (see Fig. 2.2.2)

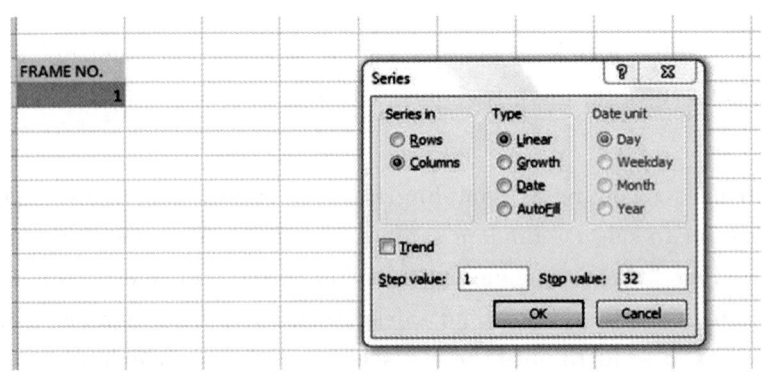

Fig. 2.2.2　Dialogue Box for Fill/Series/Columns/Step Value/Stop Value Commands

OK

Then, save this file as: Random2. You should obtain the result in Fig. 2.2.3.

Now, create a column next to these frame numbers in this manner.

B3: DUPLICATE FRAME NO.

B4: 1

Next, use the Home/Fill command again, so that the 32 frame numbers begin in cell B4 and end in cell B35. Be sure to widen the columns A and B so that all of the information in these columns fits inside the column width. Then, center the information inside both Column A and Column B on your spreadsheet. You should obtain the information given in Fig. 2. 2. 4.

FRAME NO.
1
2
3
4
5
6
7
8
9
10
11
12
13
14
15
16
17
18
19
20
21
22
23
24
25
26
27
28
29
30
31
32

Fig. 2. 2. 3   Frame Numbers from 1 to 32

FRAME NO.	DUPLICATE FRAME NO.
1	1
2	2
3	3
4	4
5	5
6	6
7	7
8	8
9	9
10	10
11	11
12	12
13	13
14	14
15	15
16	16
17	17
18	18
19	19
20	20
21	21
22	22
23	23
24	24
25	25
26	26
27	27
28	28
29	29
30	30
31	31
32	32

Fig. 2. 2. 4   Duplicate Frame Numbers from 1 to 32

Save this file as: Random3

You are probably wondering why you created the same information in both Column A and Column B of your spreadsheet. This is to make sure that before you sort the frame numbers that you have exactly 32 of them when you finish sorting them into a random sequence of 32 numbers. Now, let's add a random number to each of the duplicate frame numbers as follows.

2. 2. 2   Creating Random Numbers in an Excel Worksheet

C3: RANDOM NO.

(Then widen columns A, B, C so that their labels fit inside the columns; then center the information in A3: C35)

C4: =RAND ()

Next, hit the Enter key to add a random number to cell C4.

Note that you need both an open parenthesis and a closed parenthesis after=RAND (). The RAND command "looks to the left of the cell with the RAND () COMMAND in it" and assigns a random number to that cell.

Now, put the pointer using your mouse in cell C4 and then move the pointer to the bottom right corner of that cell until you see a "plus sign" in that cell. Then, click and drag the pointer down to cell C35 to add a random number to all 32 ID frame numbers (see Fig. 2.2.5).

FRAME NO.	DUPLICATE FRAME NO.	RANDOM NO.
1	1	0.690332931
2	2	0.022334603
3	3	0.89452184
4	4	0.981573849
5	5	0.698381228
6	6	0.611413628
7	7	0.013551391
8	8	0.036862479
9	9	0.412932328
10	10	0.460808373
11	11	0.533416136
12	12	0.988470378
13	13	0.097821358
14	14	0.881481661
15	15	0.352287507
16	16	0.344014139
17	17	0.084570168
18	18	0.467909507
19	19	0.904917153
20	20	0.252482436
21	21	0.788783634
22	22	0.592964999
23	23	0.946665187
24	24	0.214249616
25	25	0.509340791
26	26	0.439105519
27	27	0.086378662
28	28	0.975489923
29	29	0.120077924
30	30	0.216062043
31	31	0.353995884
32	32	0.558171248

Fig. 2.2.5 Example of Random Numbers Assigned to the Duplicate Frame Numbers

Then, click on any empty cell to deselect C4: C35 to remove the darker color highlighting these cells.

Save this file as: Random3A

Now, let's sort these duplicate frame numbers into a random sequence.

2.2.3 Sorting Frame Numbers into a Random Sequence

Objective: To sort the duplicate frame numbers into a random sequence

Highlight cells B3: C35 (include the labels at the top of columns B and C) Data (top of screen)

Sort (click on this word at the top center of your screen; see Fig. 2.2.6)

Sort by: RANDOM NO. (click on the down arrow) Smallest to Largest (see Fig. 2.2.7)

OK

Click on any empty cell to deselect B3: C35. Save this files as: Random4

Print this file now.

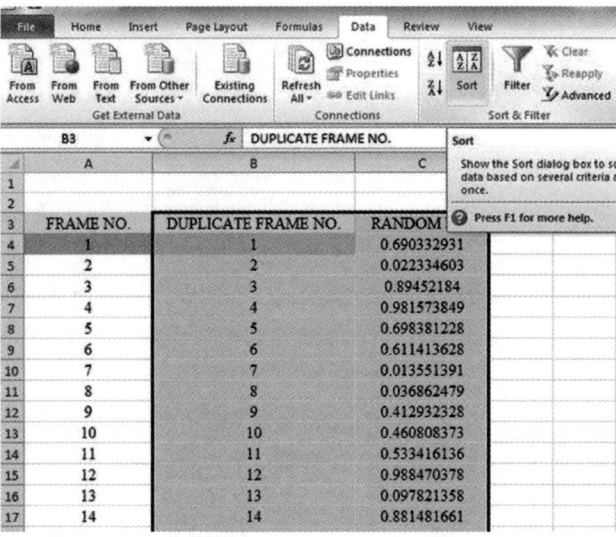

Fig. 2. 2. 6　Dialogue Box for Data/Sort Commands

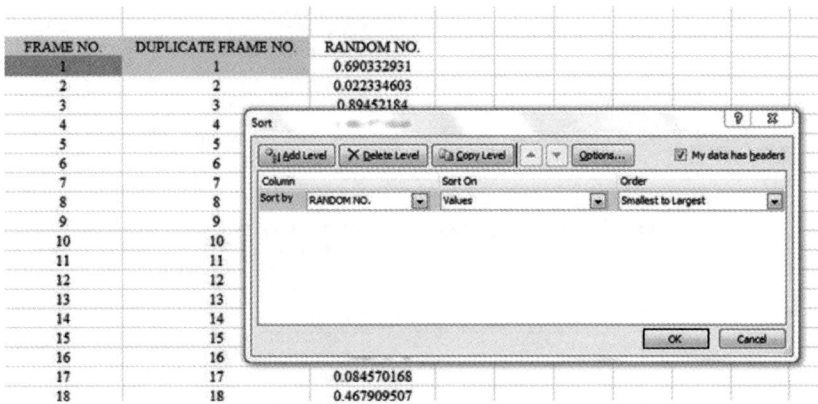

Fig. 2. 2. 7　Dialogue Box for Data/Sort/RANDOM NO. /Smallest to Largest Commands

These steps will produce Fig. 2. 2. 8 with the DUPLICATE FRAME NUMBERS sorted into a random order.

Important note: Because Excel randomly assigns these random numbers, your Excel commands will produce a different sequence of random numbers from everyone else who reads this book!

Because your objective at the beginning of this chapter was to select randomly 5 of your company's 32 salespeople for a personal interview, you now can do that by selecting the first five ID numbers in DUPLICATE FRAME NO. column after the sort.

Although your first five random numbers will be different from those we have selected in the random sort that we did in this chapter, we would select these five IDs of salespeople to interview by using Fig. 2. 2. 9.

7, 2, 8, 17, 27

FRAME NO.	DUPLICATE FRAME NO.	RANDOM NO.
1	7	0.343261283
2	2	0.929607291
3	8	0.914304212
4	17	0.903618324
5	27	0.257228182
6	13	0.456204036
7	29	0.390622986
8	24	0.222210116
9	30	0.432155483
10	20	0.219982266
11	16	0.842461398
12	15	0.3781508
13	31	0.694049089
14	9	0.939764564
15	26	0.075689667
16	10	0.302227714
17	18	0.468687794
18	25	0.148502036
19	11	0.49462371
20	32	0.87719372
21	22	0.413151766
22	6	0.094310793
23	1	0.962115342
24	5	0.528964967
25	21	0.401140496
26	14	0.403327013
27	3	0.865025638
28	19	0.517332393
29	23	0.968085821
30	28	0.647609375
31	4	0.670143403
32	12	0.09483352

Fig. 2.2.8　Duplicate Frame Numbers Sorted by Random Number

FRAME NO.	DUPLICATE FRAME NO.	RANDOM NO.
1	7	0.343261283
2	2	0.929607291
3	8	0.914304212
4	17	0.903618324
5	27	0.257228182
6	13	0.456204036
7	29	0.390622986
8	24	0.222210116
9	30	0.432155483
10	20	0.219982266
11	16	0.842461398
12	15	0.3781508
13	31	0.694049089
14	9	0.939764564
15	26	0.075689667
16	10	0.302227714
17	18	0.468687794
18	25	0.148502036
19	11	0.49462371
20	32	0.87719372
21	22	0.413151766
22	6	0.094310793
23	1	0.962115342
24	5	0.528964967
25	21	0.401140496
26	14	0.403327013
27	3	0.865025638
28	19	0.517332393
29	23	0.968085821
30	28	0.647609375
31	4	0.670143403
32	12	0.09483352

Fig. 2.2.9　First Five Salespeople Selected Randomly

Remember, your five ID numbers selected after your random sort will be different from the five ID numbers in Fig. 2.2.9 because Excel assigns a different random number each time the= RAND () command is given.

Before we leave this chapter, you need to learn how to print a file so that all of the information on that file fits onto a single page without "dribbling over" onto a second or third page.

2.2.4 Printing an Excel File So That All of the Information Fits onto One Page

Objective: To print a file so that all of the information fits onto one page

Note that the three practice problems at the end of this chapter require you to sort random numbers when the files contain 63 customers, 114 counties of the state of Missouri, and 76 key accounts, respectively. These files will be "too big" to fit onto one page when you print them unless you format these files so that they fit onto a single page when you print them.

Let's create a situation where the file does not fit onto one printed page unless you format it first to do that.

Go back to the file you just created, Random 4, and enter the name: Jennifer into cell: A52. If you printed this file now, the name, Jennifer, would be printed onto a second page because it "dribbles over" outside of the page range for this file in its current format.

So, you would need to change the page format so that all of the information, including the name, Jennifer, fits onto just one page when you print this file by using the following steps:

Page Layout (top left of the computer screen).

(Notice the "Scale to Fit" section in the center of your screen; see Fig. 2.2.10)

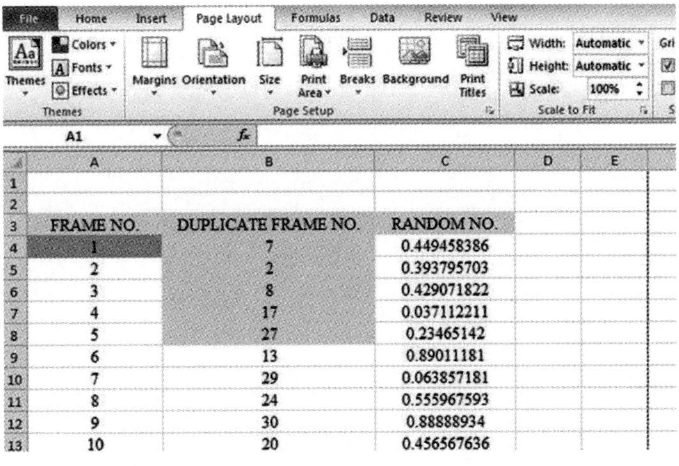

Fig. 2.2.10 Dialogue Box for Page Layout/Scale to Fit Commands

Hit the down arrow to the right of 100% once to reduce the size of the page to 95%.

Now, note that the name, Jennifer, is still on a second page on your screen because her name is below the horizontal dotted line on your screen in Fig. 2.2.11 (the dotted lines tell you outline dimensions of the file if you printed it now).

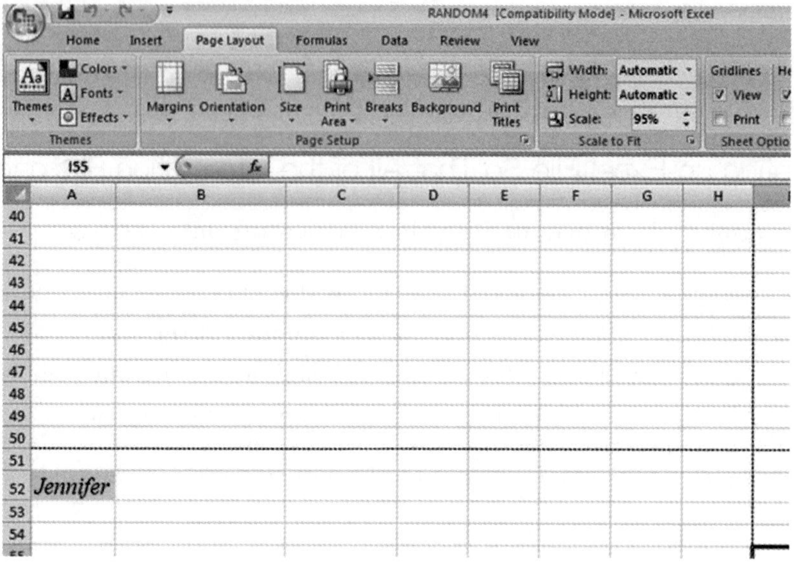

Fig. 2.2.11 Example of Scale Reduced to 95% with "Jennifer" to Be Printed on a Second Page

So, you need to repeat the "scale change steps" by hitting the down arrow on the right once more to reduce the size of the worksheet to 90% of its normal size.

Notice that the "dotted lines" on your computer screen in Fig. 2.2.12 are now below Jennifer's name to indicate that all of the information, including her name, is now formatted to fit onto just one page when you print this file.

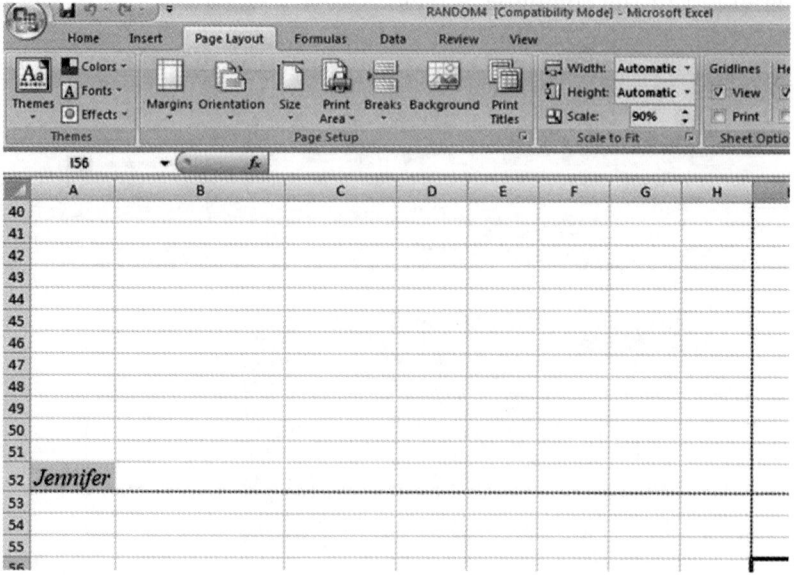

Fig. 2.2.12 Example of Scale Reduced to 90% with "Jennifer" to Be Printed on the First Page (Note the Dotted Line below Jennifer on Your Screen)

Save the file as: Random4A

Print the file. Does it all fit onto one page? (see Fig. 2. 2. 13).

FRAME NO.	DUPLICATE FRAME NO.	RANDOM NO.
1	7	0.661660768
2	2	0.408218127
3	8	0.360146461
4	17	0.547997374
5	27	0.821419485
6	13	0.654126828
7	29	0.704348993
8	24	0.687297652
9	30	0.577967707
10	20	0.0981433
11	16	0.609199142
12	15	0.287862572
13	31	0.435789306
14	9	0.104459646
15	26	0.805430237
16	10	0.039516242
17	18	0.734135176
18	25	0.566571959
19	11	0.381795818
20	32	0.11660887
21	22	0.891887278
22	6	0.370903093
23	1	0.109567029
24	5	0.94724966
25	21	0.650861462
26	14	0.678153692
27	3	0.081214079
28	19	0.421424271
29	23	0.817358479
30	28	0.573849656
31	4	0.597010138
32	12	0.853493587

Jennifer

Fig. 2. 2. 13 Final Spreadsheet of 90% Scale to Fit

2. 2. 5 End-of-chapter Practice Problems

(1) Suppose that you wanted to do a "customer satisfaction phone survey" of 15 from 63 customers who purchased at least $1,000 worth of merchandise from your company during the last 60 days.

(a) Set up a spreadsheet of frame numbers for these customers with the heading: FRAME NUMBERS using the Home/Fill commands.

(b) Then, create a separate column to the right of these frame numbers which duplicates these frame numbers with the title: Duplicate frame numbers.

(c) Then, create a separate column to the right of these duplicate frame numbers and use the =RAND () function to assign random numbers to all of the frame numbers in the duplicate frame numbers column, and change this column format so that 3 decimal places appear for each random number.

(d) Sort the duplicate frame numbers and random numbers into a random order.

(e) Print the result so that the spreadsheet fits onto one page.

(f) Circle on your printout the ID number of the first 15 customers that you would call in your phone survey.

(g) Save the file as: RAND9.

Important note: Note that everyone who does this problem will generate a different random order of customer ID numbers since Excel assigns a different random number each time the =RAND () command is used. For this reason, the answer to this problem given in this Excel Guide will have a completely different sequence of random numbers from the random sequence that you generate. This is normal and what is to be expected.

(2) Suppose that you wanted to do a random sample of 10 from the 114 counties in the state of Missouri as requested by a political pollster who wants to select registered voters by county in Missouri for a phone survey of their voting preferences in the next election. You know that there are 114 counties in Missouri because you have accessed the Web site for the U. S. census (U. S. Census Bureau 2000). For your information, the United States has a total of 3,140 counties in its 50 states (U. S. Census Bureau 2000).

(a) Set up a spreadsheet of frame numbers for these counties with the heading: FRAME NO.

(b) Then, create a separate column to the right of these frame numbers which duplicates these frame numbers with the title: Duplicate frame no.

(c) Then, create a separate column to the right of these duplicate frame numbers entitled "Random number" and use the=RAND () function to assign random numbers to all of the frame numbers in the duplicate frame number column. Then, change this column format so that 3 decimal places appear for each random number.

(d) Sort the duplicate frame numbers and random numbers into a random order.

(e) Print the result so that the spreadsheet fits onto one page.

(f) Circle on your printout the ID number of the first 10 counties that the pollster would call in his phone survey.

(g) Save the file as: RANDOM6.

(3) Suppose that your sales department at your company wants to do a "customer satisfaction survey" of 20 from your company's 76 "key accounts". Suppose, further, that your

Sales Vice-President has defined a key account as a customer who purchased at least $30,000 worth of merchandise from your company in the past 90 days.

(a) Set up a spreadsheet of frame numbers for these customers with the heading: FRAME NUMBERS.

(b) Then, create a separate column to the right of these frame numbers which duplicates these frame numbers with the title: Duplicate frame numbers.

(c) Then, create a separate column to the right of these duplicate frame numbers entitled "Random numbers" and use the =RAND () function to assign random numbers to all of the frame numbers in the duplicate frame number column. Then, change this column format so that 3 decimal places appear for each random number.

(d) Sort the duplicate frame numbers and random numbers into a random order.

(e) Print the result so that the spreadsheet fits onto one page.

(f) Circle on your printout the ID number of the first 20 customers that your Sales Vice-President would call for his phone survey.

(g) Save the file as: RAND5.

2.3 Confidence Interval about the Mean by Using the TINV Function and Hypothesis Testing

This chapter focuses on two ideas: (1) finding the 95% confidence interval about the mean, and (2) hypothesis testing.

Let's talk about the confidence interval first.

2.3.1 Confidence Interval about the Mean

In statistics, we are always interested in estimating the population mean. How do we do that?

2.3.1.1 How to Estimate the Population Mean

Objective: To estimate the population mean μ

Remember that the population mean is the average of all of the people in the target population. For example, if we were interested in how well adults aged 25—44 liked a new flavor of Ben & Jerry's ice cream, we could never ask this question of all of the people in the U.S. who were in that age group. Such a research study would take too much time to complete and the cost of doing that study would be prohibitive.

So, instead of testing everyone in the population, we take a sample of people in the population and use the results of this sample to estimate the mean of the entire population. This saves both time and money. When we use the results of a sample to estimate the population mean, this is called "inferential statistics" because we are inferring the population mean from the sample mean.

When we study a sample of people in a business research, we know the size of our sample (n), the mean of our sample (X), and the standard deviation of our sample (STDEV). We use these figures to estimate the population mean with a test called the "confidence interval about the mean".

2. 3. 1. 2   Estimating the Lower Limit and the Upper Limit of the 95 Percent Confidence Interval about the Mean

The theoretical background of this test is beyond the scope of this book, and you can learn more about this test from studying any good statistics textbook (e. g. Levine 2011) but the basic ideas are as follows.

We assume that the population mean is somewhere in an interval which has a "lower limit" and an "upper limit" to it. We also assume in this book that we want to be "95% confident" that the population mean is inside this interval somewhere. So, we intend to make the following type of statement:

"We are 95% confident that the population mean in miles per gallon (mpg) for the Chevy Impala automobile is between 26. 92 miles per gallon and 29. 42 miles per gallon."

If we want to create a billboard for this car that claims that this car gets 28 miles per gallon (mpg), we can do that because 28 is inside the 95% confidence interval in our research study in the above example. We do not know exactly what the population mean is, only that it is somewhere between 26. 92 mpg and 29. 42 mpg, and 28 is inside this interval.

But we are only 95% confident that the population mean is inside this interval, and 5% of the time we will be wrong in assuming that the population mean is 28 mpg.

But, for our purposes in business research, we are happy to be 95% confident that our assumption is accurate. We should also point out that 95% is an arbitrary level of confidence for our results. We could choose to be 80% confident, or 90% confident, or even 99% confident in our results if we wanted to do that. But, in this book, we will always assume that we want to be 95% confident of our results. If so, you will not have to guess how confident you want to be in any of the problems in this book. We will always want to be 95% confident of our results in this book.

So how do we find the 95% confidence interval about the mean for our data? In words, we will find this interval this way:

"Take the sample mean (X), and add to it 1. 96 times the standard error of the mean (se) to get the upper limit of the confidence interval. Then, take the sample mean, and subtract from it 1. 96 times the standard error of the mean to get the lower limit of the confidence interval."

You will remember (See Section 2.1.3) that the standard error of the mean (se) is found by dividing the standard deviation of our sample (STDEV) by the square root of our sample size, n.

In mathematical terms, the formula for the 95% confidence interval about the mean is:

$$\overline{X} \pm 1.96 \text{se}$$

Note that the "$\pm$ sign" stands for "plus or minus", and this means that you first add 1.96 times the se to the mean to get the upper limit of the confidence interval, and then subtract 1.96 times the se from the mean to get the lower limit of the confidence interval. Also, the symbol 1.96 se means that you multiply 1.96 times the standard error of the mean to get this part of the formula for the confidence interval.

Let's try a simple example to illustrate this formula.

2.3.1.3 Estimating the Confidence Interval for the Chevy

Let's suppose that you asked owners of the Chevy Impala to keep track of their mileage and the number of gallons used for two tanks of gas. Let's suppose that 49 owners did this, and that they average 27.83 miles per gallon (mpg) with a standard deviation of 3.01 mpg. The standard error (se) would be 3.01 divided by the square root of 49 (i.e., 7) which gives an se equal to 0.43. The 95% confidence interval for these data would be:

$$27.83 \pm 1.96(0.43)$$

The upper limit of this confidence interval uses the plus sign of the $\pm$ sign in the formula. Therefore, the upper limit would be:

$$27.83 + 1.96(0.43) = 27.83 + 0.84 = 28.67 \text{ mpg}$$

Similarly, the lower limit of this confidence interval uses the minus sign of the $\pm$ sign in the formula. Therefore, the lower limit would be:

$$27.83 - 1.96(0.43) = 27.83 - 0.84 = 26.99 \text{ mpg}$$

The result of our research study would, therefore, be the following:

"We are 95% confident that the population mean for the Chevy Impala is somewhere between 26.99 mpg and 28.67 mpg."

If we were planning to create a billboard that claimed that this car got 28 mpg, we would be able to do that based on our data, since 28 is inside of this 95% confidence interval for the population mean.

2.3.1.4 Where Did the Number "1.96" Come from?

A detailed mathematical answer to that question is beyond the scope of this book, but here is the basic idea.

We make an assumption that the data in the population are "normally distributed" in the sense that the population data would take the shape of a "normal curve" if we could test all of the people in the population. The normal curve looks like the outline of the Liberty Bell that sits in front of Independence Hall in Philadelphia, Pennsylvania. The normal curve is "symmetric" in the sense that if we cut it down the middle, and folded it over to one side, the half that we folded over would fit perfectly onto the half on the other side.

A discussion of integral calculus is beyond the scope of this book, but essentially we want to find the lower limit and the upper limit of the population data in the normal curve so that 95% of the area under this curve is between these two limits. If we have more than 40 people in our research study, the value of these limits is plus or minus 1.96 times the standard error of the mean (se) of our sample. The number 1.96 times the se of our sample gives us the upper limit and the lower limit of our confidence interval. If you want to learn more about this idea, you can consult a good statistics book (e.g. Salkind 2010).

The number 1.96 would change if we wanted to be confident of our results at a different level from 95% as long as we have more than 40 people in our research study.

For example:

(a) If we wanted to be 80% confident of our results, this number would be 1.282.

(b) If we wanted to be 90% confident of our results, this number would be 1.645.

(c) If we wanted to be 99% confident of our results, this number would be 2.576.

But since we always want to be 95% confident of our results in this book, we will always use 1.96 in this book whenever we have more than 40 people in our research study.

By now, you are probably asking yourself: "Is this number in the confidence interval about the mean always 1.96?" The answer is: "No!", and we will explain why this is true now.

2.3.1.5 Finding the Value for t in the Confidence Interval

Objective: To find the value for t in the confidence interval formula

The correct formula for the confidence interval about the mean for different sample sizes is the following:

$$\overline{X} \pm t\,\text{se}$$

To use this formula, you find the sample mean, $\overline{X}$, and add to it the value of t times the se to get the upper limit of this 95% confidence interval. Also, you take the sample mean, $\overline{X}$, and subtract from it the value of t times the se to get the lower limit of this 95% confidence interval. And, you find the value of t in the table given in Appendix of this book in the following way:

Objective: To find the value of t in the t-table in Appendix

Before we get into an explanation of what is meant by "the value of t", let's give you practice in finding the value of t by using the t-table in Appendix.

Keep your finger on Appendix as we explain how you need to "read" that table.

Since the test in this chapter is called the "confidence interval about the mean test", you will use the first column on the left in Appendix to find the critical value of t for your research study (note that this column is headed: " sample size n").

To find the value of t, you go down this first column until you find the sample size in your research study, and then you go to the right and read the value of t for that sample size in the "critical t column" of the table (note that this column is the column that you would use for the 95% confidence interval about the mean).

For example, if you have 14 people in your research study, the value of t is 2.160. If you have 26 people in your research study, the value of t is 2.060.

If you have more than 40 people in your research study, the value of t is always 1.96. Note that the "critical t column" in Appendix represents the value of t that you need to use to obtain to be 95% confident of your results as "significant" results.

Throughout this book, we are assuming that you want to be 95% confident in the results of your statistical tests. Therefore, the value of t in the t-table in Appendix tells you which value you should use for t when you use the formula for the 95% confidence interval about the mean.

Now that you know how to find the value of t in the formula for the confidence interval about the mean, let's explore how you find this confidence interval by using Excel.

2.3.1.6 Using Excel's TINV Function to Find the Confidence Interval About the Mean

Objective: To use the TINV function in Excel to find the confidence interval about the mean

When you use Excel, the formulas for finding the confidence interval are:

Lower limit: $=\overline{X}-\text{TINV}(1-0.95, n-1) * se$

Upper limit: $=\overline{X}+\text{TINV}(1-0.95, n-1) * se$

Note that the " * symbol" in this formula tells Excel to use the multiplication step in the formula, and it stands for "times" in the way we talk about multiplication.

You will recall from Chapter 2.1 that n stands for the sample size, and so $n-1$ stands for the sample size minus one.

You will also recall from Chapter 2.1 that the standard error of the mean, se, equals the STDEV divided by the square root of the sample size, n (see Section 2.1.3).

Let's try a sample problem by using Excel to find the 95% confidence interval about the mean for a problem.

Suppose that General Motors wanted to claim that its Chevy Impala gets 28 miles per gallon (mpg), and that it wanted to advertise on a billboard in St. Louis at the Vandeventer entrance to Route 44: "The new Chevy Impala gets 28 miles to the gallon." Let's call 28 mpg the "reference value" for this car.

Suppose that you work for Ford Motor Co. and that you want to check this claim to see if it holds up based on some research evidence. You decide to collect some data and to use a two-side 95% confidence interval about the mean to test your results.

2.3.1.7 Using Excel to Find the 95 Percent Confidence Interval for a Car's mpg Claim

Objective: To analyze the data by using a two-side 95% confidence interval about the mean

You select a sample of new car owners for this car and they agree to keep track of their mileage for two tanks of gas and to record the average miles per gallon they achieve on these two tanks of gas. Your research study produces the results given in Fig. 2.3.1.

Chevy Impala
Miles per gallon
30.9
24.5
31.2
28.7
35.1
29.0
28.8
23.1
31.0
30.2
28.4
29.3
24.2
27.0
26.7
31.0
23.5
29.4
26.3
27.5
28.2
28.4
29.1
21.9
30.9

Fig. 2.3.1 Worksheet Data for Chevy Impala (Practical Example)

Create a spreadsheet with these data and use Excel to find the sample size (n), the mean, the standard deviation (STDEV), and the standard error of the mean (se) for these data by using the following cell references.

A3: Chevy Impala

A5: Miles per gallon

A6: 30.9

Enter the other mpg data in cells A7: A30

Now, highlight cells A6: A30 and format these numbers in number format (one decimal place). Center these numbers in Column A. Then, widen columns A and B by making both of them twice as wide as the original width of column A. Then, widen column C so that it is three times as wide as the original width of column A so that your table looks more professional.

C7: n

C10: Mean

C13: STDEV

C16: se

C19: 95% confidence interval

D21: Lower limit:

D23: Upper limit: (see Fig. 2.3.2)

Chevy Impala				
Miles per gallon				
30.9				
24.5		n		
31.2				
28.7				
35.1		Mean		
29.0				
28.8				
23.1		STDEV		
31.0				
30.2				
28.4		se		
29.3				
24.2				
27.0		95% confidence interval		
26.7				
31.0			Lower limit:	
23.5				
29.4			Upper limit:	
26.3				
27.5				
28.2				
28.4				
29.1				
21.9				
30.9				

Fig. 2.3.2 Example of Chevy Impala Format for the Confidence Interval about the Mean Labels

B26: Draw a picture below this confidence interval

B28: 26.92

B29: lower (then right-align this word)

B30: limit (then right-align this word)

C28: '--------28 ------ —28.17 ------------ [note that you need to begin cell C28 with a single quotation mark (') to tell Excel that this is a label, and not a number]

D28: '-------------------- (note the single quotation mark at the beginning)

E28: '29.42 (note the single quotation mark)

C29: ref. Mean

C30: value

E29: upper

E30: limit

B33: Conclusion:

Now, align the labels underneath the picture of the confidence interval so that they look like Fig. 2.3.3.

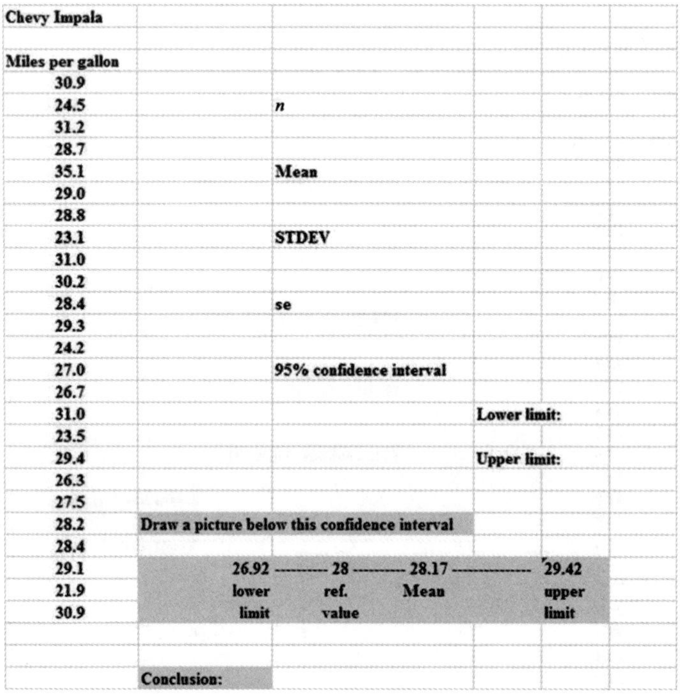

Fig. 2.3.3 Example of Drawing a Picture of a Confidence Interval about the Mean Result

Next, name the range of data from A6: A30 as: miles

D7: Use Excel to find the sample size

D10: Use Excel to find the mean

D13: Use Excel to find the STDEV

D16: Use Excel to find the se

Now, you need to find the lower limit and the upper limit of the 95% confidence interval for this study.

We will use Excel's TINV function to do this. We will assume that you want to be 95% confident of your results.

$$F21: = D10 - TINV(1 - 0.95, 24) * D16$$

Note that this TINV formula uses 24 since 24 is one less than the sample size of 25 (i.e., 24 is $n-1$). Note that D10 is the mean, while D16 is the standard error of the mean. The above formula gives the lower limit of the confidence interval, 26.92.

$$F23: = D10 + TINV(1 - 0.95, 24) * D16$$

The above formula gives the upper limit of the confidence interval, 29.42.

Now, use number format (two decimal places) in your Excel spreadsheet for the mean, standard deviation, standard error of the mean, and for both the lower limit and the upper limit of your confidence interval. If you printed this spreadsheet now, the lower limit of the confidence interval (26.92) and the upper limit of the confidence interval (29.42) would "dribble over" onto a second printed page because the information on the spreadsheet is too large to fit onto one page in its present format.

So, you need to use Excel's "Scale to Fit" commands that we discussed in Chapter 2.2 (see Section 2.2.4) to reduce the size of the spreadsheet to 95% of its current size using the Page Layout/Scale to Fit function. Do that now, and notice that the dotted line to the right of 26.92 and 29.42 indicates that these numbers would now fit onto one page when the spreadsheet is printed out (see Fig. 2.3.4).

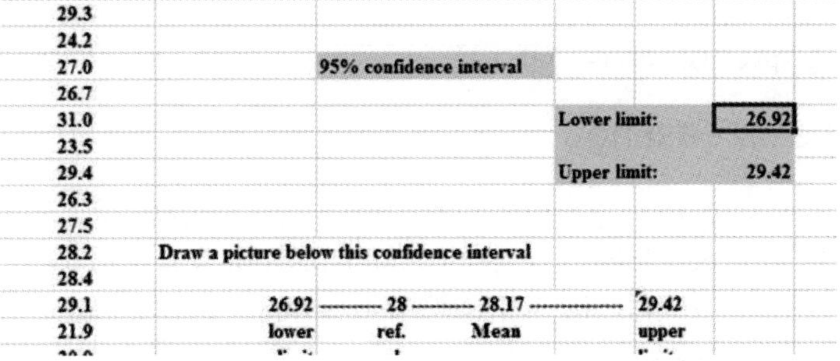

Fig. 2.3.4 Result of Using the TINV Function to Find the Confidence Interval about the Mean

Note that you have drawn a picture of the 95% confidence interval beneath cell B26, including the lower limit, the upper limit, the mean, and the reference value of 28 mpg given in the claim that the company wants to make about the car's miles per gallon performance.

Now, let's write the conclusion to your research study on your spreadsheet:

C33: Since the reference value of 28 is inside

C34: the confidence interval, we accept that

C35: the Chevy Impala does get 28 mpg.

Your research study accepted the claim that the Chevy Impala did get 28 miles per gallon. The average miles per gallon in your study was 28.17 (see Fig. 2.3.5).

Chevy Impala				
Miles per gallon				
30.9				
24.5		n	25	
31.2				
28.7				
35.1		Mean	28.17	
29.0				
28.8				
23.1		STDEV	3.03	
31.0				
30.2				
28.4		se	0.61	
29.3				
24.2				
27.0		95% confidence interval		
26.7				
31.0			Lower limit:	26.92
23.5				
29.4			Upper limit:	29.42
26.3				
27.5				
28.2	Draw a picture below this confidence interval			
28.4				
29.1	26.92 ---------- 28 ---------- 28.17 ----------		29.42	
21.9	lower	ref.	Mean	upper
30.9	limit	value		limit
	Conclusion:	Since the reference value of 28 is inside the confidence interval, we accept that the Chevy Impala does get 28 mpg.		

Fig. 2.3.5   Final Spreadsheet for the Chevy Impala Confidence Interval about the Mean

Save your resulting spreadsheet as: CHEVY7

2.3.2 Hypothesis Testing

One of the important activities of researchers, whether they are in a business research, a marketing research, a psychological research, an educational research, or in any of the social sciences is that they attempt to "check" their assumptions about the world by testing these assumptions in the form of hypotheses.

A typical hypothesis is in the form: "If x, then y."

Some examples would be:

(1) "If we raise our price by 5 percent, then our sales dollars for our product will decrease by 8 percent."

(2) "If we increase our advertising budget by $400,000 for our product, then our market share will go up by two points."

(3) "If we use this new method of teaching math to ninth graders in algebra, then our math achievement scores will go up by 10 percent."

(4) "If we change the raw materials for this product, then our production cost per unit will decrease by 5 percent."

A hypothesis, then, to a social science researcher is a "guess" about what we think is true in the real world. We can test these guesses by using statistical formulas to see if our predictions come true in the real world.

So, in order to perform these statistical tests, we must first state our hypotheses so that we can test our results against our hypotheses to see if our hypotheses match reality.

So, how do we generate hypotheses in business?

2.3.2.1 Hypotheses Always Refer to the Population of People or Events That You Are Studying

The first step is to understand that our hypotheses always refer to the population of people under study. For example, if we are interested in studying 18—24-year-olds in St. Louis as our target market, and we select a sample of people in this age group in St. Louis, depending on how we select our sample, we are hoping that our results of this study are useful in generalizing our findings to all 18—24-year-olds in St. Louis, and not just to the particular people in our sample.

The entire group of 18—24-year-olds in St. Louis would be the population that we are interested in studying, while the particular group of people in our study are called the sample from this population.

Since our sample sizes typically contain only a few people, we are interested in the results of our sample only insofar as the results of our sample can be "generalized" to the population in which we are really interested.

That is why our hypotheses always refer to the population, and never to the sample of people in our study.

You will recall from Chapter 2.1 that we used the symbol X to refer to the mean of the sample we use in our research study (see Section 2.1.1).

We will use the symbol μ (the Greek letter "mu") to refer to the population mean. In testing our hypotheses, we are trying to decide which one of two competing hypotheses about the population mean we should accept given our data set.

2.3.2.2 The Null Hypothesis and the Research (Alternative) Hypothesis

These two hypotheses are called the null hypothesis and the alternative hypothesis. Statistics textbooks typically refer to the null hypothesis with the notation H_0. The alternative hypothesis is typically referred to with the notation H_1, and it is sometimes called the alternative hypothesis.

Let's explain first what is meant by the null hypothesis and the alternative hypothesis.

(1) The null hypothesis is what we accept as true unless we have compelling evidence that it is not true.

(2) The alternative hypothesis is what we accept as true whenever we reject the null hypothesis as true.

This is similar to our legal system in America where we assume that a supposed criminal is innocent until he or she is proven guilty in the eyes of a jury. Our null hypothesis is that this defendant is innocent, while the alternative hypothesis is that he or she is guilty.

In the great state of Missouri, every license plate has the state slogan: "Show me." This means that people in Missouri think of themselves as not gullible enough to accept everything that someone says as true unless that person's actions indicate the truth of his or her claim. In other words, people in Missouri believe strongly that a person's actions speak much louder than that person's words.

Since both the null hypothesis and the alternative hypothesis cannot both be true, the task of hypothesis testing using statistical formulas is to decide which one you will accept as true, and which one you will reject as true.

Sometimes in business research a series of rating scales is used to measure people's attitudes toward a company, toward one of its products, or toward their intention-to-buy that company's products. These rating scales are typically 5-point, 7-point, or 10-point scales, although other scale values are often used as well.

Determining the Null Hypothesis and the Alternative Hypothesis

When rating scales are used, here is a typical example of a 7-point scale in an attitude research in customer satisfaction studies (see Fig. 2.3.6):

How would you rate your overall experience in purchasing your new car?						
1 Poor	2	3	4	5	6	7 Excellent

Fig. 2.3.6 Example of a Rating Scale Item for a New Car Purchase (Practical Example)

So, how do we decide what to use as the null hypothesis and the alternative hypothesis whenever rating scales are used?

Objective: To decide on the null hypothesis and the alternative hypothesis whenever rating scales are used

In order to make this determination, we will use a simple rule.

Rule: Whenever rating scales are used, we will use the "middle" of the scale as the null hypothesis and the alternative hypothesis.

In the above example, since 4 is the number in the middle of the scale (i. e., three numbers are below it, and three numbers are above it), our hypotheses become:

$$\text{Null hypothesis}: \mu = 4$$
$$\text{Alternative hypothesis}: \mu = 4$$

In the above rating scale example, if the result of our statistical test for this one attitude scale item indicates that our population mean is "close to 4," we say that we accept the null hypothesis that our new car purchase experience was neither positive nor negative.

In the above example, if the result of our statistical test indicates that the population mean is significantly different from 4, we reject the null hypothesis and accept the alternative hypothesis by stating either that:

"The new car purchase experience was significantly positive" (this is true whenever our sample mean is significantly greater than our expected population mean of 4).

Or "The new car purchase experience was significantly negative" (this is accepted as true whenever our sample mean is significantly less than our expected population mean of 4).

Both of these conclusions cannot be true. We accept one of the hypotheses as "true" based on the data set in our research study, and the other one as "not true" based on our data set.

The job of the business researcher, then, is to decide which of these two hypotheses, the null hypothesis or the alternative hypothesis, he or she will accept as true given the data set in the research study.

Let's try some examples of rating scales so that you can practice figuring out what the null hypothesis and the alternative hypothesis are for each rating scale. In the spaces in Fig. 2.3.7, write in the null hypothesis and the alternative hypothesis for the rating scales.

How did you do?

Here are the answers to these three questions:

① The null hypothesis is 3, and the alternative hypothesis is not equal to 3 on this 5-point scale (i. e. the "middle" of the scale is 3).

② The null hypothesis is 4, and the alternative hypothesis is not equal to 4 on this 7-point scale (i. e., the "middle" of the scale is 4).

1. Webster University is an excellent university.					
	1 Strongly Disagree	2 Disagree	3 Undecided	4 Agree	5 Strongly Agree
Null hypothesis:			$\mu =$ ____		
Research hypothesis:			$\mu \neq$ ____		

2. How would you rate the quality of teaching at Webster University?							
poor	1	2	3	4	5	6	7 excellent
Null hypothesis:			$\mu =$ ____				
Research hypothesis:			$\mu \neq$ ____				

3. How would you rate the quality of the faculty at Webster University?									
1 very poor	2	3	4	5	6	7	8	9	10 very good
Null hypothesis:				$\mu =$ ____					
Research hypothesis:				$\mu \neq$ ____					

Fig. 2. 3. 7 Examples of Rating Scales for Determining the Null Hypothesis and the Research Hypothesis

③ The null hypothesis is 5.5, and the alternative hypothesis is not equal to 5.5 on this 10-point scale (i.e., the "middle" of the scale is 5.5 since there are 5 numbers below 5.5 and 5 numbers above 5.5).

As another example, Holiday Inn Express in its Stay Smart Experience Survey uses 4-point scales where:

$$1 = \text{Not So Good}$$
$$2 = \text{Average}$$
$$3 = \text{Very Good}$$
$$4 = \text{Great}$$

On this scale, the null hypothesis is: $\mu = 2.5$ and the alternative hypothesis is: $\mu = 2.5$, because there are two numbers below 2.5, and two numbers above 2.5 on that rating scale.

Now, let's discuss the 7 STEPS of hypothesis testing for using the confidence interval about the mean.

2. 3. 2. 3　The 7 Steps for Hypothesis-testing by Using the Confidence Interval about the Mean

Objective: To learn the 7 steps of hypothesis-testing by using the confidence interval about the mean

There are seven basic steps of hypothesis-testing for this statistical test.

Step 1: State the null hypothesis and the alternative hypothesis

If you are using numerical scales in your survey, you need to remember that these hypotheses refer to the "middle" of the numerical scale. For example, if you are using 7-point scales with 1=poor and 7=excellent, these hypotheses would refer to the middle of these scales and would be:

$$\text{Null hypothesis } H_0: \mu = 4$$
$$\text{Alternative hypothesis } H_1: \mu \neq 4$$

Step 2: Select the appropriate statistical test

In this chapter we are studying the confidence interval about the mean, and so we will select that test.

Step 3: Calculate the formula for the statistical test

You will recall (see Section 2.3.1.5) that the formula for the confidence interval about the mean is:

$$\overline{X} \pm t\,\text{se}$$

We discussed the procedure for computing this formula for the confidence interval about the mean by using Excel earlier in this chapter, and the steps involved in using that formula are:

① Use Excel's =COUNT function to find the sample size.

② Use Excel's =AVERAGE function to find the sample mean, $\overline{X}$.

③ Use Excel's =STDEV function to find the standard deviation, STDEV.

④ Find the standard error of the mean (se) by dividing the standard deviation (STDEV) by the square root of the sample size, n.

⑤ Use Excel's TINV function to find the lower limit of the confidence interval.

⑥ Use Excel's TINV function to find the upper limit of the confidence interval.

Step 4: Draw a picture of the confidence interval about the mean, including the mean, the lower limit of the interval, the upper limit of the interval, and the reference value given in the null hypothesis, H_0

Step 5: Decide on a decision rule

(a) If the reference value is inside the confidence interval, accept the null hypothesis, H_0

(b) If the reference value is outside the confidence interval, reject the null hypothesis, H_0, and accept the alternative hypothesis, H_1

Step 6: State the result of your statistical test

There are two possible results when you use the confidence interval about the mean, and only one of them can be accepted as "true". So your result would be one of the following:

Either since the reference value is inside the confidence interval, we accept the null hypothesis, H_0 or since the reference value is outside the confidence interval, we reject the null hypothesis, H_0, and accept the alternative hypothesis, H_1.

Step 7: State the conclusion of your statistical test in plain English!

In practice, this is more difficult than it sounds because you are trying to summarize the result of your statistical test in simple English that is both concise and accurate so that someone who has never had a statistics course (such as your boss, perhaps) can understand the conclusion of your test. This is a difficult task, and we will give you lots of practice doing this last and most important step throughout this book.

Objective: To write the conclusion of the confidence interval about the mean test

Let's set some basic rules for sating the conclusion of a hypothesis test.

Rule #1: Whenever you reject H_0 and accept H_1, you must use the word "significantly" in the conclusion to alert the reader that this test found an important result.

Rule #2: Create an outline in words of the "key terms" you want to include in your conclusion so that you do not forget to include some of them.

Rule #3: Write the conclusion in plain English so that the reader can understand it even if that reader has never taken a statistics course.

Let's practice these rules by using the Chevy Impala Excel spreadsheet that you created earlier in this chapter, but first we need to state the hypotheses for that car.

Since the billboard wants to claim that the Chevy Impala gets 28 miles per gallon, the hypotheses would be: $H_0 : \mu = 28$ mpg $H_1 : \mu = 28$ mpg.

You will remember that the reference value of 28 mpg was inside the 95% confidence interval about the mean for your data, so we would accept H_0 for the Chevy Impala that the car does get 28 mpg.

Objective: To state the result when you accept H_0

Result: Since the reference value of 28 mpg is inside the confidence interval, we accept the null hypothesis, H_0

Let's try our three rules now:

Objective: To write the conclusion when you accept H_0

Rule #1: Since the reference value was inside the confidence interval, we cannot use the word "significantly" in the conclusion. This is a basic rule we are using in this chapter for every problem.

Rule #2: The key terms in the conclusion would be:

—Chevy Impala

—reference value of 28 mpg

Rule #3: The Chevy Impala did get 28 mpg.

The process of writing the conclusion when you accept H_0 is relatively straight-forward since you put into words what you said when you wrote the null hypothesis.

However, the process of stating the conclusion when you reject H_0 and accept H_1 is more difficult, so let's practice writing that type of conclusion with three practice case examples.

Objective: To write the result and conclusion when you reject H_0

CASE #1: Suppose that an ad in *Business Week* claimed that the Ford Escape Hybrid got 34 miles per gallon. The hypotheses would be: $H_0 : \mu = 34$ mpg

$H_1 : \mu = 34$ mpg

Suppose that your research yields the following confidence interval:

```
     30          31         32          34
lower limit    mean    upper limit   ref. value
```

Result: Since the reference value is outside the confidence interval we reject the null hypothesis and accept the alternative hypothesis

The three rules for stating the conclusion would be:

Rule #1: We must include the word "significantly" since the reference value of 34 is outside the confidence interval.

Rule #2: The key terms would be:

—Ford Escape Hybrid

—significantly

—either "more than" or "less than"

—and probably closer to

Rule #3: The Ford Escape Hybrid got significantly less than 34 mpg, and it was probably closer to 31 mpg.

Note that this conclusion says that the mpg was less than 34 mpg because the sample mean was only 31 mpg. Note, also, that when you find a significant result by rejecting the null hypothesis, it is not sufficient to say only: "significantly less than 34 mpg", because that does not tell the reader "how much less than 34 mpg" the sample mean was from 34 mpg. To make the conclusion clearer, you need to add "probably closer to 31 mpg" since the sample mean was only 31 mpg.

CASE #2: Suppose that you have been hired as a consultant by the St. Louis Symphony Orchestra (SLSO) to analyze the data from an Internet survey of attendees for a concert in Powell Symphony Hall in St. Louis last month. You have decided to practice your data analysis skills on Question #7 given in Fig. 2.3.8.

Question #7:	"Overall, how satisfied have you been with your experience(s) at SLSO concerts?"						
	1 Extremely dissatisfied	2	3	4	5	6	7 Extremely satisfied

Fig. 2.3.8 Example of a Survey Item Used by the St. Louis Symphony Orchestra (SLSO)

The hypotheses for this one item would be:

$$H_0: \mu = 4$$

$$H_1: \mu \neq 4$$

Essentially, the null hypothesis equal to 4 states that if the obtained mean score for this question is not significantly different from 4 on the rating scale, then attendees, overall, were neither satisfied nor dissatisfied with their SLSO concerts.

Suppose that your analysis produced the following confidence interval for this item on the survey.

$$1.8 \quad 2.8 \quad 3.8 \quad 4$$
lower limit   mean   upper limit   ref. value

Result: Since the reference value is outside the confidence interval we reject the null hypothesis and accept the alternative hypothesis.

Rule #1: You must include the word "significantly" since the reference value is outside the confidence interval.

Rule #2: The key terms would be:

—attendees

—SLSO Internet survey

—significantly

—last month

—either satisfied or dissatisfied (since the result is significant)

—experiences at concerts

—overall

Rule #3: Attendees were significantly dissatisfied, overall, on last month's Internet survey with their experiences at concerts of the SLSO.

Note that you need to use the word "dissatisfied" since the sample mean of 2.8 was on the dissatisfied side of the middle of the rating scale.

CASE #3: Suppose that Marriott Hotel at the St. Louis Airport location had the results of one item in its Guest Satisfaction Survey from last week's customers that was the following (see Fig. 2.3.9).

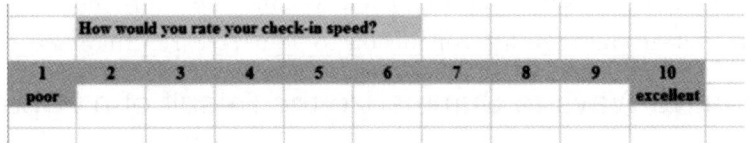

Fig. 2.3.9 Example of a Survey Item from Marriott Hotels

This item would have the following hypotheses: $H_0 : \mu = 5.5 \quad H_1 : \mu \neq 5.5$

Suppose that your research produced the following confidence interval for this item on the survey:

          5.5   5.7   5.8   5.9
ref. value lower limit mean upper limit

Result: Since the reference value is outside the confidence interval we reject the null hypothesis and accept the alternative hypothesis.

The three rules for stating the conclusion would be:

Rule #1: You must include the word "significantly" since the reference value is outside the confidence interval.

Rule #2: The key terms would be:

—Marriott Hotel

—St. Louis Airport

—significantly

—check-in speed

—survey

—last week

—customers

—either "positive" or "negative" (we will explain this)

Rule #3: Customers at the St. Louis Airport Marriott Hotel last week rated their check-in speed in a survey as significantly positive.

Note two important things about this conclusion above: (1) people when speaking English do not normally say "significantly excellent" since something is either excellent or is not excellent without any modifier, and (2) since the mean rating of the check-in speed (5.8) was significantly greater than 5.5 on the positive side of the scale, we would say "significantly positive" to indicate this fact.

The three practice problems at the end of this chapter will give you additional practice in stating the conclusion of your result, and this book will include many more examples that will help you to write a clear and accurate conclusion to your research findings.

2.3.3 Alternative Ways to Summarize the Result of a Hypothesis Test

It is important for you to understand that in this book we are summarizing an hypothesis test in one of two ways: (1) We accept the null hypothesis, or (2) we reject the null hypothesis and accept the alternative hypothesis. We are consistent in the use of these words so that you can understand the concept underlying hypothesis testing.

However, there are many other ways to summarize the result of an hypothesis test, and all of them are correct theoretically, even though the terminology differs. If you are taking a course with a professor who wants you to summarize the results of a statistical test of hypotheses in the language which is different from the language we are using in this book, do not panic! If you understand the concept of hypothesis testing as described in this book, you can then translate your understanding to use the terms that your professor wants you to use to reach the same conclusion to the hypothesis test.

Statisticians and professors of business statistics all have their own language that they like to use to summarize the results of an hypothesis test. There is no one set of words that these statisticians and professors will ever agree on, and so we have chosen the one that we believe to be easier to understand in terms of the concept of hypothesis testing.

To convince you that there are many ways to summarize the results of an hypothesis test, we present the following quotes from prominent statistics and research books to give you an idea of different ways that are possible.

2.3.3.1 Different Ways to Accept the Null Hypothesis

The following quotes are typical of the language used in statistics and research books when the null hypothesis is accepted:

"The null hypothesis is not rejected." (Black 2010)

"The null hypothesis cannot be rejected." (McDaniel and Gates 2010)

"The null hypothesis...claims that there is no difference between groups." (Salkind 2010)

"The difference is not statistically significant." (McDaniel and Gates 2010)

"…the obtained value is not extreme enough for us to say that the difference between Groups 1 and 2 occurred by anything other than chance." (Salkind 2010)

"If we do not reject the null hypothesis, we conclude that there is not enough statistical evidence to infer that the alternative (hypothesis) is true." (Keller 2009)

"The alternative hypothesis is not supported." (Zikmund and Babin 2010)

2.3.3.2 Different Ways to Reject the Null Hypothesis

The following quotes are typical of the quotes used in statistics and research books when the null hypothesis is rejected:

"The null hypothesis is rejected." (McDaniel and Gates 2010)

"If we reject the null hypothesis, we conclude that there is enough statistical evidence to infer that the alternative hypothesis is true." (Keller 2009)

"If the test statistic's value is inconsistent with the null hypothesis, we reject the null hypothesis and infer that the alternative hypothesis is true." (Keller 2009)

"Because the observed value …is greater than the critical value …the decision is to reject the null hypothesis." (Black 2010)

"If the obtained value is more extreme than the critical value, the null hypothesis cannot be accepted." (Salkind 2010)

"The critical t-value…must be surpassed by the observed t-value if the hypothesis test is to be statistically significant …" (Zikmund and Babin 2010)

"The calculated test statistic…exceeds the upper boundary and falls into this rejection region. The null hypothesis is rejected." (Weirs 2011)

You should note that all of the above quotes are used by statisticians and professors when discussing the results of a hypothesis test, and so you should not be surprised if someone asks you to summarize the results of a statistical test using a different language than the one we are using in this book.

2.3.4 End-of-chapter Practice Problems

(1) Suppose that you have been asked by the manager of the St. Louis Post-Dispatch to analyze the data from a recent survey of past subscribers who have cancelled their newspaper subscription in the past three months. A random sample of this group was called by phone and asked a series of questions about the newspaper. The hypothetical data for survey question #4 appear in Fig. 2.3.10.

Suppose, further, that top management wants to charge $3.80 for this new subscription price. Is this a reasonable price to charge based on the results of this survey question?

St. Louis Post-Dispatch Phone Survey	
Question #4:	"How much would you be willing to pay per week for a six-month weekday/weekend subscription to the Post-Dispatch?"

Subscription Price/$
4.15
3.75
3.80
4.10
3.60
3.60
3.65
4.40
3.15
4.00
3.75
4.00
3.25
3.75
3.30
3.75
3.65
4.00
4.10
3.90
3.50
3.75

Fig. 2.3.10 Worksheet Data for Chapter 2.3: Practice Problem #1

(Hint: $3.80 is the null hypothesis for this price.)

(a) To the right of this table, use Excel to find the sample size, mean, standard deviation, and standard error of the mean for the price figures. Label your answers. Use currency format (two decimal places) for the mean, standard deviation, and standard error of the mean.

(b) Enter the null hypothesis and the alternative hypothesis onto your spreadsheet.

(c) Use Excel's TINV function to find the 95% confidence interval about the mean for these figures. Label your answers. Use currency format (two decimal places).

(d) Enter your result onto your spreadsheet.

(e) Enter your conclusion in plain English onto your spreadsheet.

(f) Print the final spreadsheet to fit onto one page (if you need help to remember how to do this, see the objectives at the end of Chapter 2.2 in Section 2.2.4).

(g) On your printout, draw a diagram of this 95% confidence interval by hand.

(h) Save the file as: POST9.

(2) Suppose that you have been asked by the human resources department (HR) at your company to analyze the data from a recent "morale survey" of its managers to find out how managers think about working at your company. You want to test out your Excel skills on a small sample of managers with one item from the survey. You select a random sample of managers and the hypothetical data from Item #24 are given in Fig. 2.3.11.
Create an Excel spreadsheet with these data.

HUMAN RESOURCES DEPARTMENT							
MORALE SURVEY OF MANAGERS							
Item #24: "How would you rate the quality of leadership shown by top management in this company?"							
1 very weak	2	3	4	5	6	7 very strong	
			Rating				
			5				
			6				
			3				
			4				
			7				
			2				
			3				
			4				
			2				
			5				
			3				
			4				
			2				
			2				
			3				
			6				
			5				
			7				
			4				
			6				
			4				
			3				
			4				
			2				
			3				
			5				
			4				

Fig. 2.3.11 Worksheet Data for Chapter 2.3: Praclce Problem #2

(a) Use Excel to the right of the table to find the sample size, mean, standard deviation, and standard error of the mean for these data. Label your answers, and use two decimal places for the mean, standard deviation, and standard error of the mean.

(b) Enter the null hypothesis and the alternative hypothesis for this item on your spreadsheet.

(c) Use Excel's TINV function to find the 95% confidence interval about the mean for these data. Label your answers on your spreadsheet. Use two decimal places for the lower limit and the upper limit of the confidence interval.

(d) Enter the result of the test on your spreadsheet.

(e) Enter the conclusion of the test in plain English on your spreadsheet.

(f) Print your final spreadsheet so that it fits onto one page (if you need help to remember how to do this, see the objectives at the end of Chapter 2.2 in Section 2.2.4).

(g) Draw a picture of the confidence interval, including the reference value, onto your spreadsheet.

(h) Save the final spreadsheet as: top 8.

(3) Suppose that you have been asked to conduct three focus groups in different cities with adult women (aged 25-44) to determine how much they liked a new design of a blouse that was created by a well-known designer. The designer is hoping to sell this blouse in department stores at a retail price of $68.00. You conduct a one-hour focus group discussion with three groups of adult women in this age range, and the last question on the survey at the end of the discussion period produced the hypothetical results given in Fig. 2. 3. 12.

FOCUS GROUP PRICING STUDY
Question #10: "How much would you be willing to pay for this blouse?"
$ _____
Groups 1,2,3 in $
62
55
73
53
46
48
57
59
65
68
64
72
62
67
59
71
65
63
69
71
70
58
67
65
63
59
70
67
64
65

Fig. 2. 3. 12　Worksheet Data for Chapter 2. 3: Practice Problem #3

Create an Excel spreadsheet with these data.

(a) Use Excel to the right of the table to find the sample size, mean, standard deviation, and standard error of the mean for these data. Label your answers, and use two decimal places and currency format for the mean, standard deviation, and standard error of the mean.

(b) Enter the null hypothesis and the alternative hypothesis for this item onto your spreadsheet.

(c) Use Excel's TINV function to find the 95% confidence interval about the mean for these data. Label your answers on your spreadsheet. Use two decimal places in currency format for the lower limit and the upper limit of the confidence interval.

(d) Enter the result of the test on your spreadsheet.

(e) Enter the conclusion of the test in plain English on your spreadsheet.

(f) Print your final spreadsheet so that it fits onto one page (if you need help remembering how to do this, see the objectives at the end of Chapter 2.2 in Section 2.2.4).

(g) Draw a picture of the confidence interval, including the reference value, onto your spreadsheet.

(h) Save the final spreadsheet as: blouse 9.

2.4 One-group *t*-test for the Mean

In this chapter, you will learn how to use one of the most popular and most helpful statistical tests in business research: the one-group *t*-test for the mean.

The formula for the one-group *t*-test is as follows.

$$t = \frac{\overline{X} - \mu}{\text{se}}$$

Where $\text{se} = \dfrac{s}{\sqrt{n}}$

This formula asks you to take the mean ($\overline{X}$) and subtract the population mean (μ) from it, and then divide the answer by the standard error of the mean (se). The standard error of the mean equals the standard deviation divided by the square root of *n* (the sample size).

Let's discuss the 7 steps of hypothesis testing using the one-group *t*-test so that you can understand how this test is used.

2.4.1 The 7 Steps for Hypothesis-testing by Using the One-group *t*-test

Objective: To learn the 7 steps of hypothesis-testing by using the one-group *t*-test

Before you can try out your Excel skills on the one-group *t*-test, you need to learn the basic steps of hypothesis-testing for this statistical test. There are 7 steps in this process.

2.4.1.1 Step 1: State the Null Hypothesis and the Alternative Hypothesis

If you are using numerical scales in your survey, you need to remember that these hypotheses refer to the "middle" of the numerical scale. For example, if you are using 7-point scales with 1=poor and 7=excellent, these hypotheses would refer to the middle of these scales and would be:

Null hypothesis $H_0 : \mu = 4$

Alternative hypothesis $H_1 : \mu \neq 4$

As a second example, suppose that you worked for Honda Motor Company and that you wanted to place a magazine ad that claimed that the new Honda Fit got 35 miles per gallon (mpg). The hypotheses for testing this claim on actual data would be:

$$H_0: \mu = 35 \text{ mpg}$$
$$H_1: \mu \neq 35 \text{ mpg}$$

2.4.1.2　Step 2: Select the Appropriate Statistical Test

In this chapter we will be studying the one-group t-test, and so we will select that test.

2.4.1.3　Step 3: Decide on a Decision Rule for the One-group t-test

(a) If the absolute value of t is less than the critical value of t, accept the null hypothesis.

(b) If the absolute value of t is greater than the critical value of t, reject the null hypothesis and accept the alternative hypothesis.

You are probably saying to yourself: "That sounds fine, but how do I find the absolute value of t?"

Finding the absolute value of a number

To do that, we need another objective:

Objective: To find the absolute value of a number

If you took a basic algebra course in high school, you may remember the concept of "absolute value". In mathematical terms, the absolute value of any number is always that number expressed as a positive number.

For example, the absolute value of 2.35 is +2.35.

And the absolute value of minus 2.35 (i.e. 2.35) is also +2.35.

This becomes important when you are using the t-table in Appendix of this book. We will discuss this table later when we get to Step 5 of the one-group t-test where we explain how to find the critical value of t using Appendix.

2.4.1.4　Step 4: Calculate the Formula for the One-group t-test

Objective: To learn how to use the formula for the one-group t-test

The formula for the one-group t-test is as follows.

$$t = \frac{\overline{X} - \mu}{se}$$

$$\text{Where } se = \frac{s}{\sqrt{n}}$$

This formula makes the following assumptions about the data (Foster et al. 1998): (1) The data are independent of each other (i.e., each person receives only one score), (2) The population of the data is normally distributed, and (3) the data have a constant variance (note that the standard deviation is the square root of the variance).

To use this formula, you need to follow these steps:

(1) Take the sample mean in your research study and subtract the population mean μ from it (remember that the population mean for a study involving numerical rating scales is the "middle" number in the scale).

(2) Then take your answer from the above step, and divide your answer by the standard error of the mean for your research study (you will remember that you learned how to find the standard error of the mean in Chapter 2.1; to find the standard error of the mean, just take the standard deviation of your research study and divide it by the square root of n, where n is the number of people used in your research study).

(3) The number you get after you complete the above step is the value for t that results when you use the formula stated above.

2.4.1.5 Step 5: Find the Critical Value of t in the t-Table in Appendix

Objective: To find the critical value of t in the t-table in Appendix

Before we get into an explanation of what is meant by "the critical value of t", let's give you practice in finding the critical value of t by using the t-table in Appendix.

Keep your finger on Appendix as we explain how you need to "read" that table. Since the test in this chapter is called the "one-group t-test", you will use the first column on the left in Appendix to find the critical value of t for your research study (note that this column is headed "sample size n").

To find the critical value of t, you go down this first column until you find the sample size in your research study, and then you go to the right and read the critical value of t for that sample size in the critical t column in the table (note that this is the column that you would use for both the one-group t-test and the 95% confidence interval about the mean).

For example, if you have 27 people in your research study, the critical value of t is 2.056.

If you have 38 people in your research study, the critical value of t is 2.026.

If you have more than 40 people in your research study, the critical value of t is always 1.96.

Note that the "critical t column" in Appendix represents the value of t that you need to obtain to be 95% confident of your results as "significant" results.

The critical value of t is the value that tells you whether or not you have found a "significant result" in your statistical test.

The t-table in Appendix represents a series of "bell-shaped normal curves" (they are called bell-shaped because they look like the outline of the Liberty Bell that you can see in Philadelphia outside of Independence Hall).

The "middle" of these normal curves is treated as if it were zero point on the x-axis [the technical explanation of this fact is beyond the scope of this book, but any good statistics book (e. g. Zikmund and Babin 2010) will explain this concept to you if you are interested in learning more about it].

Thus, values of t that are to the right of this zero point are positive values that use a plus sign before them, and values of t that are to the left of this zero point are negative values that use a minus sign before them. Thus, some values of t are positive, and some are negative.

However, every statistics book that includes a t-table only reprints the positive side of the t-curves because the negative side is the mirror image of the positive side; this means that the negative side contains the exact same numbers as the positive side, but all the negative numbers have a minus sign in front of them.

Therefore, to use the t-table in Appendix, you need to take the absolute value of the t-value you found when you use the t-test formula since the t-table in Appendix only has the values of t that are the positive values for t.

Throughout this book, we are assuming that you want to be 95% confident in the results of your statistical tests. Therefore, the value for t in the t-table in Appendix tells you whether or not the t-value you obtained when you used the formula for the one-group t-test is within the 95% interval of the t-curve range which that t-value would be expected to occur with 95% confidence.

If the t-value you obtained when you used the formula for the one-group t-test is inside of the 95% confidence range, we say that the result you found is not significant (note that this is equivalent to accepting the null hypothesis).

If the t-value you found when you used the formula for the one-group t-test is outside of this 95% confidence range, we say that you have found a significant result that would be expected to occur less than 5% of the time (note that this is equivalent to rejecting the null hypothesis and accepting the alternative hypothesis).

2. 4. 1. 6 Step 6: State the Result of Your Statistical Test

There are two possible results when you use the one-group t-test, and only one of them can be accepted as "true".

Either: Since the absolute value of t that you found in the t-test formula is less than the critical value of t in Appendix, you accept the null hypothesis.

Or: Since the absolute value of t that you found in the t-test formula is greater than the critical value of t in Appendix, you reject the null hypothesis, and accept the alternative hypothesis.

2.4.1.7 Step 7: State the Conclusion of Your Statistical Test in Plain English

In practice, this is more difficult than it sounds because you are trying to summarize the result of your statistical test in simple English that is both concise and accurate so that someone who has never had a statistics course (such as your boss, perhaps) can understand the result of your test. This is a difficult task, and we will give you lots of practice doing this last and most important step throughout this book.

If you have read this far, you are ready to sit down at your computer and perform the one-group t-test by using Excel on some hypothetical data from the Guest Satisfaction Survey used by Marriott Hotels.

Let's give this a try.

2.4.2 One-group t-test for the Mean

Suppose that you have been hired as a statistical consultant by Marriott Hotel in St. Louis to analyze the data from a Guest Satisfaction survey that they give to all customers to determine the degree of satisfaction of these customers for various activities of the hotel.

The survey contains a number of items, but suppose item #7 is the one in Fig. 2.4.1.

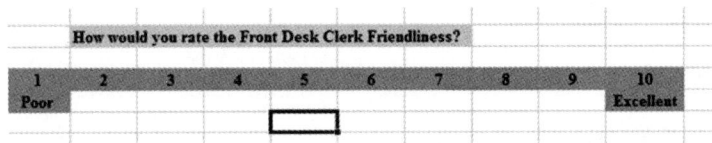

Fig. 2.4.1 Sample Survey Item for Marriot Hotel (Practical Example)

Suppose further, that you have decided to analyze the data from last week's customers by using the one-group t-test.

Important note: You would need to use this test for each of the survey items separately.

Suppose that the hypothetical data for Item #7 from last week at the St. Louis Marriott Hotel were based on a sample size of 124 guests who had a mean score on this item of 6.58 and a standard deviation on this item of 2.44.

Objective: To analyze the data for each question separately by using the one-group t-test for each survey item

Create an Excel spreadsheet with the following information:

B11: Null hypothesis

B14: Alternative hypothesis

Note: Remember that when you are using a rating scale item, both the null hypothesis and the research hypothesis refer to the "middle of the scale". In the 10-point scale in this example, the middle of the scale is 5.5 since five numbers are below 5.5 (i.e., 1~5) and five numbers are above 5.5 (i. e. 6~10). Therefore, the hypotheses for this rating scale item are:

$$H_0 : \mu = 5.5$$
$$H_1 : \mu \neq 5.5$$

B17: n

B20: mean

B23: STDEV

B26: se

B29: critical t

B32: t-test

B36: Result:

B41: Conclusion:

Now, use Excel:

D17: enter the sample size

D20: enter the mean

D23: enter the STDEV (see Fig. 2.4.2)

D26: compute the standard error by using the formula in Chapter 2.1

D29: find the critical t value of t in the t-table in Appendix

Now, enter the following formula in cell D32 to find the t-test result: =(D20−5.5)/D26

This formula takes the sample mean (D20) and subtracts the population hypothesized mean of 5.5 from the sample mean, and THEN divides the answer by the standard error of the mean (D26). Note that you need to enter D20 5.5 with an open-parenthesis before D20 and a closed-parenthesis after 5.5 so that the answer of 1.08 is THEN divided by the standard error of 0.22 to get the t-test result of 4.93. Now, use two decimal places for both the se and the t-test result (see Fig. 2.4.3).

Now, write the following sentence in D36-D39 to summarize the result of the t-test:

D36: Since the absolute value of t of 4.93 is

D37: greater than the critical t of 1.96, we

D38: reject the null hypothesis and accept

D39: the alternative hypothesis.

Part II Statistical Application with Excel 111

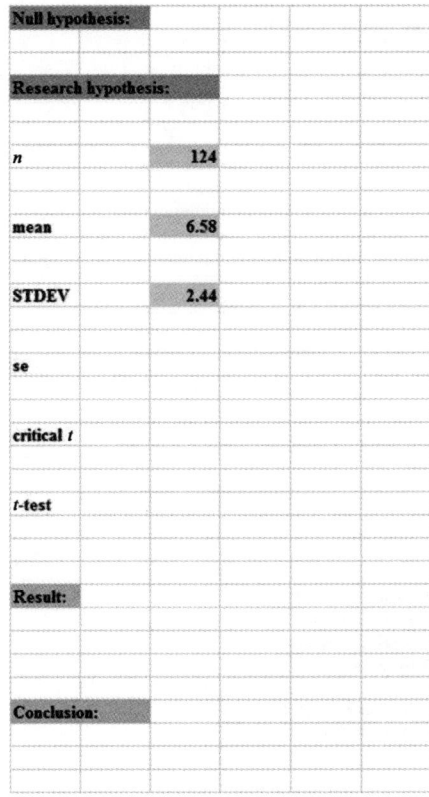

Fig. 2.4.2 Basic Data Table for
Front Desk Clerk Friendliness

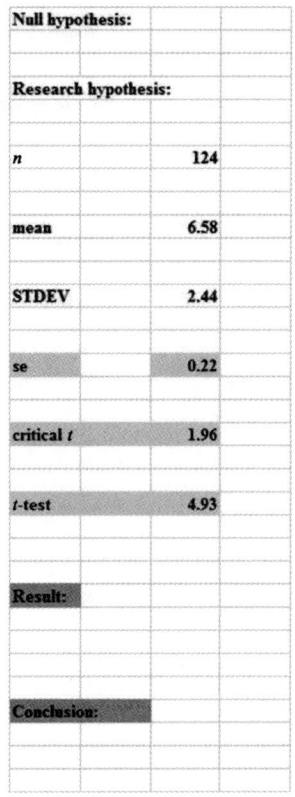

Fig. 2.4.3 t-test Formula Result
for Front Desk Clerk Friendliness

Lastly, write the following sentence in D41-D43 to summarize the conclusion of the result for Item #7 of the Marriott Guest Satisfaction Survey:

D41: St. Louis Marriott Hotel guests rated the

D42: Front Desk Clerks as significantly

D43: friendly last week.

Save your file as MARRIOTT 3

Print the final spreadsheet so that it fits onto one page as given in Fig. 2.4.4. Enter the null hypothesis and the alternative hypothesis by hand on your spreadsheet.

Important note: It is important for you to understand that "technically" the above conclusion in statistical terms should state:

"St. Louis Marriott Hotel Guests rated the Front Desk Clerks as friendly last week, and this result was probably not obtained by chance."

However, throughout this book, we are using the term "significantly" in writing the conclusion of statistical tests to alert the reader that the result of the statistical test was proba-

Null hypothesis:		μ = 5.5	
Research hypothesis:		μ ≠ 5.5	
n		124	
mean		6.58	
STDEV		2.44	
se		0.22	
critical t		1.96	
t-test		4.93	
Result:		Since the absolute value of t of 4.93 is greater than the critical t of 1.96, we reject the null hypothesis and accept the research hypothesis.	
Conclusion:		St. Louis Marriott Hotel guests rated the Front Desk Clerks as significantly friendly last week.	

Fig. 2.4.4 Final Spreadsheet for Front Desk Clerk Friendliness

bly not a chance finding, but instead of writing all of those words each time, we use the word "significantly" as a shorthand to the longer explanation. This makes it much easier for the reader to understand the conclusion when it is written "in plain English", instead of a technical, statistical language.

2.4.3 Can You Use Either the 95 Percent Confidence Interval about the Mean or the One-group t-test When Testing Hypothesis?

Both the confidence interval about the mean and the one-group t-test are used often in a business research on the types of problems described so far in this book. Both of these tests produce the same result and the same conclusion from the data set!

Both of these tests are explained in this book because some managers prefer the confidence interval about the mean test, others prefer the one-group t-test, and still others prefer to use both tests on the same data to make their results and conclusions clearer to the reader of their research reports. Since we do not know which of these tests your manager prefers, we have explained both of them so that you are competent in the use of both tests in the analysis of statistical data.

Now, let's try your Excel skills on the one-group t-test on these three problems at the end of this chapter.

2.4.4 End-of-chapter Practice Problems

(1) Subaru of America rates the customer satisfaction of its dealers on a weekly basis on its Purchase Experience Survey, and demands that dealers achieve a 93% satisfaction score, or the dealers are required to take additional training to improve their customer satisfaction scores. Suppose that you have selected a random sample of rating forms submitted by new car purchasers (either online or through the mail) for the St. Louis Subaru dealers from a recent week and that you have prepared the hypothetical table in Fig. 2.4.5 for Question #1d.

SUBARU Customer Satisfaction Survey							
Question #1d: "The salesperson was knowledgeable about the Subaru model line."							
	1 Completely Disagree	2	3	4	5	6	7 Completely Agree
		Rating					
		5					
		7					
		6					
		4					
		3					
		5					
		6					
		7					
		2					
		3					
		5					
		7					
		4					
		7					
		7					
		5					
		6					
		6					
		4					
		3					
		5					
		5					

Fig. 2.4.5 Worksheet Data for Chapter 2.4: Practice Problem #1

(a) Write the null hypothesis and the alternative hypothesis on your spreadsheet.

(b) Use Excel to find the sample size, mean, standard deviation, and standard error of the mean to the right of the data set. Use number format (2 decimal places) for the mean, standard deviation, and standard error of the mean.

(c) Enter the critical t from the t-table in Appendix onto your spreadsheet, and label it.

(d) Use Excel to compute the t-value for these data (use 2 decimal places) and label it on your spreadsheet.

(e) Type the result on your spreadsheet, and then type the conclusion in plain English on your spreadsheet.

(f) Save the file as subaru 4.

(2) Suppose that you work in the human resources department of your company and that top management has asked your department to conduct a Morale Survey of managers to determine their attitude toward working in this company. To check your Excel skills, you have drawn a random sample of the results of the survey from the managers on one question, and the data from Item #35 appear in Fig. 2.4.6.

HUMAN RESOURCES DEPARTMENT MORALE SURVEY OF MANAGERS								
Item #35: "How would you rate the intellectual challenge provided by your job?"								
1 very low	2	3	4	5	6	7	8	9 very high
				Rating				
				5				
				6				
				4				
				7				
				8				
				2				
				4				
				3				
				6				
				4				
				7				
				9				
				2				
				4				
				3				
				5				
				3				
				4				
				6				
				5				
				7				
				4				
				3				
				5				
				2				

Fig. 2.4.6 Worksheet Data for Chapter 2.4: Practice Problem #2

(a) On your Excel spreadsheet, write the null hypothesis and the alternative hypothesis for these data.

(b) Use Excel to find the sample size, mean, standard deviation, and standard error of the mean for these data (two decimal places for the mean, standard deviation, and standard error of the mean).

(c) Use Excel to perform a one-group t-test on these data (two decimal places).

(d) On your printout, type the critical value of t (0.05 level) given in your t-table in Appendix.

(e) On your spreadsheet, type the result of the t-test.

(f) On your spreadsheet, type the conclusion of your study in plain English.

(g) Save the file as: challenge4.

(3) Suppose that you have been hired as a marketing consultant by the Missouri Botanical Garden and have been asked to re-design the Comment Card survey that they have been asking visitors to The Garden to fill out after their visit. The Garden has been using a 5-point rating scale with 1=poor and 5=excellent. Suppose, further, that you have convinced The Garden staff to change to a 9-point scale with 1=poor and 9=excellent so that the data will have a larger standard deviation. The hypothetical results of a recent week for Question #10 of your revised survey appear in Fig. 2.4.7.

MISSOURI BOTANICAL GARDEN

VISITOR SURVEY

Item #10 "How would you rate the helpfulness of The Garden staff?"

1   2   3   4   5   6   7   8   9
poor   excellent

Rating
8
6
5
7
9
5
6
4
8
7
6
8
6
7
9
7
6
3
8
7
6

Fig. 2.4.7 Worksheet Data for Chapter 2.4: Practice Problem #3

(a) Write the null hypothesis and the alternative hypothesis on your spreadsheet.

(b) Use Excel to find the sample size, mean, standard deviation, and standard error of the mean to the right of the data set. Use number format (2 decimal places) for the mean, standard deviation, and standard error of the mean.

(c) Enter the critical t from the t-table in Appendix onto your spreadsheet, and label it.

(d) Use Excel to compute the t-value for these data (use 2 decimal places) and label it on your spreadsheet.

(e) Type the result on your spreadsheet, and then type the conclusion in plain English on your spreadsheet.

(f) Save the file as Garden 5.

2.5 Two-group t-test of the Difference of the Means for Independent Groups

Up until now in this book, you have been dealing with the situation in which you have had only one group of people in your research study and only one measurement "number" on each of these people. We will now change gears and deal with the situation in which you are measuring two groups of people instead of only one group of people.

Whenever you have two completely different groups of people (i.e., no one person is in both groups, but every person is measured on only one variable to produce one "number" for each person), we say that the two groups are "independent of one another". This chapter deals with just that situation and that is why it is called the two-group t-test for independent groups.

The assumptions underlying the two-group t-test are the following (Zikmund and Babin 2010): (1) Both groups are sampled from a normal population, and (2) the variances of the two populations are approximately equal. Note that the standard deviation is merely the square root of the variance. (There are different formulas to use when each person is measured twice to create two groups of data, and this situation is called "dependent", but those formulas are beyond the scope of this book.) This book only deals with two groups that are independent of one another so that no person is in both groups of data.

When you are testing for the difference between the means for two groups, it is important to remember that there are two different formulas that you need to use depending on the sample sizes of the two groups:

(1) Use Formula #1 in this chapter when both of the groups have more than 30 people in them.

(2) Use Formula #2 in this chapter when either group, or both groups, have sample sizes fewer than 30 people in them.

We will illustrate both of these situations in this chapter. But, first, we need to understand the steps involved in hypothesis-testing when two groups of people are involved before we dive into the formulas for this test.

2.5.1 The 9 Steps for Hypothesis-testing by Using the Two-group t-test

Objective: To learn the 9 steps of hypothesis-testing by using two groups of people and the two-group t-test

You will see that these steps parallel the steps used in the previous chapter that dealt with the one-group t-test, but there are some important differences between the steps that you need to understand clearly before we dive into the formulas for the two-group t-test.

2.5.1.1 Step 1: Name One Group Group 1, and the Other Group Group 2

The formulas used in this chapter will use the numbers 1 and 2 to distinguish between the two groups. If you define which group is Group 1 and which group is Group 2, you can use these numbers in your computations without having to write out the names of the groups.

For example, if you are testing teenage boys on their preference for the taste of Coke or Pepsi, you could call the groups "Coke" and "Pepsi". But this would require your writing out the words "Coke" or "Pepsi" whenever you wanted to refer to one of these groups. If you call the Coke group Group 1, and the Pepsi group Group 2, this makes it much easier to refer to the groups because it saves your writing time.

As a second example, you could be comparing the test market results for Kansas City versus Indianapolis, but if you had to write out the names of those cities whenever you wanted to refer to them, it would take you more time than it would if, instead, you named one city Group 1, and the other city Group 2.

Note, also, that it is completely arbitrary which group you call Group 1, and which group you call Group 2. You will achieve the same result and the same conclusion from the formulas since you decide to define these two groups.

2.5.1.2 Step 2: Create a Table That Summarizes the Sample Size, Mean Score, and Standard Deviation of Each Group

This step makes it easier for you to make sure that you are using the correct numbers in the formulas for the two-group t-test. If you get the numbers "mixed-up", your entire formula work will be incorrect and you will botch the problem terribly.

For example, suppose that you tested teenage boys on their preference for the taste of Coke versus Pepsi in which the boys were randomly assigned to taste just one of these brands and then rate its taste on a 100-point scale from 0 = poor to 100 = excellent. After the research study was completed, suppose that the Coke group had 52 boys in it, their mean taste rating was 55 with a standard deviation of 7, while the Pepsi group had 57 boys in it and their average taste rating was 64 with a standard deviation of 13.

The formulas for analyzing these data to determine if there was a significant difference in the taste rating for teenage boys for these two brands require you to use six numbers correctly in the formulas: the sample size, the mean, and the standard deviation of each of the two groups. All six of these numbers must be used correctly in the formulas if you what analyze the data correctly.

If you create a table to summarize these data, a good example of the table, using both Step 1 and Step 2, would be the data presented in Fig. 2.5.1.

For example, if you decide to call Group 1 the Coke group and Group 2 the Pepsi group, the following table would place the six numbers from your research study into the proper calls of the table as in Fig. 2.5.2.

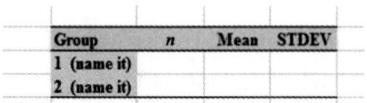

Fig. 2.5.1 Basic Table Format for the Two-group t-test

Fig. 2.5.2 Results of Entering the Data Needed for the Two-group t-test

You can now use the formulas for the two-group t-test with more confidence that the six numbers will be placed in the proper place in the formulas.

Note that you could just as easily call Group 1 the Pepsi group and Group 2 the Coke group; it makes no difference how you decide to name the two groups; this decision is up to you.

2.5.1.3 Step 3: State the Null Hypothesis and the Alternative Hypothesis for the Two-group t-test

If you have completed Step 1 above, this step is very easy because the null hypothesis and the alternative hypothesis will always be stated in the same way for the two-group t-test. The null hypothesis states that the population means of the two groups are equal, while the alternative hypothesis states that the population means of the two groups are not equal. In notation format, this becomes:

$$H_0: \mu_1 = \mu_2$$

$$H_1: \mu_1 \neq \mu_2$$

You can now see that this notation is much simpler than having to write out the names of the two groups in all of your formulas.

2.5.1.4 Step 4: Select the Appropriate Statistical Test

Since this chapter deals with the situation in which you have two groups of people but only one measurement on each person in each group, we will use the two-group t-test throughout this chapter.

2.5.1.5 Step 5: Decide on a Decision Rule for the Two-group t-test

The decision rule is exactly what it was in the previous chapter (see Section 2.4.1.3) when we dealt with the one-group t-test.

(a) If the absolute value of t is less than the critical value of t, accept the null hypothesis.

(b) If the absolute value of t is greater than the critical value of t, reject the null hypothesis and accept the research hypothesis. Since you learned how to find the absolute value of t in the previous chapter (see Section 2.4.1.3), you can use that knowledge in this chapter.

2.5.1.6 Step 6: Calculate the Formula for the Two-group t-test

Since we are using two different formulas in this chapter for the two-group t-test depending on the sample size of the people in the two groups, we will explain how to use those formulas later in this chapter.

2.5.1.7 Step 7: Find the Critical Value of t in the t-table in Appendix

In the previous chapter we dealt with the one-group t-test, we found the critical value of t in the t-table in Appendix by finding the sample size for the one group of people in the first column of the table, and then read the critical value of t across from it on the right in the "critical t column" in the table (see Section 2.4.1.5). This process was fairly simple once you have had some practice in doing this step.

However, for the two-group t-test, the procedure for finding the critical value of t is more complicated because you have two different groups of people in your study, and they often have different sample sizes in each group.

To use Appendix correctly in this chapter, you need to learn how to find the "degrees of freedom" for your study. We will discuss that process now.

Finding the Degrees of Freedom (df) for the two-group t-test

Objective: To find the degrees of freedom for the two-group t-test and to use it to find the critical value of t in the t-table in Appendix

The mathematical explanation of the concept of the "degrees of freedom" is beyond the scope of this book, but you can find out more about this concept by reading any good statistics book (e.g. Keller 2009). For our purposes, you can easily understand how to find the degrees of freedom and to use it to find the critical value of t in Appendix. The formula for the degrees of freedom (df) is:

$$\text{degrees of freedom} = df = n_1 + n_2 - 2$$

In other words, you add the sample size for Group 1 to the sample size for Group 2 and then subtract 2 from this total to get the number of degrees of freedom to use in Appendix.

Take a look at Appendix.

Instead of using the first column as we did in the one-group t-test that is based on the sample size, n, of one group of people, we need to use the second-column of this table (df) to find the critical value of t for the two-group t-test.

For example, if you had 13 people in Group 1 and 17 people in Group 2, the degrees of freedom would be: $13+17-2=28$, and the critical value of t would be 2.048 since you look down the second column which contains the degrees of freedom until you come to the number

28, and then read 2.048 in the "critical t column" in the table to find the critical value of t when $df=28$.

As a second example, if you had 52 people in Group 1 and 57 people in Group 2, the degrees of freedom would be: $52+57-2=107$. When you go down the second column in Appendix for the degrees of freedom, you find that once you go beyond the degrees of freedom equal to 39, the critical value of t is always 1.96, and that is the value you would use for the critical t with this example.

2.5.1.8 Step 8: State the Result of Your Statistical Test

The result follows the exact same result format that you found for the one-group t-test in the previous chapter (see Section 2.4.1.6).

Either: Since the absolute value of t that you found in the t-test formula is less than the critical value of t in Appendix, you accept the null hypothesis.

Or: Since the absolute value of t that you found in the t-test formula is greater than the critical value of t in Appendix, you reject the null hypothesis and accept the alternative hypothesis.

2.5.1.9 Step 9: State the Conclusion of Your Statistical Test in Plain English

Writing the conclusion for the two-group t-test is more difficult than writing the conclusion for the one-group t-test because you have to decide what the difference was between the two groups.

When you accept the null hypothesis, the conclusion is simple to write: "There is no difference between the two groups in the variable that was measured."

But when you reject the null hypothesis and accept the alternative hypothesis, you need to be careful about writing the conclusion so that it is both accurate and concise.

Let's give you some practice in writing the conclusion of a two-group t-test.

(1) Writing the conclusion of the two-group t-test when you accept the null hypothesis

Objective: To write the conclusion of the two-group t-test when you have accepted the null hypothesis

Suppose that you have been hired as a statistical consultant by Marriott Hotel in St. Louis to analyze the data from a Guest Satisfaction Survey that they give to all customers to determine the degree of satisfaction of these customers for various activities of the hotel. The survey contains a number of items, but suppose Item #7 is the one in Fig. 2.5.3.
Suppose further, that you have decided to analyze the data from last week's customers comparing men and women using the two-group t-test.

Important note: You would need to use this test for each of the survey items separately.

Suppose that the hypothetical data for Item #7 from last week at the St. Louis Marriott Hotel were based on a sample size of 124 men who had a mean score on this item of 6.58 and a

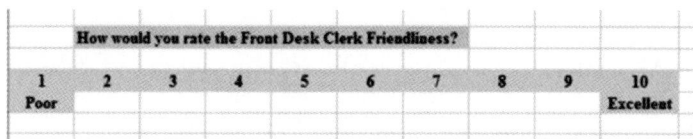

Fig. 2.5.3   Marriott Hotel Guest Satisfaction Survey Item #7

standard deviation on this item of 2.44. Suppose that you also had data from 86 women from last week who had a mean score of 6.45 with a standard deviation of 1.86.

We will explain later in this chapter how to produce the results of the two-group t-test using its formulas, but, for now, let's "cut to the chase" and tell you that those formulas would produce the following in Fig. 2.5.4.

degrees of freedom: 208

critical t: 1.96 (in Appendix)

t-test formula: 0.44 (when you use your calculator)

Result: Since the absolute value of 0.44 is less than the critical t of 1.96, we accept the null hypothesis.

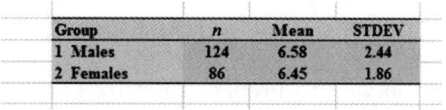

Fig. 2.5.4   Worksheet Data for Males vs. Females for the St. Louis Marriott Hotel for Accepting the Null Hypothesis

Conclusion: There was no difference between male and female guests last week in their rating of the friendliness of the front-desk clerk at the St. Louis Marriott Hotel.

Now, let's see what happens when you reject the null hypothesis (H_0) and accept the alternative hypothesis (H_1).

(2) Writing the conclusion of the two-group t-test when you reject the null hypothesis and accept the alternative hypothesis

Objective: To write the conclusion of the two-group t-test when you have rejected the null hypothesis and accepted the alternative hypothesis

Let's continue with this same example of the Marriott Hotel, but with the result that we reject the null hypothesis and accept the alternative hypothesis.

Let's assume that this time you have data on 85 males from last week and their mean score on this question was 7.26 with a standard deviation of 2.35. Let's further suppose that you also have data on 48 females from last week and their mean score on this question was 4.37 with a standard deviation of 3.26.

Group	n	Mean	STDEV
1 Males	85	7.26	2.35
2 Females	48	4.37	3.26

Fig. 2.5.5   Worksheet Data for St. Louis Marriott Hotel for Obtaining a Significant Difference Between Males and Females

Without going into the details of the formulas for the two-group t-test, these data would produce the following result and conclusion based on Fig. 2.5.5.

Null Hypothesis: $\mu_1 = \mu_2$

Alternative Hypothesis: $\mu_1 \neq \mu_2$

degrees of freedom: 131

critical t: 1.96 (in Appendix)

t-test formula: 5.40 (when you use your calculator)

Result: Since the absolute value of 5.40 is greater than the critical t of 1.96, we reject the null hypothesis and accept the alternative hypothesis.

Now, you need to compare the ratings of the men and women to find out which group had the more positive rating of the friendliness of the front-desk clerk using the following rule.

Rule: To summarize the conclusion of the two-group t-test, just compare the means of the two groups, and be sure to use the word "significantly" in your conclusion if you rejected the null hypothesis and accepted the alternative hypothesis.

A good way to prepare to write the conclusion of the two-group t-test when you are using a rating scale is to place the mean scores of the two groups on a drawing of the scale so that you can visualize the difference of the mean scores. For example, for our Marriott Hotel example above, you would draw this "picture" of the scale in Fig. 2.5.6.

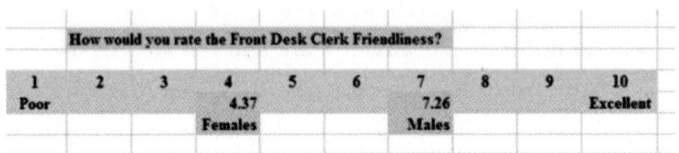

Fig. 2.5.6 Example of Drawing a "Picture" of the Means of the Two Groups on the Rating Scale

This drawing tells you visually that males had a higher positive rating than females on this item (7.26 vs. 4.37). And, since you rejected the null hypothesis and accepted the alternative hypothesis, you know that you have found a significant difference between the two mean scores. So, our conclusion needs to contain the following key words:

—Male guests

—Female guests

—Marriott Hotel

—St. Louis

—last week

—significantly

—Front Desk Clerks

—more friendly or less friendly

—either (7.26 vs. 4.37) or (4.37 vs. 7.26)

We can use these key words to write either of two conclusions which are logically identical:

Either: Male guests at the Marriott Hotel in St. Louis last week rated the Front Desk Clerks as significantly more friendly than female guests (7.26 vs. 4.37).

Or: Female guests at the Marriott Hotel in St. Louis last week rated the Front Desk Clerks as significantly less friendly than male guests (4.37 vs. 7.26).

Both of these conclusions are accurate, so you can decide which one you want to write. It is up to you.

Also, note that the mean scores in parentheses at the end of these conclusions must match the sequence of the two groups in your conclusion. For example, if you say that "Male guests rated the Front Desk Clerks as significantly more friendly than female guests", the end of this conclusion should be 7.26 vs. 4.37 since you mentioned males first and females second.

Alternately, if you wrote that "Female guests rated the Front Desk Clerks as significantly less friendly than male guests", the end of this conclusion should be 4.37 vs. 7.26 since you mentioned females first and males second.

Putting the two mean scores at the end of your conclusion saves the reader from having to turn back to the table in your research report to find these mean scores to see how far apart the mean scores were.

Now, let's discuss FORMULA #1 that deals with the situation in which both groups have more than 30 people in them.

Objective: To use FORMULA #1 for the two-group t-test when both groups have a sample size greater than 30 people.

2.5.2 Formula #1: Both Groups Have More Than 30 People in Them

The first formula we will discuss will be used when you have two groups of people with more than 30 people in each group and one measurement on each person in each group. This formula for the two-group t-test is:

$$t = \frac{\overline{X}_1 - \overline{X}_2}{S_{\overline{X}_1 - \overline{X}_2}}$$

$$\text{where} \quad S_{\overline{X}_1 - \overline{X}_2} = \sqrt{\frac{S_1^2}{n_1} + \frac{S_2^2}{n_2}}$$

and where degrees of freedom $= df = n_1 + n_2 - 2$

This formula looks daunting when you first see it, but let's explain some of the parts of this formula:

We have explained the concept of "degrees of freedom" earlier in this chapter, and so you should be able to find the degrees of freedom needed for this formula in order to find the critical value of t in Appendix.

In the previous chapter, the formula for the one-group t-test was the following:

$$t = \frac{\overline{X} - \mu}{se}$$

Where $se = \frac{s}{\sqrt{n}}$

For the one-group t-test, you found the mean score and subtracted the population mean from it, and then divided the result by the standard error of the mean (se) to get the result of the t-test. You then compared the t-test result to the critical value of t to see if you either accepted the null hypothesis, or rejected the null hypothesis and accepted the alternative hypothesis.

The two-group t-test requires a different formula because you have two groups of people, each with a mean score on some variable. You are trying to determine whether to accept the null hypothesis that the population means of the two groups are equal (in other words, there is no difference statistically between these two means), or whether the difference between the means of the two groups is "sufficiently large" that you would accept that there is a significant difference in the mean scores of the two groups.

The numerator of the two-group t-test asks you to find the difference of the means of the two groups:

$$\overline{X}_1 - \overline{X}_2$$

The next step in the formula for the two-group t-test is to divide the answer you get when you subtract the two means by the standard error of the difference of the two means, and this is a different standard error of the mean that you found for the one-group t-test because there are two means in the two-group t-test.

The standard error of the mean when you have two groups of people is called the "standard error of the difference of the means" between the two groups. This formula looks less scary when you break it down into four steps:

(1) Square the standard deviation of Group 1, and divide this result by the sample size for Group 1 (n_1).

(2) Square the standard deviation of Group 2, and divide this result by the sample size for Group 2 (n_2).

(3) Add the results of the above two steps to get a total score.

(4) Take the square root of this total score to find the standard error of the difference of the means between the two groups, $S_{\overline{X}_1 - \overline{X}_2} = \sqrt{\frac{S_1^2}{n_1} + \frac{S_2^2}{n_2}}$.

This last step is the one that gives students the most difficulty when they are finding this standard error using their calculator, because they are in such a hurry to get to the answer that they forget to carry the square root sign down to the last step, and thus get a larger number than they should for the standard error.

An Example of Formula #1 for the Two-group t-test

Now, let's use Formula #1 in a situation in which both groups have a sample size greater than 30 people.

Suppose that you have been hired by Pepsi Co to do a taste test with teenage boys (aged 13-18) to determine if they like the taste of Pepsi the same as the taste of Coke. The boys are not told the brand name of the soft drink that they taste.

You select a group of boys in this age range, and randomly assign them to one of two groups: (1) Group 1 tastes Coke, and (2) Group 2 tastes Pepsi. Each group rates the taste of their soft drink on a 100-point scale using the following scale in Fig. 2.5.7.

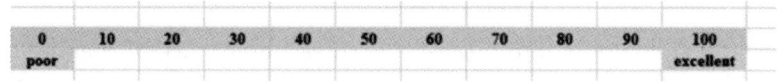

Fig. 2.5.7   Example of a Rating Scale for a Soft Drink
Taste Test (Practical Example)

Suppose you collect these ratings and determine (using your new Excel skills) that the 52 boys in the Coke group had a mean rating of 55 with a standard deviation of 7, while the 57 boys in the Pepsi group had a mean rating of 64 with a standard deviation of 13.

Note that the two-group t-test does not require that both groups have the same sample size. This is another way of saying that the two-group t-test is "robust" (a fancy term that statisticians like to use).

Group	n	Mean	STDEV
1 Coke	52	55	7
2 Pepsi	57	64	13

Fig. 2.5.8   Worksheet Data for
Soft Drink Taste Test

Your data then produce the following table in Fig. 2.5.8.

Create an Excel spreadsheet, and enter the following information:

B3: Group

B4: 1 Coke

B5: 2 Pepsi

C3: n

D3: Mean E3: STDEV

C4: 52

D4: 55

E4: 7

C5: 57

D5: 64

E5: 13

B8: Null hypothesis:

B10: Alternative hypothesis:

Fig. 2.5.9 Results of Widening Column B and Centering the Numbers in the Cells

Now, widen column B so that it is twice as wide as column A, and center the six numbers and their labels in your table (see Fig. 2.5.9)

Since both groups have a sample size greater than 30, you need to use Formula #1 for the t-test for the difference of the means of the two groups.

Let's "break this formula down into pieces" to reduce the chance of making a mistake.

B13: STDEV1 squared/n_1 (note that you square the standard deviation of Group 1, and then divide the result by the sample size of Group 1)

B16: STDEV2 squared/n_2

B19: D13+D16

B22: se

B25: critical t

B28: t-test

B31: Result:

B36: Conclusion: (see Fig. 2.5.10)

You now need to compute the values of the above formulas in the following cells:

D13: the result of the formula needed to compute cell B13 (use 2 decimals)

D16: the result of the formula needed to compute cell B16 (use 2 decimals)

D19: the result of the formula needed to compute cell B19 (use 2 decimals)

D22: =SQRT(D19) (use 2 decimals)

Fig. 2.5.10 Formula Labels for the Two-group t-test

This formula should give you a standard error (se) of 1.98.

D25: 1.96 (Since $df = n_1 + n_2 - 2$, this gives $df = 109 - 2 = 107$, and the critical t is, therefore, 1.96 in Appendix.)

D28: = (D4−D5)/D22 (2 decimals)

This formula should give you a value for the t-test of: −4.55.

Next, check to see if you have rounded off all figures in D13: D28 to two decimal places (see Fig. 2.5.11).

A	B	C	D	E
13	STDEV1 squared / n_1		0.94	
16	STDEV2 squared / n_2		2.96	
19	D13 + D16		3.91	
22	se		1.98	
25	critical t		1.96	
28	t-test		-4.55	

Fig. 2.5.11 Results of the t-test Formula for the Soft Drink Taste Test

Now, write the following sentence in D31 to D34 to summarize the result of the study:

D31: Since the absolute value of −4.55

D32: is greater than the critical t of

D33: 1.96, we reject the null hypothesis

D34: and accept the alternative hypothesis.

Finally, write the following sentence in D36 to D38 to summarize the conclusion of the study in plain English.

D36: Teenage boys rated the taste of

D37: Pepsi as significantly better than

D38: the taste of Coke (64 vs. 55).

Save your file as: COKE4

Print this file so that it fits onto one page, and write by hand the null hypothesis and the alternative hypothesis on your printout.

The final spreadsheet appears in Fig. 2.5.12.
Now, let's use the second formula for the two-group t-test which whenever we use either group, or both groups, have fewer than 30 people in them.

Objective: To use Formula #2 for the two-group t-test when one group or both groups have fewer than 30 people in them.

Now, let's look at the case when one group or both groups have a sample size fewer than 30 people in them.

Group	n	Mean	STDEV
1 Coke	52	55	7
2 Pepsi	57	64	13

Null hypothesis:	$\mu_1 = \mu_2$	
Alternative hypothesis:	$\mu_1 \neq \mu_2$	
STDEV1 squared / n_1	0.94	
STDEV2 squared / n_2	2.96	
D13 + D16	3.91	
se	1.98	
critical t	1.96	
t-test	-4.55	
Result:	Since the absolute value of -4.55 is greater than the critical t of 1.96, we reject the null hypothesis and accept the alternative hypothesis.	
Conclusion:	Teenage boys rated the taste of Pepsi as significantly better than the taste of Coke (64 vs. 55)	

Fig. 2.5.12 Final Worksheet for the Coke vs. Pepsi Taste Test

2.5.3 Formula #2: One or Both Groups Have Fewer than 30 People in Them

Suppose that you work for the manufacturer of MP3 players and that you have been asked to do a pricing experiment to see if more units can be sold at a reduction in price. Suppose, further, that you have randomly selected 7 wholesalers to purchase the product at the regular price, and they purchased a mean of 117.7 units with a standard deviation of 19.9 units.

In addition, you randomly selected a different group of 8 wholesalers to purchase the product at a 10% price cut, and they purchased a mean of 125.1 units with a standard deviation of 15.1 units. You want to test to see if the two different prices produced a significant difference in the number of MP3 units sold. You have decided to use the two-group t-test for independent samples, and the following data resulted in Fig. 2.5.13.

Group	n	Mean	STDEV
1 Regular Price	7	117.7	19.9
2 Reduced price	8	125.1	15.1

Fig. 2.5.13 Worksheet Data for Wholesaler Price Comparison (Practical Example)

Null hypothesis: $\mu_1 = \mu_2$

Alternative hypothesis: $\mu_1 \neq \mu_2$

Note: Since both groups have a sample size fewer than 30 people, you need to use Formula #2 in the following steps.

Create an Excel spreadsheet, and enter the following information:

B3: Group

B4: 1 Regular Price

B5: 2 Reduced Price

C3: n

D3: Mean

E3: STDEV

Now, widen column B so that it is three times as wide as column A.

To do this, click on B at the top left of your spreadsheet to highlight all of the cells in column B. Then, move the mouse pointer to the right end of the B cell until you get a "cross" sign; then, click on this "cross" sign and drag the sign to the right until you can read all of the words on your screen. Then, stop clicking!

C4: 7

D4: 117.7

E4: 19.9

C5: 8

D5: 125.1

E5: 15.1

Next, center the information in cells C3 to E5 by highlighting these cells and then using this step.

Click on the bottom line, second from the left icon, under "Alignment" at the top-center of Home

B8: Null hypothesis

B10: Alternative hypothesis: (see Fig. 2.5.14)
Since both groups have a sample size less than 30, you need to use Formula #2 for the t-test for the difference of the means of two independent samples.

Formula #2 for the two-group t-test is the following:

$$t = \frac{\overline{X}_1 - \overline{X}_2}{S_{\overline{X}_1 - \overline{X}_2}}$$

Fig. 2.5.14 Wholesaler Price Comparison Worksheet
Data for Hypothesis Testing

$$\text{where } S_{\bar{X}_1 - \bar{X}_2} = \sqrt{\frac{(n_1-1)S_1^2 + (n_2-1)S_2^2}{n_1+n_2-2}\left(\frac{1}{n_1}+\frac{1}{n_2}\right)}$$

and where degrees of freedom $= df = n_1 + n_2 - 2$

This formula is complicated, and so it will reduce your chance of making a mistake in writing it if you "break it down into pieces" instead of trying to write the formula as one cell entry.

Now, enter these words on your spreadsheet:

B13: $(n_1-1) \times$ STDEV1 squared

B16: $(n_2-1) \times$ STDEV2 squared

B19: $n_1 + n_2 - 2$

B22: $1/n_1 + 1/n_2$

B25: se

B28: critical t

B31: t-test

B34: Result

B39: Conclusion: (see Fig. 2.5.15)

You now need to compute the values of the above formulas in the following cells.

E13: the result of the formula needed to compute cell B13 (use 2 decimals)

E16: the result of the formula needed to compute cell B16 (use 2 decimals)

E19: the result of the formula needed to compute cell B19

Fig. 2.5.15 Who Lesaler Price Comparison Formula Labels for Two-group t-test

E22: the result of the formula needed to compute cell B22 (use 2 decimals)

E25: =SQRT{[(E13+E16)/E19]×E22}

Note the three open parentheses after SQRT, and the three closed parentheses on the right side of this formula. You need three open parentheses and three closed parentheses in this formula or the formula will not work correctly.

The above formula gives a standard error of the difference of the means equal to 9.05 (two decimals).

E28: enter the critical t value from the t-table in Appendix in this cell using $df = n_1 + n_2 - 2$ to find the critical t value

E31: =(D4−D5)/E25

Note that you need an open parenthesis before D4 and a closed parenthesis after D5 so that this answer of −7.40 is then divided by the standard error of the difference of the means of 9.05, to give a t-test value of −0.82 (note the minus sign here). Use two decimal places for the t-test result (see Fig. 2.5.16).

Now write the following sentence in D34 to D37 to summarize the result of the study.

Group	n	Mean	STDEV
1 Regular Price	7	117.7	19.9
2 Reduced Price	8	125.1	15.1
Null hypothesis:			
Alternative hypothesis:			
$(n_1-1) \times$ STDEV1 squared			2376.06
$(n_2-1) \times$ STDEV2 squared			1596.07
$n_1 + n_2 - 2$			13
$1/n_1 + 1/n_2$			0.27
s e			9.05
critical t			2.160
t-test			−0.82
Result:			
Conclusion:			

Fig. 2.5.16 Wholesaler Price Comparison Two-group t-test Formula Results

D34: Since the absolute value

D35: of t of −0.82 is less than

D36: the critical t of 2.160, we

D37: accept the null hypothesis.

Finally, write the following sentence in D39 to D43 to summarize the conclusion of the study:

D39: There was no difference

D40: in the number of units of

D41: MP3 players sold at the

D42: two prices. So, you should

D43: not reduce the price!

Save your file as: MP4

Print the final spreadsheet so that it fits onto one page.

Write the null hypothesis and the alternative hypothesis by hand on your printout. The final spreadsheet appears in Figure 2.5.17.

Group	n	Mean	STDEV
1 Regular Price	7	117.7	19.9
2 Reduced Price	8	125.1	15.1

Null hypothesis:	$\mu_1 = \mu_2$
Alternative hypothesis:	$\mu_1 \neq \mu_2$
$(n_1 - 1) \times \text{STDEV1 squared}$	2376.06
$(n_2 - 1) \times \text{STDEV2 squared}$	1596.07
$n_1 + n_2 - 2$	13
$1/n_1 + 1/n_2$	0.27
s e	9.05
critical t	2.160
t-test	-0.82
Result:	Since the absolute value of t of -0.82 is less than the critical t of 2.160, we accept the null hypothesis.
Conclusion:	There was no difference in the number of units of MP3 players sold at the two prices. So, you should not reduce the price!

Fig. 2.5.17 Wholesaler Price Comparison Final Spreadsheet

2.5.4 End-of-chapter Practice Problems

(1) Suppose Boeing Company has hired you to do data analysis for its surveys that have been returned for its Morale Surveys that they had their managers answer during the past month. The items were summed to form a total score, in which a high score indicates high job satisfaction, while a low score indicates low job satisfaction.

You select a random sample of managers, 202 females who averaged 84.80 on this survey with a standard deviation of 5.10. You also select a random sample of 241 males on this survey and they averaged 88.20 with a standard deviation of 4.30.

(a) State the null hypothesis and the alternative hypothesis on an Excel spreadsheet.

(b) Find the standard error of the difference between the means using Excel.

(c) Find the critical t value by using Appendix, and enter it on your spreadsheet.

(d) Perform a t-test on these data by using Excel. What is the value of t that you obtain?

Use three decimal places for all figures in the formula section of your spreadsheet.

(e) State your result on your spreadsheet.

(f) State your conclusion in plain English on your spreadsheet.

(g) Save the file as: Boeing3.

(2) Massachusetts Mutual Financial Group (2010) placed a full-page color ad in *The Wall Street Journal* in which it used a male model hugging a two-year-old daughter. The ad had the headline and sub-headline.

WHAT IS THE SIGN OF A GOOD DECISION?

It's knowing your life insurance can help provide income for retirement. And peace of mind until you get there.

Since the majority of the subscribers to *The Wall Street Journal* are men, an interesting research question would be the following.

"Does a male model in a magazine ad affect adult men's or adult women's willingness to learn more about how life insurance can provide income for retirement?"

Suppose that you have shown one group of adult males (aged 25~39) and one group of adult females (aged 25~39) a mockup of an ad so that both groups saw the ad with a male model. The ads were identical in a copy format. The two groups were kept separate during the experiment and could not interact with one another.

At the end of a one-hour discussion of the mockup ad, the respondents were asked the question given in Fig. 2.5.18.

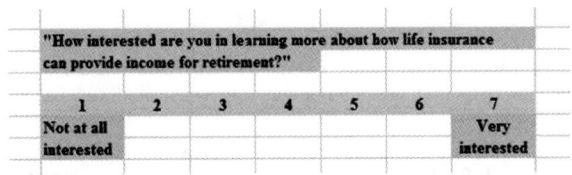

Fig. 2.5.18 Rating Scale Item for a Magazine Ad Interest Indicator

The resulting data for this question appear in Fig. 2.5.19.

(a) On your Excel spreadsheet, write the null hypothesis and the alternative hypothesis.

(b) Create a table that summarizes these data on your spreadsheet and use Excel to find the sample sizes, the means, and the standard deviations of the two groups in this table.

(c) Use Excel to find the standard error of the difference of the means.

(d) Use Excel to perform a two-group t-test. What is the value of t that you obtain (use two decimal places)?

134 Basics of Statistics and Statistical Application with Excel

Magazine ad: Male model	
Men	Women
5	3
6	4
4	6
7	5
5	2
6	3
5	1
4	3
3	2
6	4
7	3
5	5
6	6
4	3
7	4
5	2
4	5
6	3
3	4
7	5
5	4
6	3
2	2
6	4
1	3
7	5
6	1
5	3
4	2
6	3
5	2
7	5
	3
	4

Fig. 2. 5. 19 Worksheet Data for Chapter 2. 5: Practice Problem #2

(e) On your spreadsheet, type the critical value of t by using the t-table in Appendix.

(f) Type your result on the test on your spreadsheet.

(g) Type your conclusion in plain English on your spreadsheet.

(h) Save the file as: lifeinsur12.

(3) American Airlines offered an in-flight meal that passengers could purchase for $8.00, and asked these customers to fill out a survey giving their opinion of the meal. Passengers were asked to rate their likelihood of purchasing this meal on a future flight on a 5-point scale. But, suppose that you have convinced the airline to change its survey item on purchase intention to a 7-point scale instead; the intention-to-buy item would then take the form in Fig. 2. 5. 20.

Passengers were asked on the survey to indicate whether they were either business travelers or vacationers. Suppose that the average rating last month for 64 "business travelers" was 3. 23 with a standard deviation of 1. 04, while the 56 vacationers had an average rating of 2. 36 with a standard deviation of 1. 35.

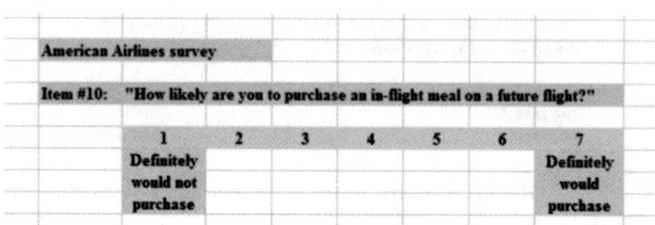

Fig. 2. 5. 20 Rating Scale Item for an In-flight Meal on an American Airlines Survey

(a) State the null hypothesis and the research hypothesis on an Excel spreadsheet.

(b) Find the standard error of the difference between the means using Excel.

(c) Find the critical t value by using Appendix, and enter it on your spreadsheet.

(d) Perform a t-test on these data by using Excel. What is the value of t that you obtain?

(e) State your result on your spreadsheet.

(f) State your conclusion in plain English on your spreadsheet.

(g) Save the file as: AAmeal3.

2.6 Correlation and Simple Linear Regression

There are many different types of "correlation coefficients", but the one we will use in this book is the Pearson product-moment correlation which we will call: r.

2.6.1 What Is a "Correlation"?

Basically, a correlation is a number between -1 and $+1$ that summarizes the relationship between two variables, which we will call X and Y.

A correlation can be either positive or negative. A positive correlation means that as X increases, Y increases. A negative correlation means that as X increases, Y decreases. In statistics books, this part of the relationship is called the direction of the relationship (i.e., it is either positive or negative).

The correlation also tells us the magnitude of the relationship between X and Y. As the correlation approaches closer to $+1$, we say that the relationship is strong and positive.

As the correlation approaches closer to -1, we say that the relationship is strong and negative.

A zero correlation means that there is no relationship between X and Y. This means that neither X nor Y can be used as a predictor of the other.

A good way to understand what a correlation means is to see a "picture" of the scatterplot of points produced in a chart by the data points. Let's suppose that you want to know if variable X can be used to predict variable Y. We will place the predictor variable X on the x-axis (the horizontal axis of a chart) and the criterion variable Y on the y-axis (the vertical axis of a chart). Suppose, further, that you have collected data given in the scatterplots below (see Fig. 2.6.1 through Fig. 2.6.6).

Fig. 2.6.1 shows the scatterplot for a perfect positive correlation of $r=+1.0$. This means that you can perfectly predict each y-value from each x-value because the data points move "upward-and-to-the-right" along a perfectly-fitting straight line (see Fig. 2.6.1)

Fig. 2.6.2 shows the scatterplot for a moderately positive correlation of $r=+0.53$. This means that each x-value can predict each y-value moderately well because you can draw a picture of a "football" around the outside of the data points that move upward-and-to-the-right, but not along a straight line (see Fig. 2.6.2).

Fig. 2.6.3 shows the scatterplot for a low, positive correlation of $r=+0.23$. This means that each x-value is a poor predictor of each y-value because the "picture" you could draw around the outside of the data points approaches a circle in shape (see Fig. 2.6.3).

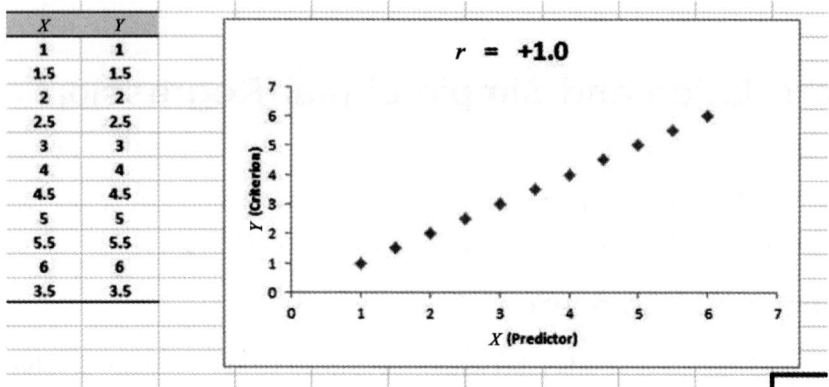

Fig. 2.6.1　Example of a Scatterplot for a Perfect Positive Correlation ($r=+1.0$)

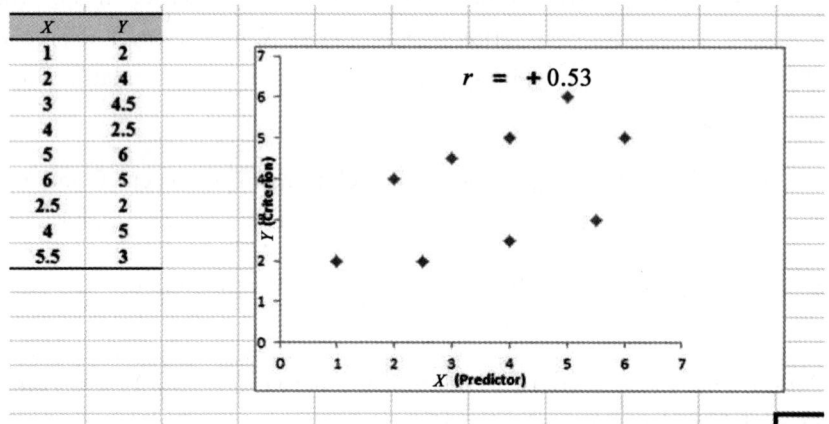

Fig. 2.6.2　Example of a Scatterplot for a Moderate Positive Correlation ($r=+0.53$)

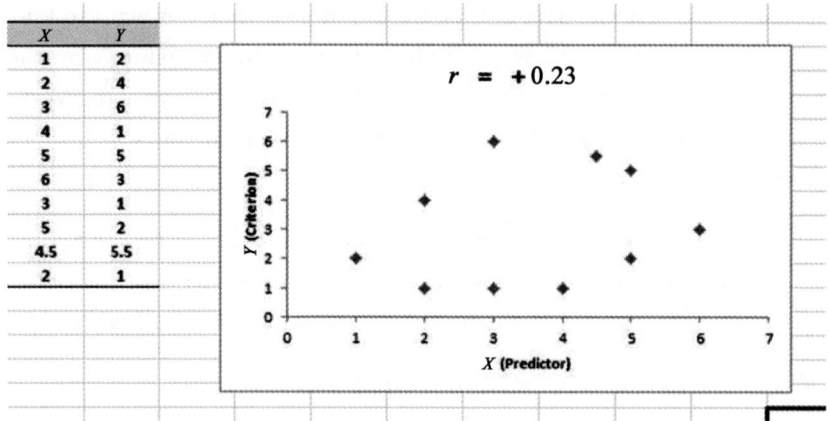

Fig. 2.6.3　Example of a Scatterplot for a Low Positive Correlation ($r=+0.23$)

We have not shown a figure of a zero correlation because it is easy to imagine what it looks like as a scatterplot. A zero correlation of $r=0.00$ means that there is no relationship between X and Y and the "picture" drawn around the data points would be a perfect circle in shape, indicating that you cannot use X to predict Y because these two variables are not correlated with one another.

Fig. 2.6.4 shows the scatterplot for a low, negative correlation of $r=-0.22$ which means that each X is a poor predictor of Y in an inverse relationship, meaning that as X increases, Y decreases. In this case, it is a negative correlation because the "football" you could draw around the data points slopes down and to the right.

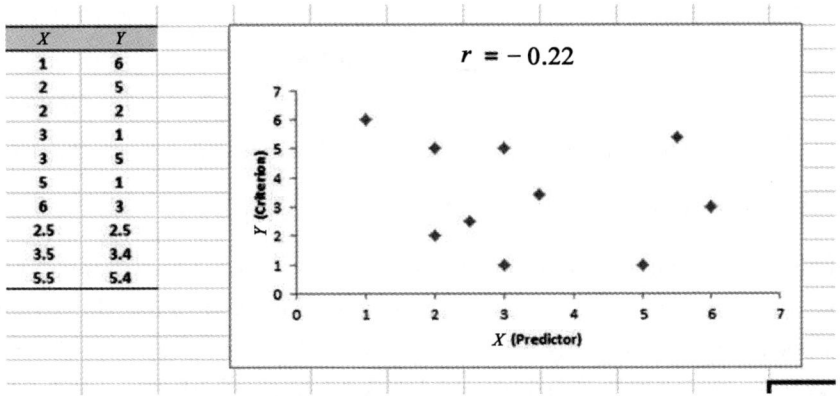

Fig. 2.6.4 Example of a Scatterplot for a Low, Negative Correlation ($r=-0.22$)

Fig. 2.6.5 shows the scatterplot for a moderate, negative correlation of $r=-0.39$ which means that X is a moderately good predictor of Y, although there is an inverse relationship between X and Y (i.e., as X increases, Y decreases). In this case, it is a negative correlation because the "football" you could draw around the data points slopes down and to the right.

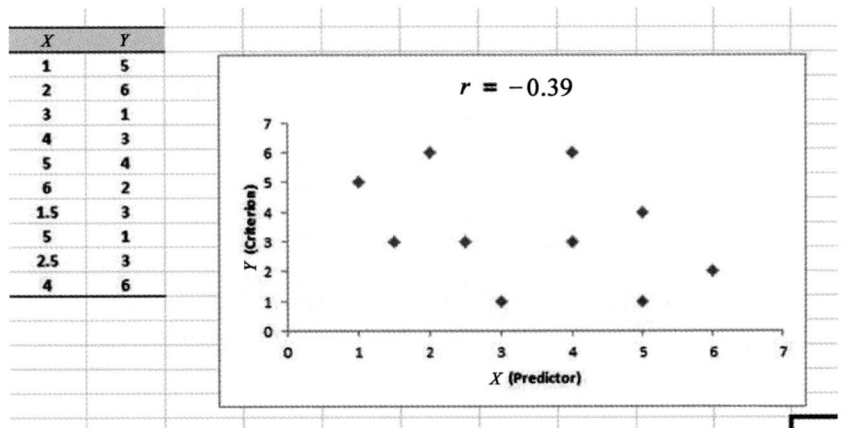

Fig. 2.6.5 Example of a Scatterplot for a Moderate, Negative Correlation ($r=-0.39$)

Fig. 2.6.6 shows a perfect negative correlation of $r=-1.0$ which means that X is a perfect predictor of Y, although in an inverse relationship where as X increases, Y decreases. The data points fit perfectly along a downward-sloping straight line (see Fig. 2.6.6).

Let's explain the formula for computing the correlation r so that you can understand where

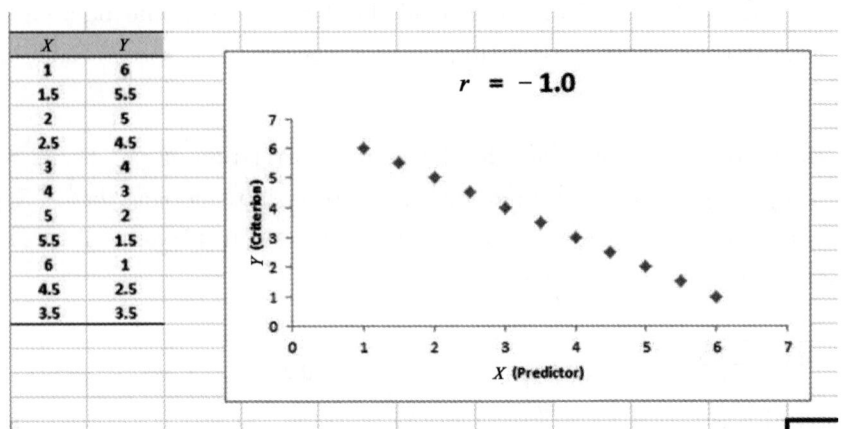

Fig. 2. 6. 6　Example of a Scatterplot for a Perfect Negative Correlation ($r = -1.0$)

the number summarizing the correlation came from.

In order to help you to understand where the correlation number that ranges from -1.0 to $+1.0$ comes from, we will walk you through the steps involved to use the formula as if you were using a pocket calculator. This is the one time in this book that we will ask you to use your pocket calculator to find a correlation, but knowing how the correlation is computed step-by-step will give you the opportunity to understand how the formula works in practice.

To do that, let's create a situation in which you need to find the correlation between two variables. Suppose that you have been hired by a manager of a supermarket chain to find the relationship between the amount of money spent weekly by the chain on television ads and the weekly sales of the supermarket chain in St. Louis. You collect the data from the past eight weeks given in Fig. 2. 6. 7.

Week	TV ad cost/$1000	Weekly Sales/$1000
1	4.8	94
2	1.9	87
3	3.8	93
4	2.3	89
5	2.9	92
6	3.3	92
7	2.4	93
8	2.8	92
n	8	8
MEAN	3.03	91.50
STDEV	0.93	2.33

Fig. 2. 6. 7　Worksheet Data for a Supermarket Chain

For the purpose of explanation, let's call the weekly cost of TV ads as the predictor variable X, and the weekly sales as the criterion variable Y. Notice that the data for the cost of TV ads for each week is in thousands of dollars ($\$1000$). For example, the TV ads for Week 6 cost $\$3,300$, and when we "move the decimal place three places to the left to change the amount to thousands of dollars", it becomes 3.3. Similarly, the weekly sales for Week 6 were really $\$92,000$ as those data are also in thousands of dollars format ($\$1000$).

Notice also that we have used Excel to find the sample size for both variables, X and Y, and the mean and STDEV of both variables. (You can practice your Excel skills by seeing if you get this same results when you create an Excel spreadsheet for these data.)

Now, let's use the above table to compute the correlation r between the weekly cost of TV ads and the weekly sales of this supermarket chain by using your pocket calculator.

2.6.1.1 Understanding the Formula for Computing a Correlation

Objective: To understand the formula for computing the correlation r

The formula for computing the correlation r is as follows.

$$r = \frac{\frac{1}{n-1}\sum_{i=1}^{n}(x_i - \overline{x})(y_i - \overline{y})}{s_x s_y}$$

This formula looks daunting at first glance, but let's "break it down into its steps" to understand how to compute the correlation r.

2.6.1.2 Understanding the Nine Steps for Computing a Correlation, r

Objective: To understand the nine steps of computing a correlation r

The nine steps are as follows.

Step   Computation Result

Step 1   Find the sample size n by noting the number of weeks

Step 2   Divide the number 1 by the sample size minus 1 (i.e., 1/7) and you get 0.14286

Step 3   For each week, take the cost of TV ads for that week and subtract the mean cost of TV ads for the 8 weeks and call this $X - \overline{X}$. (For example, for Week 6, this would be: 3.3-3.03)

Note: With your calculator, this difference is 0.27, but when Excel uses 16 decimal places for every computation, this result will be 0.28 instead of 0.27.

Step 4   For each week, take the weekly sales for that week and subtract the mean weekly sales for the 8 weeks and call this $Y - \overline{Y}$. (For example, for week 6, this would be: 92-91.50)

Step 5   Then, for each week, multiply $(X - \overline{X})$ times $(Y - \overline{Y})$. (For example, for Week 6 this would be: 0.27×0.50)

Step 6   Add the results of $(X - \overline{X})$ times $(Y - \overline{Y})$ for the 8 weeks.

Steps 1~6 would produce the Excel table given in Fig. 2.6.8.

Notice that when Excel multiplies a minus number by a minus number, the result is a plus

Week	X TV ad cost/$1000	Y Weekly Sales/$1000	$X-\bar{X}$	$Y-\bar{Y}$	$(X-\bar{X})(Y-\bar{Y})$
1	4.8	94	1.78	2.50	4.44
2	1.9	87	-1.13	-4.50	5.06
3	3.8	93	0.78	1.50	1.16
4	2.3	89	-0.73	-2.50	1.81
5	2.9	92	-0.13	0.50	-0.06
6	3.3	92	0.28	0.50	0.14
7	2.4	93	-0.63	1.50	-0.94
8	2.8	92	-0.23	0.50	-0.11
n	8	8		Total	11.50
MEAN	3.03	91.50			
STDEV	0.93	2.33			

Fig. 2.6.8 Worksheet for Computing the Correlation, r

number, for example for Week 2: $(-1.13) \times (-4.50) = +5.06$. And when Excel multiplies a minus number by a plus number, the result is a negative number, for example for Week 5: $(-0.13) \times (+0.50) = -0.06$.

Note: Excel computes all computation to 16 decimal places. So, when you check your work with a calculator, you frequently get a slightly different answer than Excel's answer.

For example, when you compute above:

$$(X-\bar{X})(Y-\bar{Y})$$ for Week 2, your calculator gives :

$$(-1.13) \times (-4.50) = +5.085$$

But, as you can see from the table, Excel's answer of 5.06 is more accurate because Excel uses 16 decimal places for every number.

You should also note that when you do Step 6, you have to be careful to add all of the positive numbers first to get $+12.61$ and then add all of the negative numbers second to get -1.11, so that when you subtract these two numbers you get $+11.50$ as your answer to Step 6.

Step 7   Multiply the answer for Step 2 above by the answer for Step 6   (0.14286×11.5)

Step 8   Multiply the STDEV of X times the STDEV of Y (0.93×2.33)

Step 9   Finally, divide the answer from Step 7 by the answer from Step 8 (1.6429 divided by 2.1669)

This number of 0.76 is the correlation between the weekly cost of TV ads (X) and the weekly sales in this supermarket chain (Y) over this 8-week period. The number $+0.76$ means that there is a strong, positive correlation between these two variables. That is, as the chain increases its spending on TV ads, its sales for that week increase. For a more detailed discussion of correlation, see Zikmund and Babin (2010).

You can also use the results of the above table in the formula for computing the correlation r in the following way:

$$\text{correlation } r = [1/(n-1) \times \Sigma(X-\overline{X})(Y-\overline{Y})]/(STDEV\ X \times STDEV\ Y)$$

$$\text{correlation } r = [(1/7) \times 11.50]/(0.93 \times 2.33)$$

$$\text{correlation } r = 0.76$$

Now, let's discuss how you can use Excel to find the correlation between two variables in a much simpler and much faster fashion than using your calculator.

2.6.2 Using Excel to Compute a Correlation Between Two Variables

Objective: To use Excel to find the correlation between two variables

Suppose that you have been hired by the owner of a supermarket chain in St. Louis to make a recommendation as to how many shelf facings of Kellogg's Corn Flakes this chain should use. A "shelf facing" is the number of boxes of the cereal that are stacked beside one another. Thus a shelf facing of 3 means that 3 boxes of Kellogg's Corn Flakes are stacked beside each other on the supermarket shelf in the cereals section.

You randomly assign supermarket locations to your study, and you randomly select the number of facings used in each supermarket location, where the number of facings ranges from 1 to 3. You track the weekly sales (in thousands of dollars) of this cereal over a ten-week period, and the resulting sales figures are given in Fig. 2.6.9.

You want to determine if there is a relationship between the number of facings of Kellogg's Corn Flakes and the weekly sales of this cereal, and you decide to use a correlation to determine this relationship. Let's call the number of facings X, and the sales figures Y.

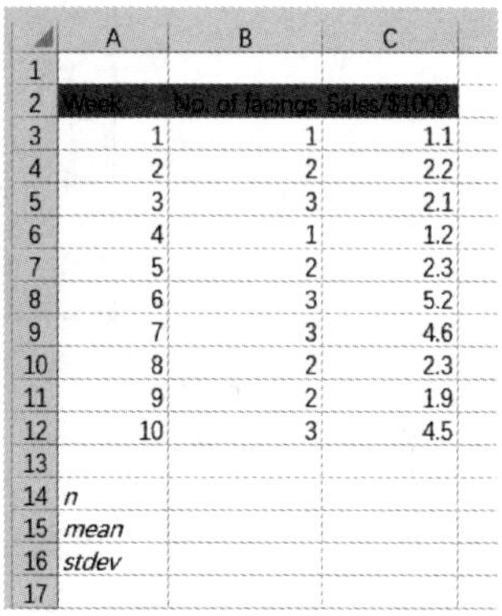

	A	B	C
1			
2	Week	No. of facings	Sales/$1000
3	1	1	1.1
4	2	2	2.2
5	3	3	2.1
6	4	1	1.2
7	5	2	2.3
8	6	3	5.2
9	7	3	4.6
10	8	2	2.3
11	9	2	1.9
12	10	3	4.5
13			
14	*n*		
15	*mean*		
16	*stdev*		
17			

Fig. 2.6.9 Worksheet Data for the Number of Facings and Sales (Practical Example)

Create an Excel spreadsheet with the following information:

A2: Week

B2: No. of facings

C2: Sales ($1000)

A3: 1

Next, change the width of Columns B and C so that the information fits inside the cells.

Now, complete the remaining figures in the table given above so that A12 is 10, B12 is 3, and C12 is 4.5 (be sure to double-check your figures to make sure that they are correct) Then, center the information in all of these cells.

A14: *n*

A15: mean

A16: STDEV

Next, define the "name" to the range of data from B3: B12 as: facings. We discussed earlier in this book (see Section 2.1.4.4) how to "name a range of data", but here is a reminder of how to do that: To give a "name" to a range of data:

Click on the top number in the range of data and drag the mouse down to the bottom number of the range.

For example, to give the name "facings" to the cells B3: B12, click on B3, and drag the pointer down to B12 so that the cells B3: B12 are highlighted on your computer screen. Then, click on:

Formulas

Define name (top center of your screen) facings (in the Name box; see Fig. 2.6.10)

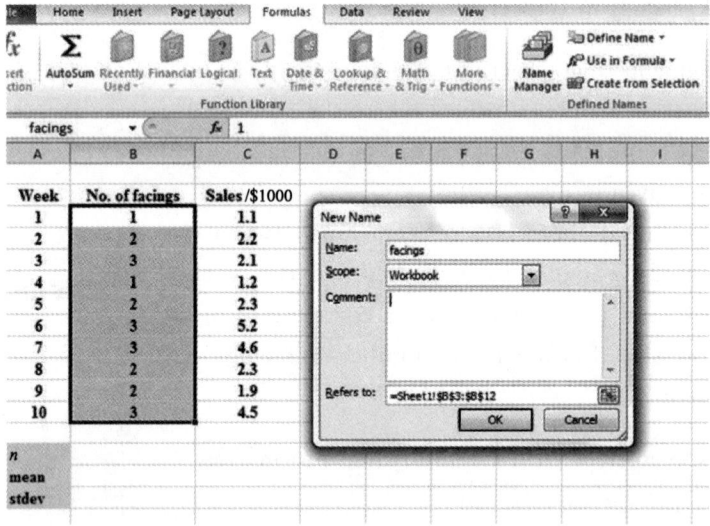

Fig. 2.6.10 Dialogue Box for Naming a Range of Data as "Facings"

OK

Now, repeat these steps to give the name: sales to C3: C12

Finally, click on any blank cell on your spreadsheet to "deselect" cells C3: C12 on your computer screen.

Now, complete the data for these sample sizes, means, and standard deviations in columns B and C so that B16 is 0.79, and C16 is 1.47 (use two decimals for the means and standard deviations; see Fig. 2.6.11).

Objective: Find the correlation between the number of facings and the weekly sales dollars

B18: correlation

C18: =correl (facings, sales). See Fig. 2. 6. 12.

Week	No. of facings	Sales /$1000
1	1	1.1
2	2	2.2
3	3	2.1
4	1	1.2
5	2	2.3
6	3	5.2
7	3	4.6
8	2	2.3
9	2	1.9
10	3	4.5
n	10	10
mean	2.20	2.74
stdev	0.79	1.47

Fig. 2. 6. 11 Example of Using Excel to Find the Sample Size, Mean, and STDEV

SUM =correl(facings,sales)

	A	B	C	D	E
1					
2	Week	No. of facings	Sales /$1000		
3	1	1	1.1		
4	2	2	2.2		
5	3	3	2.1		
6	4	1	1.2		
7	5	2	2.3		
8	6	3	5.2		
9	7	3	4.6		
10	8	2	2.3		
11	9	2	1.9		
12	10	3	4.5		
13					
14	n	10	10		
15	mean	2.20	2.74		
16	stdev	0.79	1.47		
17					
18		correlation	=correl(facings,sales)		
19					

Fig. 2. 6. 12 Example of Using Excel's=correl Function to Compute the Correlation Coefficient

Hit the Enter key to compute the correlation.

C18: format this cell to two decimals.

Note that the equal sign tells Excel that you are going to use a formula.

The correlation between the number of facings (X) and weekly sales (Y) is +0. 83, a very strong positive correlation. This means that you have evidence that there is a strong relationship between these two variables. In effect, the more facings (when1,2,3 facings are used), the higher the weekly sales dollars generated for this cereal.

Save this file as: FACINGS5

The final spreadsheet appears in Fig. 2. 6. 13.

C18 =CORREL(facings,sales)

A	B	C	D	E
Week	No. of facings	Sales /$1000		
1	1	1.1		
2	2	2.2		
3	3	2.1		
4	1	1.2		
5	2	2.3		
6	3	5.2		
7	3	4.6		
8	2	2.3		
9	2	1.9		
10	3	4.5		
n	10	10		
mean	2.20	2.74		
stdev	0.79	1.47		
	correlation	0.83		

Fig. 2. 6. 13 Final Result of Using the =correl Function to Compute the Correlation Coefficient

2. 6. 3 Creating a Chart and Drawing the Regression Line onto the Chart

This section deals with the concept of "linear regression". Technically, the use of a simple linear regression model (i. e. , the word "simple" means that only one predictor, X, is used to predict the criterion, Y) requires that the data meet the following four assumptions if that statistical model is to be used:

(1) The underlying relationship between the two

variables under study (X and Y) is linear in the sense that a straight line, and not a curved line, can fit among the data points on the chart.

(2) The errors of measurement are independent of each other (e. g. the errors from a specific time period are sometimes correlated with the errors in a previous time period).

(3) The errors fit a normal distribution of Y-values at each of the X-values.

(4) The variance of the errors is the same for all X-values (i. e. , the variability of the Y-values is the same for both low and high values of X).

A detailed explanation of these assumptions is beyond the scope of this book, but the interested reader can find a detailed discussion of these assumptions in Levine et al. (2011).

Now, let's create a chart summarizing these data.

Important note: Whenever you draw a chart, it is ESSENTIAL that you put the predictor variable (X) on the left, and the criterion variable (Y) on the right in your Excel spreadsheet, so that you know which variable is the predictor variable and which variable is the criterion variable. If you do this, you will save yourself a lot of grief whenever you do a problem involving correlation and simple linear regression using Excel!

Important note: You need to understand that in any chart that has one predictor and a criterion that there are really TWO LINES that can be drawn between the data points:

① One line uses X as the predictor, and Y as the criterion.

② A second line uses Y as the predictor, and X as the criterion. This means that you have to be very careful to note in your input data the cells that contain X as the predictor, and Y as the criterion. If you get these cells mixed up and reverse them, you will create the wrong line for your data and you will have botched the problem terribly.

This is why we STRONGLY RECOMMEND IN THIS BOOK that you always put the X data (i. e. , the predictor variable) on the LEFT of your table, and the Y data (i. e. , the criterion variable) on the RIGHT of your table on your spreadsheet so that you don't get these variables mixed up.

Also note that the correlation, r, will be exactly the same correlation no matter which variable you call the predictor variable and which variable you call the criterion variable. The correlation coefficient just summarizes the relationship between two variables, and doesn't care which one is the predictor and which one is the criterion.

Let's suppose that you would like to use the number of facings of Corn Flakes as the predictor variable, and that you would like to use it to predict the weekly sales dollars of this cereal. Since the correlation between these two variables is $+0.83$, this shows that there is a strong, positive relationship and that the number of facings is a good predictor of the weekly sales for this cereal.

Using Excel to Create a Chart and the Regression Line Through the Data Points

Objective: To create a chart and the regression line summarizing the relationship between the number of shelf facings and the weekly sales ($1000)

(1) Open the file that you saved earlier in this chapter: FACINGS5.

(2) Click and drag the mouse to highlight both columns of numbers (B3: C12), but do not highlight the labels at the top of Column B and Column C.

Highlight the data set: B3: C12

Insert (top left of screen).

Highlight: Scatter chart icon (immediately above the word "Charts" at the top center of your screen).

Click on the down arrow on the right of the chart icon.

Highlight the top left scatter chart icon (see Fig. 2.6.14).

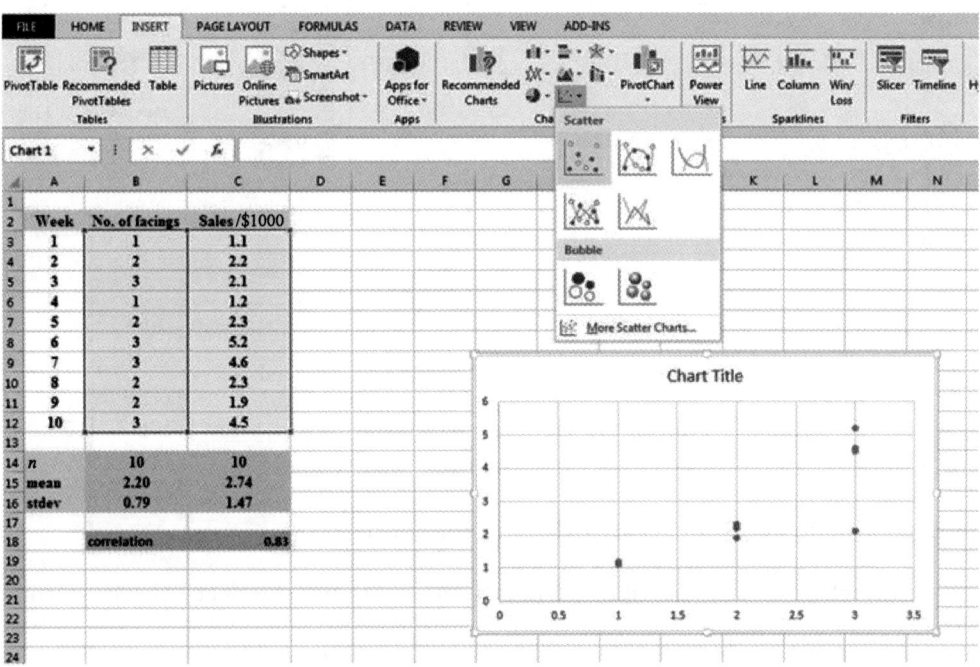

Fig. 2.6.14 Example of Selecting a Scatter Chart

Click on the top left chart to select it.

Click on the " + " icon to the right of the chart (CHART ELEMENTS).

Click on the check mark next to "Chart Title" and also next to "Gridlines" to remove these check marks (see Fig. 2.6.15).

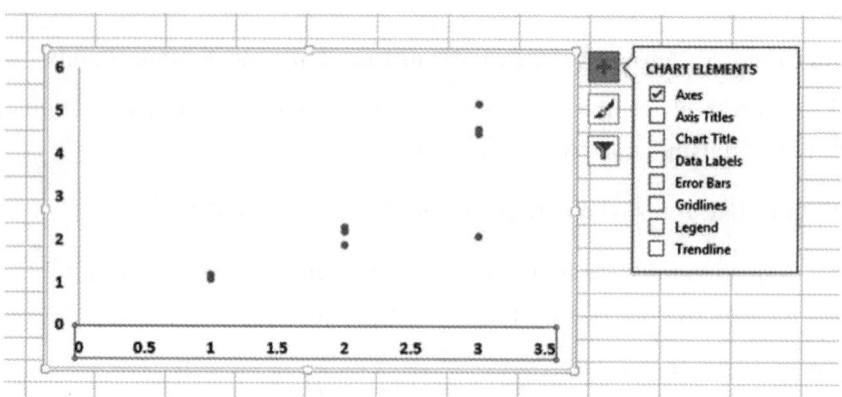

Fig. 2. 6. 15　Example of Chart Elements Selected

Click on the box next to "Chart Title" and then click on the arrow to its right. Then, click on "Above chart".

Note that the words "Chart Title" are now in a box at the top of the chart (see Fig. 2. 6. 16)

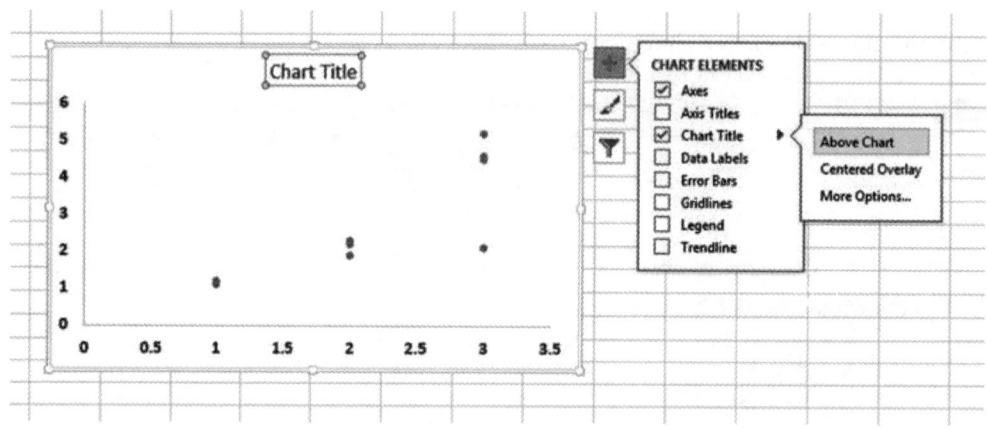

Fig. 2. 6. 16　Example of Chart Title Selected

Enter the following Chart Title to the right of f_x at the top of your screen: RELATIONSHIP BETWEEN NO. OF FACINGS AND SALES (see Fig. 2. 6. 17).

Hit the Enter Key to enter this chart title onto the chart.

Click inside the chart at the top right corner of the chart to "deselect" the box around the Chart Title (see Fig. 2. 6. 18).

Click on the "+" box to the right of the chart.

Add a check mark to the left of "Axis Titles" (This will create an "Axis Title" box on the Y-axis of the chart).

Click on the right arrow for "Axis Titles" and then click on "Primary Horizontal" to remove the check mark in its box (this will create the Y-axis title).

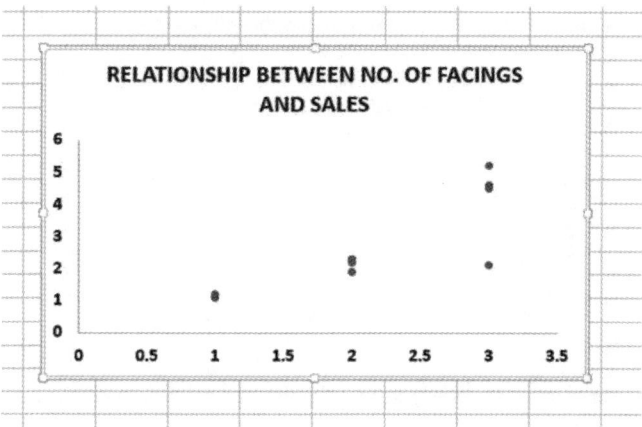

Fig. 2.6.17 Example of a Chart Title Inserted onto the Chart

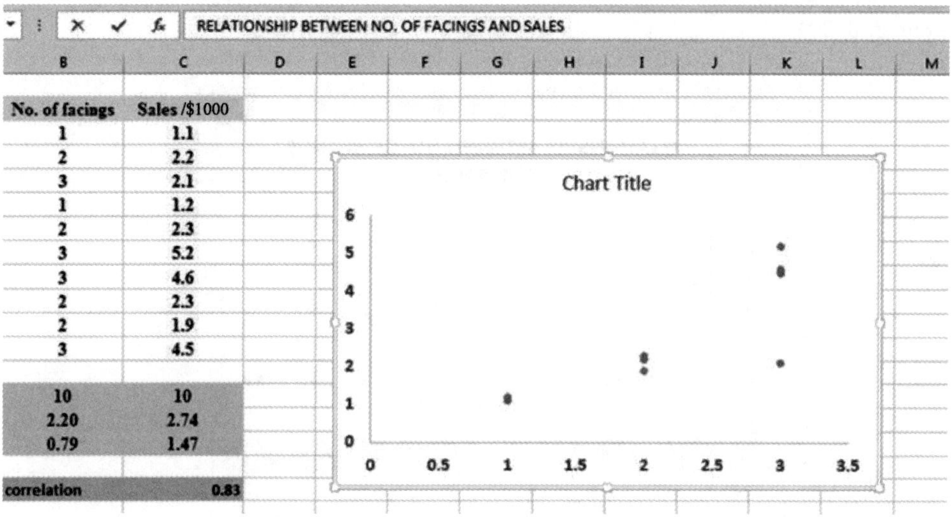

Fig. 2.6.18 Example of Creating a Chart Title

Enter the following Y-axis title to the right of f_x at the top of your screen: SALES ($1000)

Then, hit the Enter Key to enter this Y-axis title to the chart.

Click inside the chart at the top right corner of the chart to "deselect" the box around the Y-axis title (see Fig. 2.6.19).

Click on the "+" box to the right of the chart.

Highlight "Axis Titles" and click on its right arrow.

Click on the words "Primary Horizontal" to add a check mark to its box (this creates an "Axis Title" box on the X-axis of the chart).

Enter the following X-axis title to the right of f_x at the top of your screen: NO. OF FACINGS.

Then, hit the Enter Key to add this X-axis title to the chart.

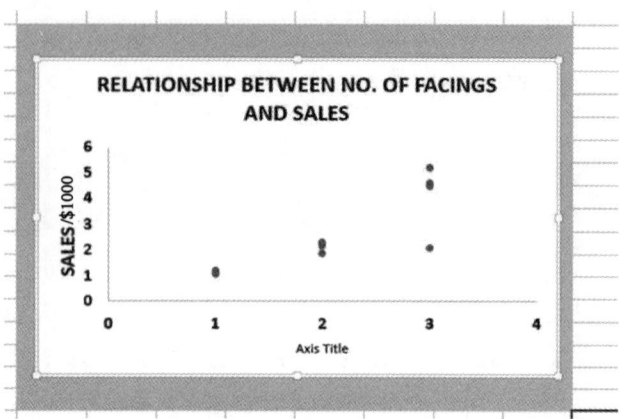

Fig. 2.6.19 Example of Adding a Y-axis Title to the Chart

Click inside the chart at the top right corner of the chart to "deselect" the box around the X-axis title (see Fig. 2.6.20)

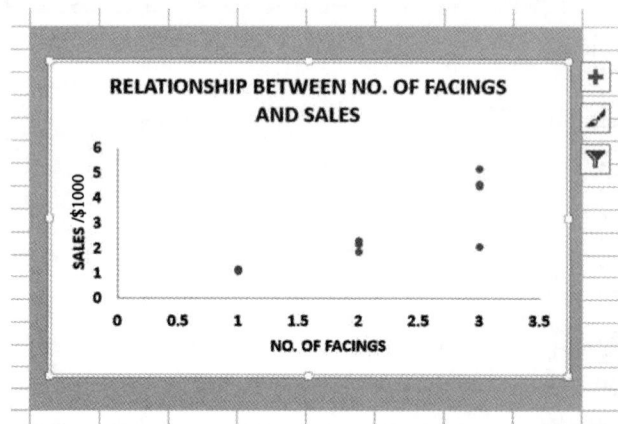

Fig. 2.6.20 Example of a Chart Title, an X-axis Title, and a Y-axis Title

(1) Drawing the regression line through the data points in the chart

Objective: To draw the regression line through the data points on the chart

Right-click on any one of the data points inside the chart.

Highlight: Add Trendline (see Fig. 2.6.21).

Click on: Add Trendline Linear (be sure the "linear" button near the top is selected on the "Format Trendline" dialog box; see Fig. 2.6.22).

Click on the X at the top right of the "Format Trendline" dialog box to close this dialog box.

Click on any blank cell outside the chart to "deselect" the chart.

Save this file as: FACINGS7.

Your spreadsheet should look like the spreadsheet in Fig. 2.6.23.

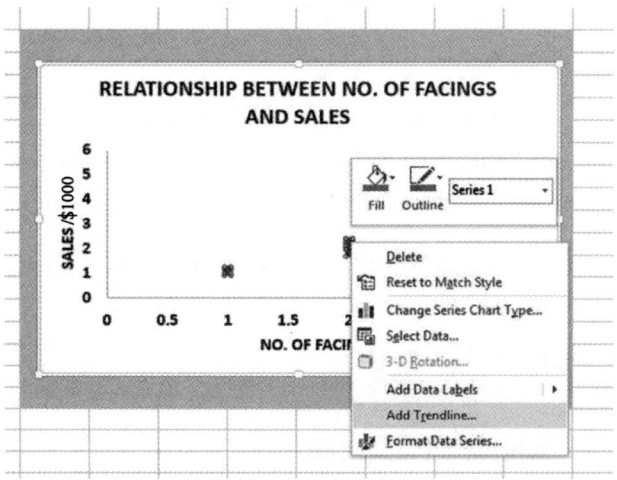

Fig. 2. 6. 21 Dialogue Box for Adding a Trendline to the Chart

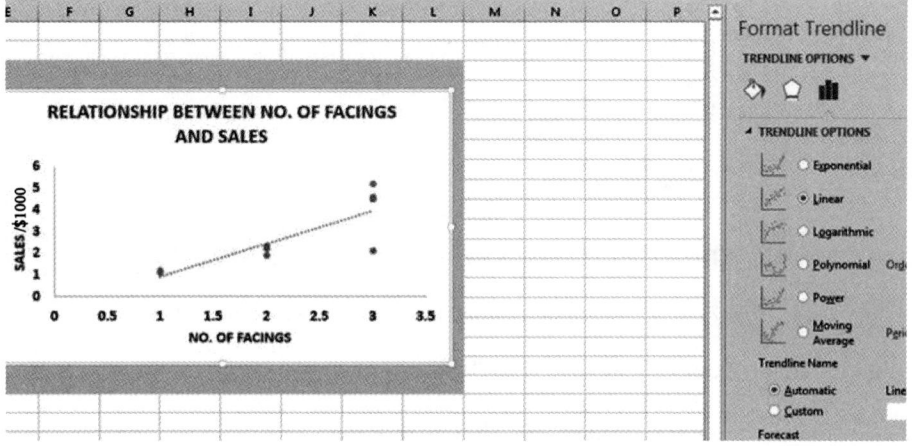

Fig. 2. 6. 22 Dialogue Box for a Linear Trendline

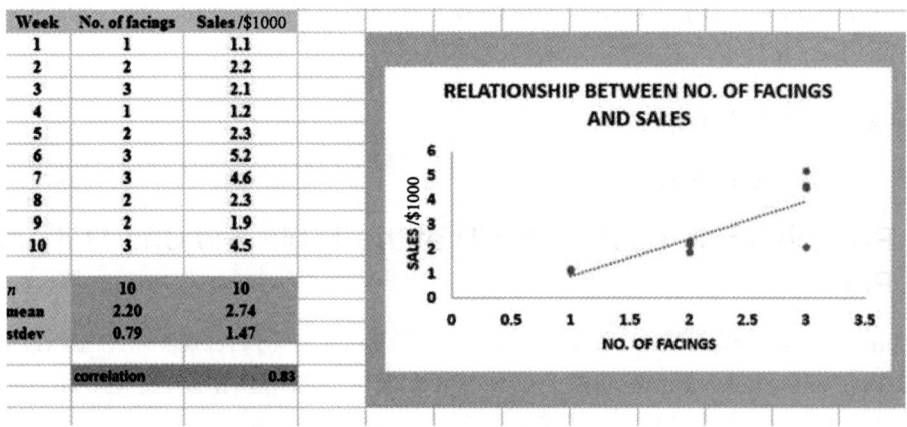

Fig. 2. 6. 23 Final Chart with the Trendline Fitted Through the Data Points of the Scatterplot

(2) Moving the chart below the table in the spreadsheet

Objective: To move the chart below the table

Left-click your mouse on any white space to the right of the top title inside the chart, keep the left-click down, and drag the chart down and to the left so that the top left corner of the chart is in cell A20, then take your finger off the left-click of the mouse (see Fig. 2.6.24).

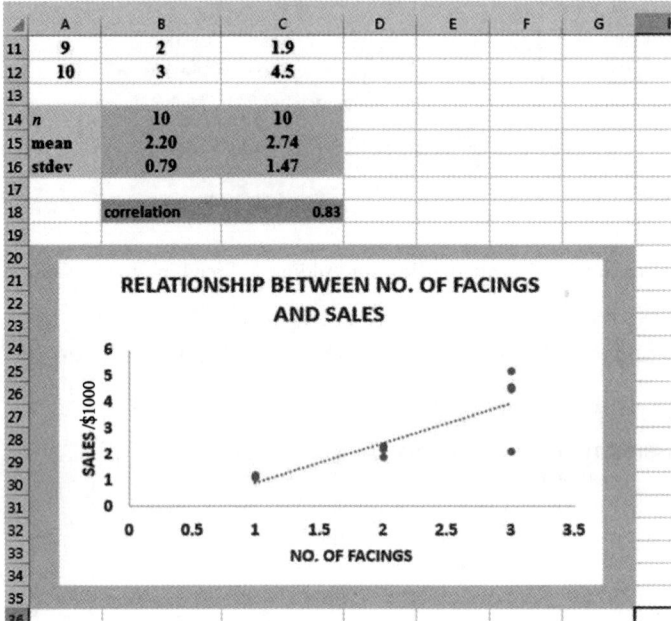

Fig. 2.6.24 Example of Moving the Chart below the Table

(3) Making the chart "longer" so that it is "taller"

Objective: To make the chart "longer" so that it is taller

Left-click your mouse on the bottom-center of the chart to create an "up-and-down- arrow" sign, hold the left-click of the mouse down and drag the bottom of the chart down to row 42 to make the chart longer, and then take your finger off the mouse.

(4) Making the chart "wider"

Objective: To make the chart "wider"

2.6.4 Printing a Spreadsheet So That the Table and Chart Fit onto One Page

Put the pointer at the middle of the right-border of the chart to create a "left-to-right arrow" sign, and then left-click your mouse and hold the left-click down while you drag the right border of the chart to the middle of Column H to make the chart wider (see Fig. 2.6.25). Now, click on any blank cell outside the chart to "deselect" the chart.

Objective: To print the spreadsheet so that the table and the chart fit onto one page

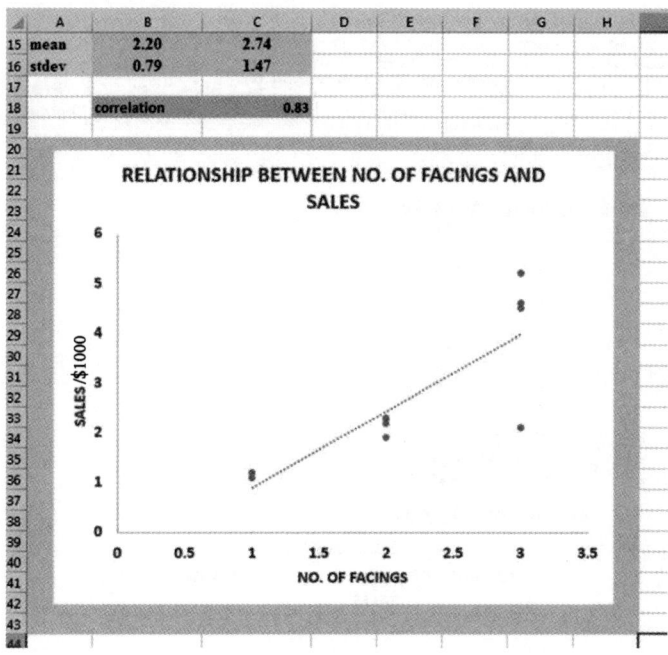

Fig. 2.6.25　Example of a Chart That Is Enlarged to Fit the Cells: A20: H42

Page Layout (top of screen).

Change the scale at the middle icon near the top of the screen "Scale to Fit" by clicking on the down-arrow until it reads "95％" so that the table and the chart will fit onto one page on your screen (see Fig. 2.6.26)

File

Print

Print (see Fig. 2.6.27)

Save your file as: FACINGS8.

2.6.5　Finding the Regression Equation

The main reason for charting the relationship between X and Y [i.e., No. of facings as X and Sales ($1000) as Y in our example] is to see if there is a strong relationship between X and Y so that the regression equation that summarizes this relationship can be used to predict Y for a given value of X.

Since we know that the correlation between the number of facings and sales is $+0.83$, this tells us that it makes sense to use the number of facings to predict the weekly sales that we can expect based on past data.

We now need to find that regression equation that is the equation of the "best-fitting straight line" through the data points.

152 Basics of Statistics and Statistical Application with Excel

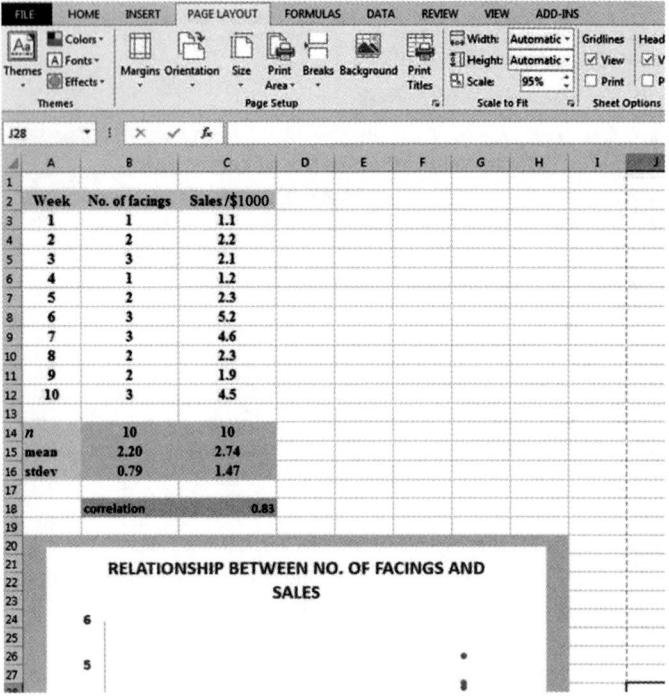

Fig. 2.6.26 Example of the Page Layout for Reducing the Scale of the Chart to 95% of Normal Size

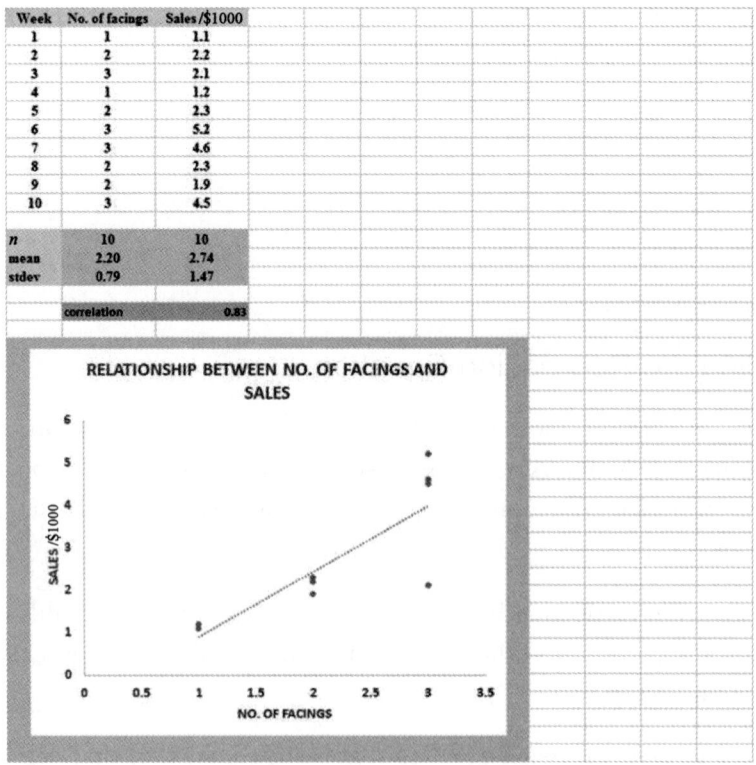

Fig. 2.6.27 Final Spreadsheet of a Table and a Chart (95% Scale to Fit Size)

Objective: To find the regression equation summarizing the relationship between X and Y.

In order to find this equation, we need to check to see if your version of Excel contains the "Data Analysis ToolPak" necessary to run a regression analysis.

2.6.5.1 Installing the Data Analysis ToolPak into Excel

Objective: To install the Data Analysis ToolPak into Excel

Since there are currently four versions of Excel in the marketplace (2003, 2007, 2010, 2013), we will give a brief explanation of how to install the Data Analysis ToolPak into each of these versions of Excel.

(1) Installing the Data Analysis ToolPak into Excel 2013

Open a new Excel spreadsheet.

Click on: Data (at the top of your screen).

Look at the top of your monitor screen. Do you see the words "Data Analysis" at the far right of the screen? If you do, the Data Analysis ToolPak for Excel 2013 was correctly installed when you installed Office 2013, and you should skip ahead to Section 2.6.5.2.

If the words "Data Analysis" are not at the top right of your monitor screen, then the Tool-Pak component of Excel 2013 was not installed when you installed Office 2013 onto your computer. If this happens, you need to follow these steps:

File

Options (bottom left of screen)

Note: This creates a dialog box with "Excel Options" (at the top left of the box)

Add-Ins (on left of screen)

Manage: Excel Add-Ins (at the bottom of the dialog box)

Go (at the bottom center of dialog box)

Highlight: Analysis ToolPak (in the Add-Ins dialog box)

Put a check mark to the left of Analysis Toolpak.

OK (at the right of this dialog box)

Data

You now should have the words "Data Analysis" at the top right of your screen to show that this feature has been installed correctly.

If you get a prompt asking you for the "installation CD", put this CD in the CD drive and click on: OK.

Note: If these steps do not work, you should try these steps instead: File/Options (bottom left) /Add-ins/Analysis ToolPak/Go/click to the left of Analysis ToolPak to add a check mark/OK.

If you need help to do this, ask your favorite "computer techie" for help. You are now ready to skip ahead to Section 2.6.5.2.

(2) Installing the data analysis ToolPak into Excel 2010

Open a new Excel spreadsheet

Click on: Data (at the top of your screen)

Look at the top of your monitor screen. Do you see the word "Data Analysis" at the far right of the screen? If you do, the Data Analysis ToolPak for Excel 2010 was correctly installed when you installed Office 2010, and you should skip ahead to Section 2.6.5.2.

If the words "Data Analysis" are not at the top right of your monitor screen, then the Tool-Pak component of Excel 2010 was not installed when you installed Office 2010 onto your computer. If this happens, you need to follow these steps:

File

Options

Excel options (creates a dialog box) Add-Ins

Manage: Excel Add-Ins (at the bottom of the dialog box)

Go

Highlight: Analysis ToolPak (in the Add-Ins dialog box)

OK

Data

(You now should have the words "Data Analysis" at the top right of your screen) If you get a prompt asking you for the "installation CD", put this CD in the CD drive and click on: OK

Note: If these steps do not work, you should try these steps instead: File/Options (bottom left) /Add-ins/Analysis ToolPak/Go/click to the left of Analysis ToolPak to add a check mark/OK.

If you need help to do this, ask your favorite "computer techie" for help. You are now ready to skip ahead to Section 2.6.5.2.

(3) Installing the data analysis ToolPak into Excel 2007

Open a new Excel spreadsheet

Click on: Data (at the top of your screen)

If the words "Data Analysis" do not appear at the top right of your screen, you need to install the Data Analysis ToolPak by taking the following steps:

Microsoft Office button (top left of your screen) Excel options (bottom of dialog box)

Add-ins (far left of dialog box)

Go (to create a dialog box for Add-Ins)

Highlight: Analysis ToolPak

OK (If Excel asks you for permission to proceed, click on: Yes)

Data (You should now have the words "Data Analysis" at the top right of your screen)

If you need help to do this, ask your favorite "computer techie" for help.

You are now ready to skip ahead to Section 2.6.5.2.

(4) Installing the data analysis ToolPak into Excel 2003

Open a new Excel spreadsheet

Click on: Tools (at the top of your screen)

If the bottom of this Tools box says "Data Analysis", the ToolPak has already been installed in your version of Excel and you are ready to find the regression equation. If the bottom of the Tools box does not say "Data Analysis", you need to install the ToolPak as follows:

Click on: File

Options (bottom left of screen) Add-ins.

Analysis ToolPak (it is directly underneath Inactive Application Add-ins near the top of the box).

Go

Click to add a check-mark to the left of analysis ToolPak.

OK

Note: If these steps do not work, try these steps instead: Tools/Add-ins/Click to the left of analysis ToolPak to add a check mark to the left/OK.

You are now ready to skip ahead to Section 2.6.5.2.

2.6.5.2 Using Excel to Find the Summary Output of Regression

You have now installed ToolPak, and you are ready to find the regression equation for the "best-fitting straight line" through the data points by using the following steps:

Open the Excel file: FACINGS8 (if it is not already open on your screen).

Note: If this file is already open, and there is a gray border around the chart, you need to click on any empty cell outside of the chart to deselect the chart.

Now that you have installed ToolPak, you are ready to find the regression equation summarizing the relationship between the number of shelf facings of Kellogg's Corn Flakes and the sales dollars in your data set.

Remember that you gave the name facings to the X data (the predictor), and the name sales to the Y data (the criterion) in a previous section of this chapter (see Section 2.6.2)

Data (top of screen)

Data analysis (far right at top of screen; see Fig. 2.6.28)

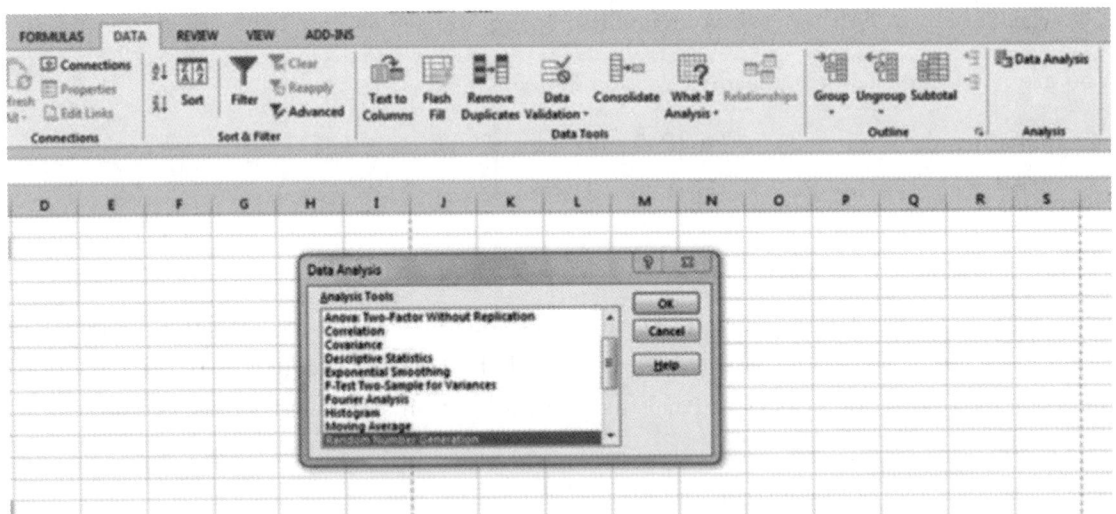

Fig. 2.6.28 Example of Using the Data/Data Analysis Function of Excel

Scroll down the dialog box by using the down arrow and highlight: Regression (see Fig. 2.6.29)

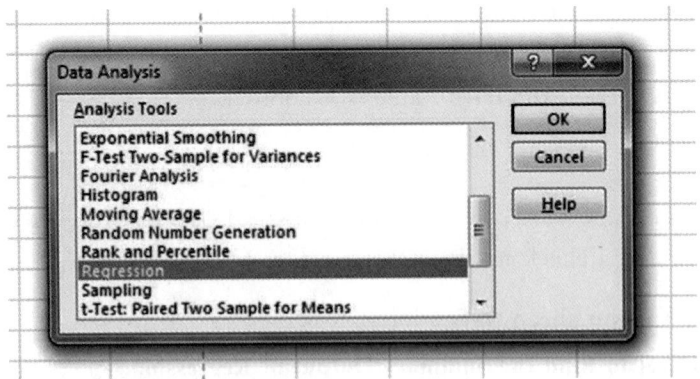

Fig. 2.6.29 Dialogue Box for Creating the Regression Function in Excel

OK

Input Y Range: sales

Input X Range: facings

Click on the "button" to the left of Output Range to select this, and enter A44 in the box as the place on your spreadsheet to insert the Regression analysis in cell A44.

OK

The SUMMARY OUTPUT should now be in cells A44 : I61.

Widen Column A so that all of the words in the SUMMARY OUTPUT are readable.

Now, change the data in the following three cells to Number format (2 decimal places) by first clicking on "Home" at the top left of your screen:

B47

B60

B61

Now, change the format for all other numbers that are in decimal format to number format, three decimal places.

Next, widen all columns so that all of the labels fit inside the column widths. Then, center all numbers in their cells.

Print the file so that it fits onto one page. (Hint: Change the scale under "Page Layout" to 70% to make it fit.) Your file should be like the file in Fig. 2. 6. 30.
Save the resulting file as: FACINGS9

Note the following problem with the summary output.

Whoever wrote the computer program for this version of Excel made a mistake and gave the name "Multiple R" to cell A47.

This is not correct. Instead, cell A47 should say "correlation r" since this is the notation that we are using for the correlation between X and Y.

You can now use your printout of the regression analysis to find the regression equation that is the best-fitting straight line through the data points.

But first, let's review some basic terms.

(1) Finding the Y-intercept, a, of the regression line

The point on the Y-axis that the regression line would intersect the Y-axis if it were extended to reach the Y-axis is called the "Y-intercept" and we will use the letter "a" to stand for the

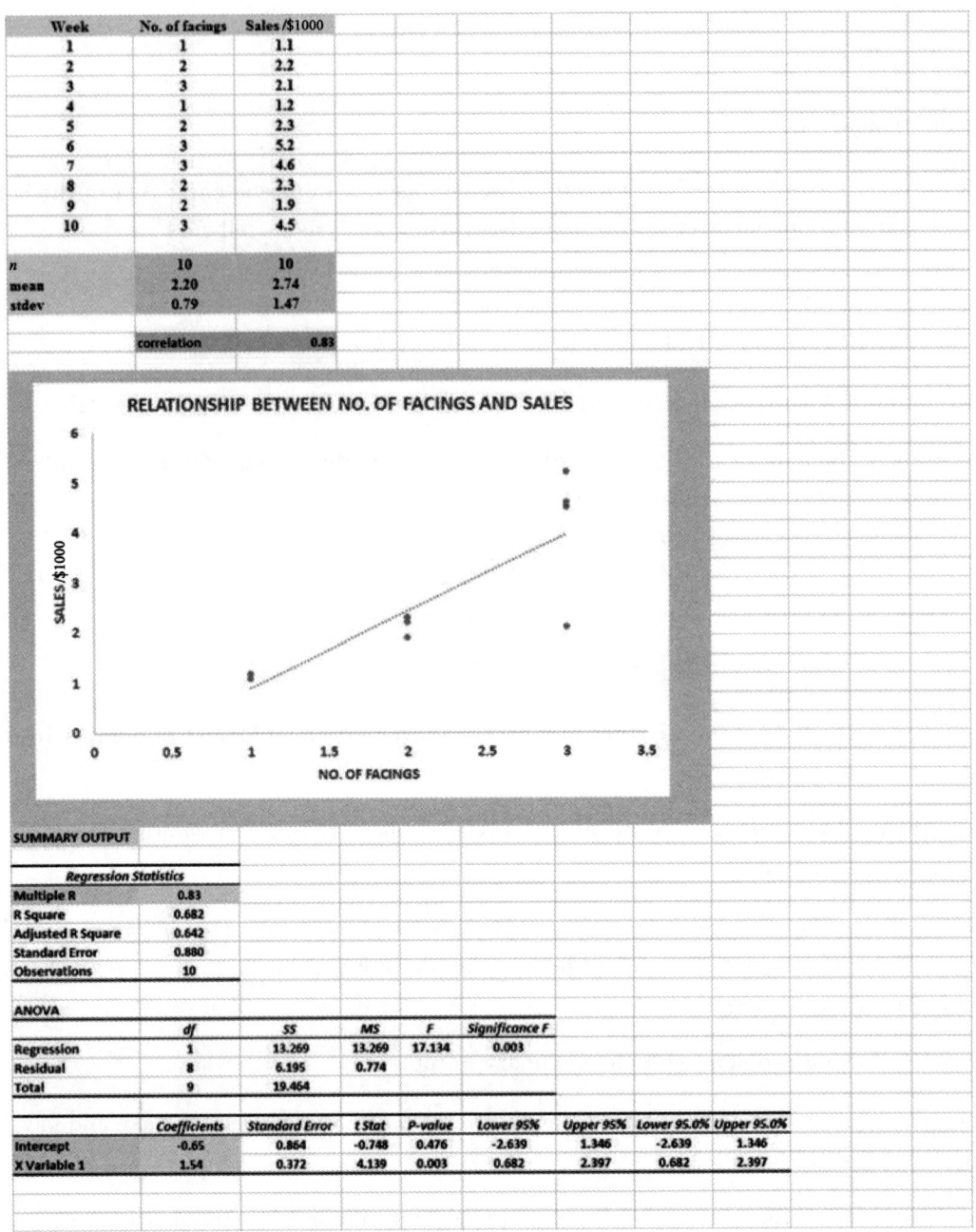

Fig. 2.6.30　Final Spreadsheet of Correlation and Simple Linear Regression Including the SUMMARY OUTPUT for the Data

Y-intercept of the regression line. The Y-intercept on the SUMMARY OUTPUT on the previous page is -0.65 and appears in cell B60 (note the minus sign). This means that if you were to draw an imaginary line continuing down the regression line toward the Y-axis that this imaginary line would cross the Y-axis at -0.65. This is why a is called the "Y-intercept".

(2) Finding the slope, b, of the regression line

The "tilt" of the regression line is called the "slope" of the regression line. It summarizes to what degree the regression line is either above or below a horizontal line through the data points. If the correlation between X and Y were zero, the regression line would be exactly horizontal to the X-axis and would have a zero slope.

If the correlation between X and Y is positive, the regression line would "slope upward to the right" above the X-axis. Since the regression line in Fig. 2.6.30 slopes upward to the right, the slope of the regression line is $+1.54$ as given in cell B61. We will use the notation "b" to stand for the slope of the regression line. (Note that Excel calls the slope of the line "X Variable 1" in the Excel printout.)

Since the correlation between the number of facings and the weekly sales dollars was $+0.83$, you can see that the regression line for these data "slopes upward to the right" through the data. Note that the SUMMARY OUTPUT of the regression line in Fig. 2.6.28 gives a correlation, r, of $+0.83$.

If the correlation between X and Y were negative, the regression line would "slope down to the right" above the X-axis. This would happen whenever the correlation between X and Y is a negative correlation that is between zero and minus one (0 and -1).

2.6.5.3 Finding the Equation for the Regression Line

To find the regression equation for the straight line that can be used to predict weekly sales from the number of facings, we only need two numbers in the SUMMARY OUTPUT in Fig. 2.6.28: B60 and B61.

The format for the regression line is: $Y = a + bX$

where a = the Y-intercept (-0.65 in our example in cell B60) and b = the slope of the line ($+1.54$ in our example in cell B61)

Therefore, the equation for the best-fitting regression line for our example is:

$$Y = a + b\ X$$

$$Y = -0.65 + 1.54X$$

Remember that Y is the weekly sales (\$1000) that we are trying to predict, using the number of facings as the predictor, X.

Let's try an example by using this formula to predict the weekly sales.

2.6.5.4 Using the Regression Line to Predict the Y-value for a Given X-value

Objective: Find the weekly sales predicted from one facing of Kellogg's Corn Flakes on the supermarket shelf.

Since the number of facings is one (i. e. , $X=1$), substituting this number into our regression equation gives:

$$Y=-0.65+1.54\ (1)$$
$$Y=-0.65+1.54$$
$$Y=0.89$$

Important note: If you look at your chart, if you go directly upwards from one facing until you hit the regression line, you see that you hit this line just under the number 1 on the Y-axis to the left (actually, it is 0.89), the result above for predicting sales from one shelf facing.

But since weekly sales are recorded in thousands of dollars ($1000), we need to multiply our answer above by 1,000 to find the weekly sales figure.

When we do that, this gives an estimated weekly sales of $890 (0.89×1,000) when we use one facing of this cereal.

Now, let's do a second example and predict what the weekly sales figure would be if we used 3 facings of Kellogg's Corn Flakes on the supermarket shelf.

$$Y=-0.65+1.54\ X$$
$$Y=-0.65+1.54\ (3)$$
$$Y=-0.65+4.62$$
$$Y=3.97$$

Important note: If you look at your chart, if you go directly upwards from three facings until you hit the regression line, you see that you hit this line just under the number 4 on the Y-axis to the left (actually it is 3.97), the result above for predicting sales from three shelf facings.

But since weekly sales are recorded in thousands of dollars ($1000), we need to multiply our answer above by 1,000 to find the weekly sales figure.

When we do that, this gives an estimated weekly sales of $3,970 when we use three facings of the cereal. For a more detailed discussion of regression, see Black (2010).

2.6.6 Adding the Regression Equation to the Chart

Objective: To Add the Regression Equation to the Chart

If you want to include the regression equation within the chart next to the regression line, you can do that, but a word of caution first.

Throughout this book, we are using the regression equation for one predictor and one criterion to be the following:

$$Y=a+b\ X$$

where $a = Y$-intercept and $b =$ slope of the line.

See, for example, the regression equation in Section 2. 6. 5. 3 where the Y-intercept was $a = -0.65$ and the slope of the line was $b = +1.54$ to generate the following regression equation:

$$Y = -0.65 + 1.54\ X$$

However, Excel 2013 uses a slightly different regression equation which is logically identical to the one used in this book when you add a regression equation to a chart:

$$Y = b\ X + a$$

where $a = Y$-intercept and $b =$ slope of the line

Note that this equation is identical to the one we are using in this book with the terms arranged in a different sequence.

For the example we used in Section 2. 6. 5. 3, Excel 2013 would write the regression equation on the chart as:

$$Y = 1.54\ X - 0.65$$

This is the format that will result when you add the regression equation to the chart using Excel 2013 by taking the following steps:

Open the file: FACINGS9 (that you saved in Section 2. 6. 5. 2).

Click just inside the outer border of the chart in the top right corner to add the "gray border" around the chart in order to "select the chart" for changes you are about to make.

Right-click on any of the data-points in the chart.

Highlight: Add Trendline, and click on it to select this command.

The "Linear button" near the top of the dialog box will already be selected (on its left).

Click on: Display Equation on chart (near the bottom of the dialog box; see Fig. 2. 6. 31). Click on the X at the top right of the Format Trendline dialogue box to remove this box.

Note that the regression equation on the chart is in the following form next to the regression line on the chart (see Fig. 2. 6. 32).

Click on any empty cell outside of the chart to deselect the chart

$$Y = 1.54X - 0.65$$

Save this file as FACINGS10 and print it out so that it fits onto one page.

2. 6. 7 How to Recognize Negative Correlations in the Summary Output Table

Important note: Since Excel does not recognize negative correlations in the SUMMARY OUTPUT

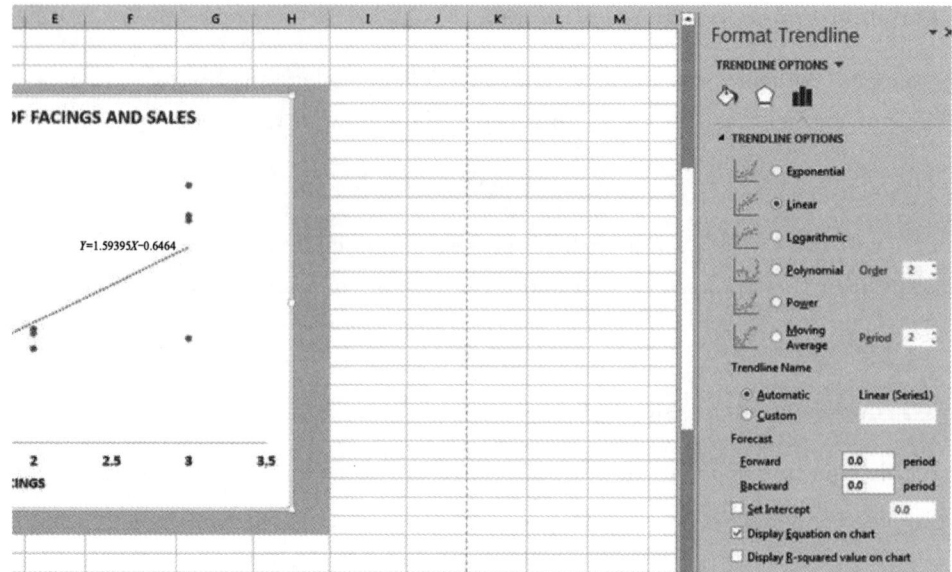

Fig. 2.6.31 Dialogue Box for Adding the Regression Equation to the Chart Next to the Regression Line on the Chart

results, but treats all correlations as if they were positive correlations (this was a mistake made by the programmer), you need to be careful to note that there may be a negative correlation between X and Y even if the printout says that the correlation is a positive correlation.

You will know that the correlation between X and Y is a negative correlation when these two things occur:

(1) THE SLOPE, b, IS A NEGATIVE NUMBER. This can only occur when there is a negative correlation.

(2) THE CHART CLEARLY SHOWS A DOWNWARD SLOPE IN THE REGRESSION LINE, which can only occur when the correlation between X and Y is negative.

2.6.8 Printing Only Part of a Spreadsheet Instead of the Entire Spreadsheet

Objective: To print part of a spreadsheet separately instead of printing the entire spreadsheet

There will be many occasions when your spreadsheet is so large in the number of cells used for your data and charts that you only want to print part of the spreadsheet separately so that the print will not be so small that you cannot read it easily.

We will now explain how to print only part of a spreadsheet onto a separate page by using three examples of how to do that by using the file FACINGS10 that you created in Section 2.6.6: (1) printing only the table and the chart on a separate page, (2) printing only the chart on a separate page, and (3) printing only the SUMMARY OUTPUT of the regression analysis on a separate page.

Note: If the file FACINGS10 is not open on your screen, you need to open it now.

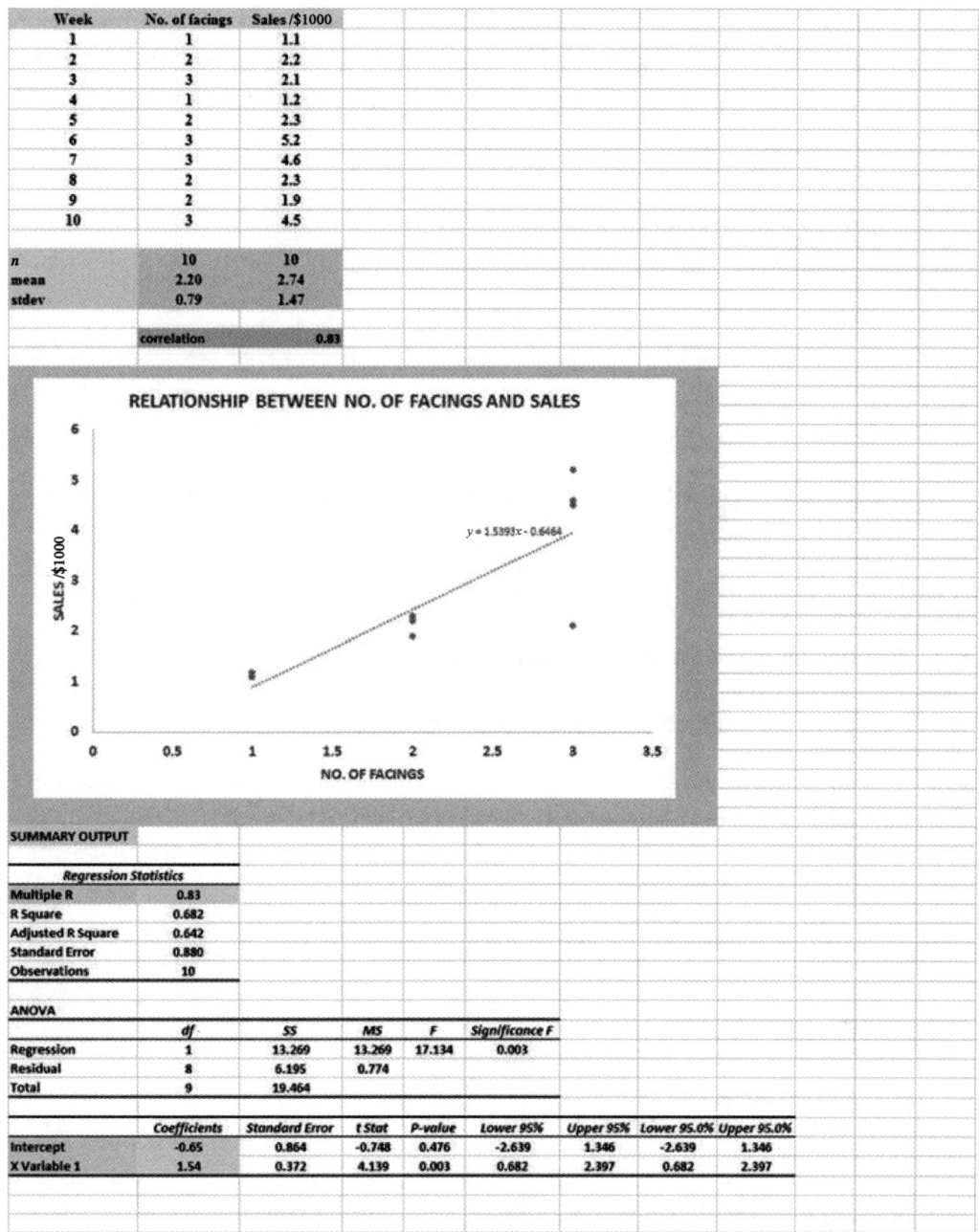

Fig. 2.6.32 Example of a Chart with the Regression Equation Displayed Next to the Regression Line

If the gray border is around the outside of the chart, click on any white space outside of the chart to deselect the chart.

Let's describe how to do these three goals with three separate objectives:

2.6.8.1 Printing Only the Table and the Chart on a Separate Page

Objective: To print only the table and the chart on a separate page

(1) Left-click your mouse starting at the top left of the table in cell A2 and drag the mouse down and to the right so that all of the table and all of the chart are highlighted in light blue on your computer screen from cell A2 to cell I43 (the highlighted cells are called the "selection" cells).

(2) File

Print

Print Active Sheets

Print Selection

Print

The resulting printout should contain only the table of the data and the chart resulting from the data.

Then, click on any empty cell in your spreadsheet to deselect the table and chart.

2.6.8.2 Printing Only the Chart on a Separate Page

Objective: To print only the chart on a separate page

(1) Click on any "white space" just inside the outside border of the chart in the top right corner of the chart to create the gray border around all of the borders of the chart in order to "select" the chart.

(2) File

Print

Print Selected Chart

Print Selected Chart (again)

Print

The resulting printout should contain only the chart resulting from the data.

Important note: After each time you print a chart by itself on a separate page, you should immediately click on any white space OUTSIDE the chart to remove the gray border from the border of the chart. When the gray border is on the borders of the chart, this tells Excel that you want to print only the chart by itself.

2.6.8.3 Printing Only the Summary Output of the Regression

Objective: To print only the SUMMARY OUTPUT of the regression analysis on a separate page

(1) Left-click your mouse at the cell just above SUMMARY OUTPUT in cell A43 on the

left of your spreadsheet and drag the mouse down and to the right until all of the regression output is highlighted in dark blue on your screen from A43 to I62. (Change the "Scale to Fit" to 75% so that the SUMMARY OUTPUT will fit onto one page when you print it out.)

(2) File

Print

Print Active Sheets

Print Selection

Print

The resulting printout should contain only the summary output of the regression analysis on a separate page.

Finally, click on any empty cell on the spreadsheet to "deselect" the regression table.

2.6.9 End-of-chapter Practice Problems

(1) Suppose that you have been hired by Blockbuster Video to develop a regression equation to predict the average number of rentals per day from stores based on average family income for families within a two-mile radius of Blockbuster's current stores in the state of Missouri. Blockbuster plans to use this equation to predict store sales for new stores that it is considering opening in Missouri. You develop the hypothetical data given in Fig. 2.6.33 to test your Excel regression skills.

Average Family Income/$1000	Rentals/d
62	705
41	525
27	309
45	498
50	623
47	425
44	314
28	203
30	465
41	540
47	605
62	690

Fig. 2.6.33 Worksheet Data for average family income and daily rental: Practice Problem #1

Create an Excel spreadsheet and enter the data by using income as the independent variable (predictor) and number of daily rentals as the dependent variable (criterion). (Hint: Remember that the independent variable, X, must be on the left column in the table, and the dependent variable, Y, must be on the right column of the table.)

Important note: When you are trying to find a correlation between two variables, it is important that you place the predictor, X, ON THE LEFT COLUMN in your Excel spreadsheet, and the criterion, Y, IMMEDIATELY TO THE RIGHT OF THE X COLUMN. You should do this every time that you want to use Excel to find a correlation between two variables to check your thinking.

(a) Use Excel's=correl function to find the correlation between these two variables, and round off the result to two decimal places.

(b) Create an XY scatterplot of these two sets of data so that:

- Top title: RELATIONSHIP BETWEEN INCOME AND RENTALS/ DAY
- X-axis title: AVERAGE FAMILY INCOME ($1,000)
- Y-axis title: RENTALS (per day)
- re-size the chart so that it is 8 columns wide and 25 rows long
- move the chart below the table

(c) Create the least-squares regression line for these data on the scatterplot.

(d) Use Excel to run the regression statistics to find the equation for the leastsquares regression line for these data and display the results below the chart on your spreadsheet. Use number format (2 decimal places) for the correlation and for the coefficients.

(e) Print just the input data and the chart so that this information fits onto one page. Then, print the regression output table on a separate page so that it fits onto that separate page.

(f) Save the file as RENTAL.

Now, answer these questions by using your Excel printout:

① What is the Y-intercept?

② What is the slope of the line?

③ What is the regression equation for these data (use two decimal places for the Y-intercept and the slope)?

④ Use the regression equation to predict the average number of daily rentals you would expect for a retail area that had an average family income of $50,000.

(2) In a large engineering company, what is the relationship between the salary of engineers as a percent of the engineers' midpoint salary (position in range) and the raise given to the engineers at the last contract? The midpoint of the range of engineers' salaries is scored as 100, and each engineer's salary is more compared to that midpoint to determine what percent of that midpoint an engineer's salary represents. The resulting number is called "position in range". Engineers whose salaries are below the midpoint have a score less than 100, and engineers whose salaries are above the midpoint have a score greater than 100. Suppose that you wanted to study this question. Analyze the hypothetical data that are given in Fig. 2.6.34.

Create an Excel spreadsheet, and enter the data.

(a) Create an XY scatterplot of these two sets of data so that:

- top title: RELATIONSHIP BETWEEN POSITION IN RANGE AND PERCENT RAISE

COMPANY XYZ	
Question: Is there a relationship between the salary of engineers as a percent of the engineers' midpoint salary (position in range) and the raise given to the engineers at the last contract?	
POSITION IN RANGE	PERCENT RAISE
83	5.5
90	5.0
100	3.0
110	1.5
86	4.0
97	3.5
102	4.0
107	1.5
112	2.0
114	2.5
116	1.5

Fig. 2.6.34 Worksheet Data for Engineer' Salary Position in Range and Percent Raise Practice Problem #2

FOR ENGINEERS

- X-axis title: POSITION IN RANGE

- Y-axis title: % RAISE

- move the chart below the table

- re-size the chart so that it is 7 columns wide and 25 rows long

(b) Create the least-squares regression line for these data on the scatterplot.

(c) Use Excel to run the regression statistics to find the equation for the least-squares regression line for these data and display the results below the chart on your spreadsheet. Add the regression equation to the chart. Use number format (2 decimal places) for the correlation and number format (3 decimal places) for the coefficients.

Print just the input data and the chart so that this information fits onto one page in portrait format.

Then, print just the regression output table on a separate page so that it fits onto that separate page in portrait format.

(d) Circle and label the value of the Y-intercept and the slope of the regression line on your printout.

(e) Write the regression equation by hand on your printout for these data (use three decimal places for the Y-intercept and the slope).

(f) Circle and label the correlation between the two sets of scores in the regression analysis summary output table on your printout.

(g) Underneath the regression equation you wrote by hand on your printout, use the regression equation to predict the PERCENT RAISE you would expect for an engineer with a POSITION IN RANGE score of 90.

(h) Read from the graph, the PERCENT RAISE you would expect for an engineer with a POSITION IN RANGE score of 110, and write your answer in the space immediately below.

(i) Save the file.

(3) Is there a relationship between the number of sales calls a sales staff make in a month on potential customers and the number of copiers sold that month by a salesperson? Suppose that you gathered the hypothetical data given below for your sales staff for the previous month. The resulting data are presented in Fig. 2.6.35.

No. of sales calls	No. of copiers sold
25	40
30	55
18	30
22	35
14	18
18	23
22	28
24	38
12	15
13	16
18	25
22	28
25	36

Fig. 2.6.35 Worksheet Data for No. of Sales Calls and No. of Copies Sold Practice Problem #3

Create an Excel spreadsheet and enter the data by using the number of sales calls as the independent variable (predictor) and the number of copiers sold last month by each salesperson as the dependent variable (criterion).

(a) Use Excel's =correl function to find the correlation between these two sets of scores, and round off the result to two decimal places.

(b) Create an XY scatterplot of these two sets of data so that:

- top title: RELATIONSHIP BETWEEN NO. OF SALES CALLS AND COPIERS SOLD

- X-axis title: NO. OF SALES CALLS

- Y-axis title: NO. OF COPIERS SOLD

- move the chart below the table

- re-size the chart so that it is 7 columns wide and 25 rows long

(c) Create the least-squares regression line for these data on the scatterplot.

(d) Use Excel to run the regression statistics to find the equation for the least-squares regression line for these data and display the results below the chart on your spreadsheet. Use number format (2 decimal places) for the correlation and for the coefficients.

(e) Print just the input data and the chart so that this information fits onto one page. Then, print the regression output table on a separate page so that it fits onto that separate page.

(f) Save the file as: copier4.

Answer the following questions by using your Excel printout:

① What is the correlation between the number of sales calls and the number of copiers sold?

② What is the Y-intercept?

③ What is the slope of the line?

④ What is the regression equation?

⑤ Use the regression equation to predict the number of copiers sold you would expect for a salesperson who made 25 sales calls last month. Show your work on a separate sheet of paper.

2.7 Multiple Correlation and Multiple Regression

There are many times in business when you want to predict a criterion, Y, but you want to find out if you can develop a better prediction model by using several predictors in combination (e. g. X_1, X_2, X_3, etc.) instead of a single predictor, X.

The resulting statistical procedure is called "multiple correlation" because it uses two or more predictors in combination to predict Y, instead of a single predictor, X. Each predictor is "weighted" differently based on its separate correlation with Y and its correlation with the other predictors. The job of multiple correlation is to produce a regression equation that will weight each predictor differently and in such a way that the combination of predictors does a better job of predicting Y than any single predictor by itself. We will call the multiple correlation R_{xy}.

Important note: You will remember from Chapter 2.6 (see Section 2.6.1) that the correlation, r, ranges from -1 to $+1$, and, therefore, can be a negative number.

However, the multiple correlation, R_{xy}, only ranges from zero to $+1$ (0 to $+1$), and can never be negative! It is very important that you remember this fact.

You will recall (see Secion 2.6.5.3) that the regression equation that predicts Y when only one predictor, X, is used is:

$$Y = a + bX$$

2.7.1 Multiple Regression Equation

The multiple regression equation follows a similar format and is:

$$Y = a + b_1 X_1 + b_2 X_2 + b_3 X_3 + \cdots b_n X_n$$

The "weight" given to each predictor in the equation is represented by the letter "b" with a subscript to correspond to the same subscript on the predictors.

Important note: In order to do multiple regression, you need to have installed the Data Analysis TookPak that was described in Chapter 2.6 (see Section 2.6.5.1). If you did not install it you need to do so now.

Let's try a practice problem.

Suppose that you have been hired by a car rental company to see if you could predict annual sales based on the number of cars that a rental car company has in its fleet and the number of locations where you can rent that company's cars in the U.S.

Let's use the following notation:

Y Annual Sales (in millions of dollars)

X_1 No. of cars in the fleet (in thousands of cars)

X_2 No. of locations in the U. S.

Suppose, further, that this rental car company supplied you with the following hypothetical data summarizing its performance along with the performance of its competitors (see Fig. 2. 7. 1).

CAR RENTAL COMPANIES		
Y	X_1	X_2
SALES /10^6	NO. OF CARS/1000	NO. OF LOCATIONS
1070	120	152
1460	180	1120
1480	85	1032
552	92	440
2105	315	2587
308	71	1697
2380	221	1153
1140	142	922
43	25	105
154	35	1483
72	15	442
81	18	251
333	42	465
91	15	492
147	18	44

Fig. 2. 7. 1   Worksheet Data for Rental Car Companies

Create an Excel spreadsheet for these data by using the following cell reference:

A3: CAR RENTAL COMPANIES

A5: Y

A6: SALES/ $ 10^6

A7: 1070

B5: X_1

B6: NO. OF CARS/1000

B7: 120

C5: X_2

C6: NO. OF LOCATIONS

C7: 152

Next, change the column width to match the above table, and change all figures to number format (zero decimal places).

Now, fill in the additional data in the chart such as:

A21: 147

B21: 18

C21: 44

Then, center the information in all cells of your table.
Important note: Be sure to double-check all of your numbers in your table to be sure that they are correct, or your spreadsheets will be incorrect.

Save this file as RENTAL5

Important note: When we use one predictor, X, to predict one criterion, Y, we say that you need to make sure that the X variable is ON THE LEFT in your table, and the Y variable is ON THE RIGHT in your table so that you know which variable is the predictor, and which variable is the criterion (see Section 2.6.3).

However, in multiple regression, you need to follow this rule which is exactly the opposite:

When you use several predictors in multiple regression, it is essential that the criterion you are trying to predict, Y, be ON THE FAR LEFT, and all of the predictors are TO THE RIGHT of the criterion, Y, in your table so that you know which variable is the criterion, Y, and which variables are the predictors.

Notice in the table above, that the criterion Y (SALES) is on the far left of the table, and the two predictors (NO. OF CARS AND NO. OF LOCATIONS) are to the right of the criterion variable. You must follow this rule or your regression equation will be completely wrong.

2.7.2 Finding the Multiple Correlation and the Multiple Regression Equation

Objective: To find the multiple correlation and multiple regression equation by using Excel

You do this by the following commands:

Click on: Date

Click on: Data Analysis (far right top of screen) and then Regression (scroll down to this in the box; see Fig. 2.7.2)

OK

Input Y Range: A6: A21

Input X Range: B6: C21

172　Basics of Statistics and Statistical Application with Excel

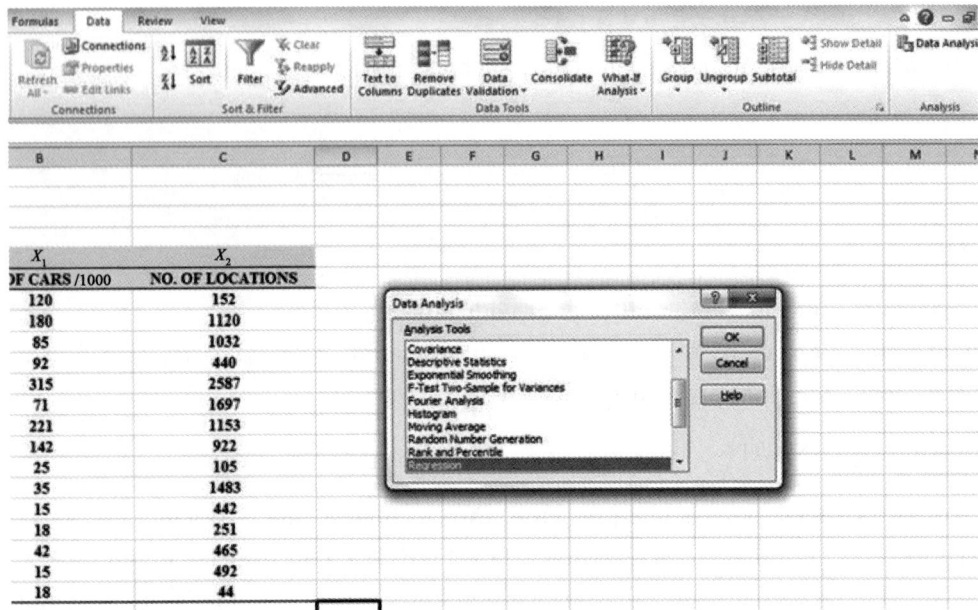

Fig. 2.7.2　Dialogue Box for Regression Function

Click on the Labels box to add a check mark to it (because you have included the column labels in row 6)

Output Range (click on the button to its left, and enter): A25 (see Fig. 2.7.3)

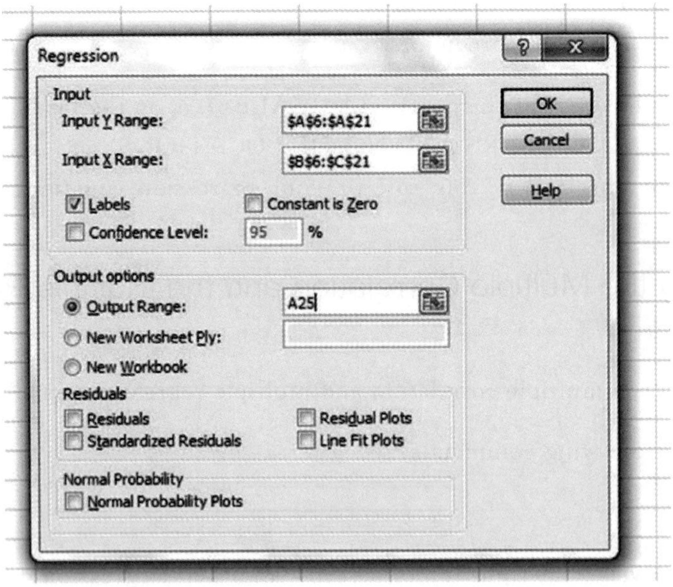

Fig. 2.7.3　Dialogue Box for Regression of Car Rental Companies Data

Important note: Excel automatically assigns a dollar sign $ in front of each column letter and each row number so that you can keep these ranges of data constant for the regression analysis.

OK (see Fig. 2.7.4 to see the resulting SUMMARY OUTPUT)

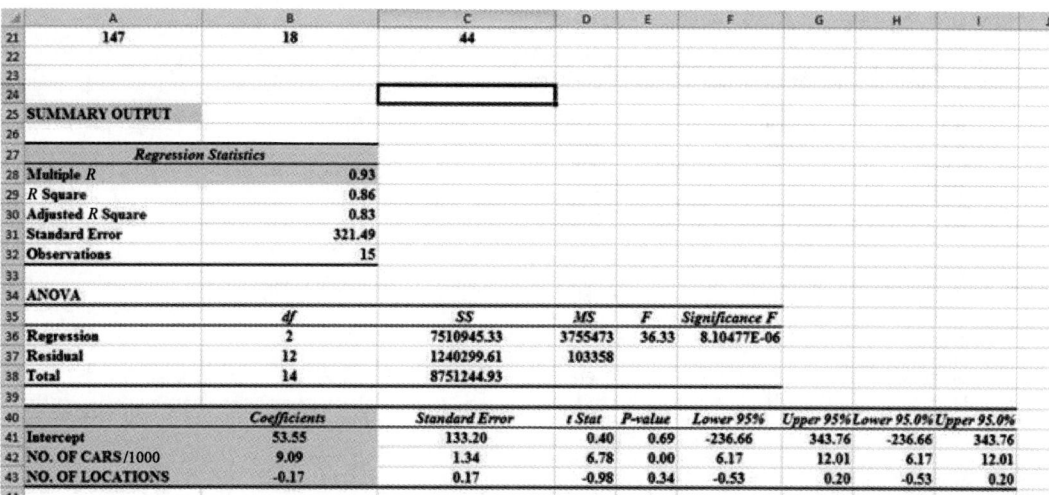

Fig. 2.7.4 Regression SUMMARY OUTPUT of Car Rental Companies Data

Next, format the following four cells in Number format (2 decimal places):

B28

B41

B42

B43

Note that both the input Y Range and the Input X Range above both include the label at the top of the columns.

Re-save the file as RENTAL5

Now, print the file so that it fits onto one page by changing the scale to 60% size. The resulting regression analysis is given in Fig. 2.7.5.

Once you have the SUMMARY OUTPUT, you can determine the multiple correlation and the regression equation that is the best-fit line through the data points by using NO. OF CARS (1000) and NO. OF LOCATIONS as the two predictors, and SALES ($\$10^6$) as the criterion.

Note on the SUMMARY OUTPUT where it says "Multiple R". This term is correct since this is the term Excel used for the multiple correlation, which is $+0.93$. This means that from these data, the combination of NO. OF CARS and NO. OF LOCATIONS together form a very strong positive relationship in predicting Annual Sales.

To find the regression equation, notice the coefficients at the bottom of the SUMMARY OUTPUT:

Intercept: a (this is the Y-intercept) 53.55

CAR RENTAL COMPANIES

Y SALES /$10⁶	X_1 NO. OF CARS/1000	X_2 NO. OF LOCATIONS
1070	120	152
1460	180	1120
1480	85	1032
552	92	440
2105	315	2587
308	71	1697
2380	221	1153
1140	142	922
43	25	105
154	35	1483
72	15	442
81	18	251
333	42	465
91	15	492
147	18	44

SUMMARY OUTPUT

Regression Statistics	
Multiple R	0.93
R Square	0.86
Adjusted R Square	0.83
Standard Error	321.49
Observations	15

ANOVA

	df	SS	MS	F	Significance F
Regression	2	7510945.33	3755473	36.33	8.10477E-06
Residual	12	1240299.61	103358		
Total	14	8751244.93			

	Coefficients	Standard Error	t Stat	P-value	Lower 95%	Upper 95%	Lower 95.0%	Upper 95.0%
Intercept	53.55	133.20	0.40	0.69	-236.66	343.76	-236.66	343.76
NO. OF CARS /1000	9.09	1.34	6.78	0.00	6.17	12.01	6.17	12.01
NO. OF LOCATIONS	-0.17	0.17	-0.98	0.34	-0.53	0.20	-0.53	0.20

Fig. 2.7.5 Final Spreadsheet for Car Rental Companies Regression Analysis

NO. OF CARS/1000: b_1 9.09

NO. OF LOCATIONS: b_2 −0.17

Since the general form of the multiple regression equation is:

$$Y = a + b_1 X_1 + b_2 X_2$$

we can now write the multiple regression equation for these data:

$$Y = 53.55 + 9.09 X_1 - 0.17 X_2$$

2.7.3 Using the Regression Equation to Predict Annual Sales

Objective: To find the predicted annual sales for a rental car company that has 80,000 cars and 900 locations

Note that X_1 (NO. OF CARS) is measured in thousands of cars in the original data set. This means, that for our example, 80,000 cars would become just 80, since 80 is 80,000 measured in thousands of cars. Plugging these two numbers into our regression equation gives us:

$$Y = 53.55 + 9.09 \times (80) - 0.17 \times (900)$$
$$Y = 53.55 + 727.2 - 153$$
$$Y = 627.75$$

But, since Annual Sales are measured in millions of dollars in the original data set, we have to convert this figure to millions of dollars. Therefore, the predicted annual sales for a rental car company that has 80,000 cars and 900 locations where customers can rent their cars is: $ 627,750,000 or $ 627.75 million.

If you want to learn more about the theory behind multiple regression, see Keller (2009).

2.7.4 Using Excel to Create a Correlation Matrix in Multiple Regression

The final step in multiple regression is to find the correlation between all of the variables that appear in the regression equation.

In our example, this means that we need to find the correlation between each of the three pairs of variables:

① number of cars and sales.

② number of locations and sales.

③ number of cars and number of locations.

To do this, we need to use Excel to create a "correlation matrix." This matrix summarizes the three correlations above.

Objective: To use Excel to create a correlation matrix between the three variables in this example

To use Excel to do this, take these steps:

Data Analysis

Correlation (scroll up to highlight this formula; see Fig. 2.7.6)

OK

Input range: A6: C21

Note that this input range includes the labels at the top of the three variables (SALES, NO. OF CARS, and NO. OF LOCATIONS) as well as all of the figures in the original data set.

Grouped by: Columns

Put a check in the box for: Labels in the First Row (since you included the labels at the top of the columns in your input range of data above)

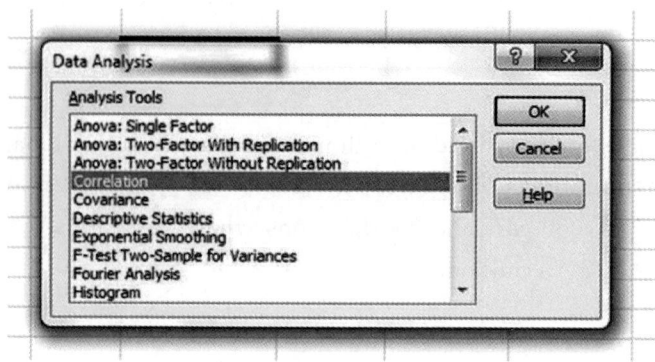

Fig. 2.7.6 Dialogue Box for Correlation Matrix for Car Rental Companies

Output range (click on the button to its left, and enter): A47 (see Fig. 2.7.7)

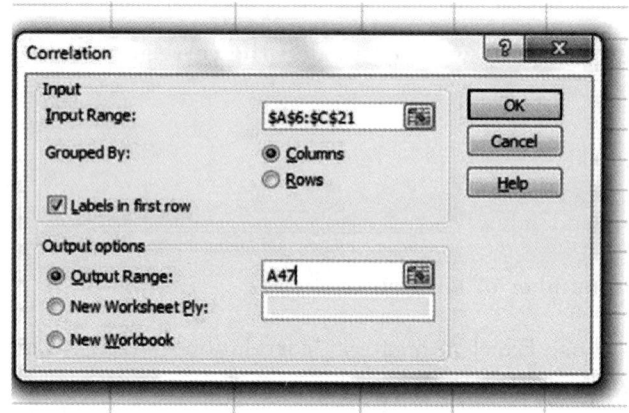

Fig. 2.7.7 Dialogue Box for Input/Output Range for Correlation Matrix

OK

The resulting correlation matrix appears in A47: D50 (see Fig. 2.7.8).

47		SALES /$10⁶	NO. OF CARS /1000	NO. OF LOCATIONS
48	SALES /$10⁶	1		
49	NO. OF CARS /1000	0.920235314	1	
50	NO. OF LOCATIONS	0.562140716	0.694488326	1
51				

Fig. 2.7.8 Resulting Correlation Matrix for Rental Car Companies Data

Next, format the three numbers in the correlation matrix that are in decimals to two decimals places. And, also, make column D wider so that the Number of Locations label fits inside cell D47.

Save this Excel file as RENTAL6

The final spreadsheet for these Car Rental Companies appears in Fig. 2.7.9.

Note that the number "1" along the diagonal of the correlation matrix means that the corre-

CAR RENTAL COMPANIES		
Y SALES/10^6	X_1 NO. OF CARS/1000	X_2 NO. OF LOCATIONS
1070	120	152
1460	180	1120
1480	85	1032
552	92	440
2105	315	2587
308	71	1697
2380	221	1153
1140	142	922
43	25	105
154	35	1483
72	15	442
81	18	251
333	42	465
91	15	492
147	18	44

SUMMARY OUTPUT

Regression Statistics	
Multiple R	0.93
R Square	0.86
Adjusted R Square	0.83
Standard Error	321.49
Observations	15

ANOVA

	df	SS	MS	F	Significance F
Regression	2	7510945.33	3755472.663	36.33	8.10477E-06
Residual	12	1240299.61	103358.3006		
Total	14	8751244.93			

	Coefficients	Standard Error	t Stat	P-value	Lower 95%	Upper 95%	Lower 95.0%	Upper 95.0%
Intercept	53.55	133.20	0.40	0.69	-236.66	343.76	-236.66	343.76
NO. OF CARS /1000	9.09	1.34	6.78	0.00	6.17	12.01	6.17	12.01
NO. OF LOCATIONS	-0.17	0.17	-0.98	0.34	-0.53	0.20	-0.53	0.20

	SALES/10^6	NO. OF CARS/1000	NO. OF LOCATIONS
SALES/10^6	1		
NO. OF CARS /1000	0.92	1	
NO. OF LOCATIONS	0.56	0.69	1

Fig. 2.7.9 Final Spreadsheet for Car Rental Companies Regression and the Correlation Matrix

lation of each variable with itself is a perfect, positive correlation of 1.0.

Correlation coefficients are always expressed in just two decimal places.

You are now ready to read the correlation between the three pairs of variables:

The correlation between NO. OF CARS and SALES is: +0.92

The correlation between NO. OF LOCATIONS and SALES is: +0.56

The correlation between NO. OF CARS and NO. OF LOCATIONS is: +0.69

This means that the better predictor of sales is NO. OF CARS with a correlation of +0.92. Adding the second predictor variable, NO. OF LOCATIONS, improved the prediction by only 0.01 to 0.93, and was, therefore, not worth the extra effort. NO. OF CARS is an excellent prediction of ANNUAL SALES all by itself.

If you want to learn more about the correlation matrix, see Levine et al. (2011).

2.7.5 End-of-chapter Practice Problems

(1) The Graduate Record Examinations (GRE) are frequently used to predict the first-year GPA of students in an MBA program.

The Graduate Record Examinations (GRE) are a standardized test that is an admission requirement for many U. S. graduate schools that offer an MBA degree. The GRE is intended to measure general academic preparedness, regardless of specialization field. The GRE test produces three subtest scores: ① GRE VERBAL REASONING (scale 130-170), ② GRE QUANTITATIVE REASONING (scale 130-170), and ③ ANALYTICAL WRITING (scale 0-6).

Suppose that you have been asked by a director of an MBA program to find out the relationship between these variables based on last year's entering graduate class and the ability of the GRE to predict first-year grade-point average (GPA).

You have decided to use the three subtest scores as the predictors, X_1, X_2, and X_3 and the first-year grade-point average (FIRST-YEAR GPA) as the criterion, Y. To test your Excel skills, you have randomly selected a small group of students from last year's entering MBA graduate class, and have recorded their scores on these variables.

But, suppose, that you want to find out what would happen if you added undergraduate GPA as a fourth predictor. What would be the multiple correlation?

Let's find out what happens when you use the hypothetical data that is presented in Fig. 2.7.10 that includes undergraduate GPA as a fourth predictor of first-year GPA for students in an MBA program.

GRADUATE RECORD EXAMINATIONS (GRE)				
How well does the GRE predict first-year GPA in an MBA program?				
FIRST-YEAR GPA	GRE VERBAL	GRE QUANTITATIVE	GRE WRITING	UNDERGRAD GPA
3.25	160	161	5	3.40
3.42	156	158	4	3.15
2.85	156	157	2	3.05
2.65	154	153	1	2.55
3.65	166	166	6	3.25
3.16	159	160	3	3.20
3.56	166	163	4	3.66
2.35	155	154	2	2.55
2.86	153	154	3	2.85
2.95	158	157	4	2.80
3.15	158	159	4	3.05
3.45	160	160	5	3.44

Fig. 2.7.10 Worksheet Data for Chapter 2.7 Practice Problem #1

(a) Create an Excel spreadsheet by using FIRST-YEAR GPA as the criterion (Y), and the other variables as the four predictors of this criterion.

(b) Use Excel's multiple regression function to find the relationship between these variables and place it below the table.

(c) Use number format (2 decimal places) for the multiple correlation on the Summary Output, use number format (three decimal places) for the coefficients, and four decimal places for all other decimal figures in the SUMMARY OUTPUT.

(d) Print the table and regression results below the table so that they fit onto one page.

(e) On this printout, circle and label by hand:

(1a) multiple correlation R_{xy}

(2b) coefficients for the Y-intercept, GRE VERBAL, GRE QUANTITATIVE, GRE WRITING, and UNDERGRAD GPA

(f) Save this file as GRE24.

(g) Now, go back to your Excel file and create a correlation matrix for these five variables, and place it underneath the SUMMARY OUTPUT. Change each correlation to just two decimals. Save this file again as: GRE24.

(h) Now, print out just this correlation matrix in portrait mode on a separate sheet of paper.

Answer the following questions by using your Excel printout:

① What is the multiple correlation R_{xy}?

② What is the Y-intercept a?

③ What is the coefficient for GRE VERBAL b_1?

④ What is the coefficient for GRE QUANTITATIVE b_2?

⑤ What is the coefficient for GRE WRITING b_3?

⑥ What is the coefficient for UNDERGRAD GPA b_4?

⑦ What is the multiple regression equation?

⑧ Underneath this regression equation by hand, predict the FIRST-YEAR GPA you would expect for a GRE VERBAL score of 159, a GRE QUANTITATIVE score of 154, a GRE WRITING score of 4, and an UNDERGRAD GPA of 3.05.

Answer the following questions by using your Excel printout. Be sure to include the plus or minus sign for each correlation:

⑨ What is the correlation between UNDERGRAD GPA and FIRST-YEAR GPA?

⑩ What is the correlation between UNDERGRAD GPA and GRE VERBAL?

⑪ What is the correlation between UNDERGRAD GPA and GRE QUANTITATIVE?

⑫ What is the correlation between UNDERGRAD GPA and GRE WRITING?

⑬ Discuss which of the four predictors is the best predictor of FIRST-YEAR GPA.

⑭ Explain in words how much better the four predictor variables combined predict FIRST-YEAR GPA than the best single predictor by itself.

(2) The Graduate Management Admission Test (GMAT) is a three-and-a-half hour exam that is accepted by almost 6,000 Business and Management programs in more than 80 countries as part of the admission application for people who want to obtain a graduate degree. This test is taken by more than 200,000 applicants each year. Suppose that a major university that offers an M. A. in Human Resources Management requires a GMAT score as part of the application process to this program, and wants to know how well GMAT scores of applicants predict their Grade-Point Average (GPA) at the end of their first year of graduate school. The GMAT has four subtest scores:
①Verbal (score range 0~60), ②Quantitative (score range 0~60), ③Analytical writing (score range 0~6 in 0.5 intervals), and ④Integrated Reasoning (score range 1~8). You have decided to use these four subtest scores as predictors of first-year GPA, and to check your skills in Excel, you have created the hypothetical data given in Fig. 2.7.11.

GRADUATE MANAGEMENT ADMISSION TEST (GMAT)

How well does the GMAT predict first-year GPA in an HRM program?

FIRST-YEAR GPA	VERBAL	QUANTITATIVE	ANALYTICAL WRITING	INTEGRATED REASONING
3.25	50	45	4.0	4
3.67	56	48	4.5	6
2.8	54	51	5.0	5
3.05	52	53	5.5	4
3.45	51	54	4.0	3
3.33	48	58	3.0	7
2.75	46	59	4.5	8
2.95	45	57	5.5	5
2.6	52	51	6.0	6
3.67	57	50	4.5	4
3.75	53	48	3.0	7
3.42	46	46	4.0	6
3.15	42	48	5.0	7
3.26	38	49	4.0	5
2.96	41	52	5.5	4

Fig. 2.7.11 Worksheet Data for Correlationship between GMAT and First-year GPA: Practice Problem #2

(a) Create an Excel spreadsheet by using FIRST-YEAR GPA as the criterion (Y), and the other variables as the four predictors of this criterion (X_1 = VERBAL, X_2 = QUANTITATIVE, X_3 = ANALYTICAL WRITING, and X_4 = INTEGRATED REASONING).

(b) Use Excel's multiple regression function to find the relationship between these five variables and place the SUMMARY OUTPUT below the table.

(c) Use number format (2 decimal places) for the multiple correlation on the Summary Output, and use three decimal places for the coefficients in the SUMMARY OUTPUT.

(d) Save the file as: GMAT26.

(e) Print the table and regression results below the table so that they fit onto one page.

Answer the following questions by using your Excel printout:

① What is the multiple correlation R_{xy}?

② What is the Y-intercept a?

③ What is the coefficient for VERBAL, b_1?

④ What is the coefficient for QUANTITATIVE, b_2?

⑤ What is the coefficient for ANALYTICAL WRITING, b_3?

⑥ What is the coefficient for INTEGRATED REASONING, b_4?

⑦ What is the multiple regression equation?

⑧ Predict the FIRST-YEAR GPA you would expect for a VERBAL score of 52, a QUANTITATIVE score of 48, an ANALYTICAL WRITING score of 4.5, and an INTEGRATED REASONING score of 6.

(f) Now, go back to your Excel file and create a correlation matrix for these five variables, and place it underneath the SUMMARY OUTPUT.

(g) Re-save this file as: GMAT26.

(h) Now, print out just this correlation matrix on a separate sheet of paper.

Answer the following questions by using your Excel printout. (Be sure to include the plus or minus sign for each correlation)

⑨ What is the correlation between VERBAL and FIRST-YEAR GPA?

⑩ What is the correlation between QUANTITATIVE and FIRST-YEAR GPA?

⑪ What is the correlation between ANALYTICAL WRITING and FIRST-YEAR GPA?

⑫ What is the correlation between INTEGRATED REASONING and FIRST-YEAR GPA?

⑬ What is the correlation between VERBAL and QUANTITATIVE?

⑭ What is the correlation between QUANTITATIVE and ANALYTICAL WRITING?

⑮ What is the correlation between ANALYTICAL WRITING and INTEGRATED REASONING?

⑯ What is the correlation between QUANTITATIVE and INTEGRATED REASONING?

⑰ Discuss which of the four predictors is the best predictor of FIRST-YEAR GPA.

⑱ Explain in words how much better the four predictor variables combined predict FIRST-YEAR GPA than the best single predictor by itself.

(3) Suppose that you are the marketing manager for 7-Eleven stores in Missouri and that you want to see if a proposed store location would generate sufficient yearly sales volume to support the idea of building a new store at that location. You have checked the data available at your company to generate the following table for a random sample of 20 7-Eleven stores in Missouri based on last year's data to create the hypothetical data given in Fig. 2. 7. 12.

Store ID	Y Annual Sales /$1000	X_1 Average Daily Traffic	X_2 Population (2-mile radius)	X_3 Average Income in Area
1	1,121	61,655	17,880	$28,991
2	766	35,236	13,742	$14,731
3	595	35,403	19,741	$8,114
4	899	52,832	23,246	$15,324
5	915	40,809	24,485	$11,438
6	782	40,820	20,410	$11,730
7	833	49,147	28,997	$10,589
8	571	24,953	9,981	$10,706
9	692	40,828	8,982	$23,591
10	1,005	39,195	18,814	$15,703
11	589	34,574	16,941	$9,015
12	671	26,639	13,319	$10,065
13	903	55,083	21,482	$17,365
14	703	37,892	26,524	$7,532
15	556	24,019	14,412	$6,950
16	657	27,791	13,896	$9,855
17	1,209	53,438	22,444	$21,589
18	997	54,835	18,096	$22,659
19	844	32,919	16,458	$12,660
20	883	29,139	16,609	$11,618

Fig. 2. 7. 12 Worksheet Data for 7-Eleven's Yearly Sales Volumn: Practice Problem #3

(a) Create an Excel spreadsheet by using the annual sales figures as the criterion and the average daily traffic, population, and income figures as the predictors.

(b) Use Excel's multiple regression function to find the relationship between these four variables and place the SUMMARY OUTPUT below the table.

(c) Use number format (2 decimal places) for the multiple correlation on the Summary Output, and use this same number format for the coefficients in the summary output.

(d) Save the file as: multiple2.

(e) Print the table and regression results below the table so that they fit onto one page.

Answer the following questions by using your Excel printout:

① What is multiple correlation R_{xy}?

② What is the Y-intercept a?

③ What is the coefficient for Average Daily Traffic b_1?

④ What is the coefficient for Population b_2?

⑤ What is the coefficient for Average Income in Area b_3?

⑥ What is the multiple regression equation?

⑦ Predict the annual sales you would expect for Average Daily Traffic of 42,000, a population of 23,000, and Average Income in Area of $22,000.

(f) Now, go back to your Excel file and create a correlation matrix for these four variables, and place it underneath the SUMMARY OUTPUT on your spreadsheet.

(g) Save this file as: multiple3.

(h) Now, print out just this correlation matrix on a separate sheet of paper.

Answer the following questions by using your Excel printout. (Be sure to include the plus or minus sign for each correlation):

⑧ What is the correlation between traffic and sales?

⑨ What is the correlation between population and sales?

⑩ What is the correlation between income and sales?

⑪ What is the correlation between traffic and population?

⑫ What is the correlation between population and income?

⑬ Discuss which of the three predictors is the best predictor of Yearly Sales.

⑭ Explain in words how much better the three predictor variables combined predict annual sales than the best single predictor by itself.

2.8　One-way Analysis of Variance (ANOVA)

So far in this 2013 Excel Guide, you have learned how to use a one-group t-test to compare the sample mean to the population mean, and a two-group t-test to test the difference between two sample means. But what should you do when you have more than two groups and you want to determine if there is a significant difference between the means of these groups?

The answer to this question is: Analysis of Variance (ANOVA).

The ANOVA test allows you to test for the difference between the means when you have three or more groups in your research study.

Important note: In order to do One-way Analysis of Variance, you need to have installed the "Data Analysis Toolpak" that was described in Chapter 2.6 (see Section 2.6.5.1). If you did not install it, you need to do that now.

Let's suppose that you are interested in comparing prices between three major supermarket chains in St. Louis: ①Dierberg's, ②Schnuck's, and ③Shop'n Save. Suppose, further, that you have selected the 28 specific items listed in the table below as your "market basket of products" to compare prices at these three supermarkets. You have also specified the package size of each of these items in your checklist. Item #14, for example, might be: Tide Liquid laundry detergent, 16 ounces.

Suppose that you have selected zip code 63119 in St. Louis, as this zip code has one store of each of these three supermarket chains. You drive to each of these three supermarkets in this zip code area, and you have obtained the hypothetical data given in Fig. 2.8.1 summarizing the prices of the items in your market basket of products:

	SUPERMARKET PRICE COMPARISONS		
ITEM	DIERBERG'S	SCHNUCK'S	SHOP 'n SAVE
1	1.85	1.45	1.25
2	3.95	3.35	3.04
3	2.25	1.75	1.45
4	2.85	2.35	2.25
5	1.65	1.10	0.85
6	3.65	2.95	2.45
7	2.45	1.85	1.45
8	1.95	1.56	1.44
9	1.83	1.25	1.15
10	2.64	2.14	2.04
11	2.84	2.25	2.15
12	1.84	1.20	0.55
13	1.65	1.25	1.15
14	2.75	2.10	2.04
15	2.71	1.86	1.75
16	1.55	0.94	0.85
17	1.85	1.30	1.01
18	0.95	0.55	0.45
19	1.55	1.28	1.06
20	1.44	0.85	0.74
21	1.65	1.25	1.15
22	1.64	1.28	1.04
23	4.21	3.75	3.36
24	1.20	0.71	0.61
25	4.55	3.90	3.25
26	3.45	2.84	2.65
27	5.85	5.30	5.14
28	1.65	1.25	1.04

Fig. 2.8.1 Worksheet Data for Supermarket Price Comparisons

Create an Excel spreadsheet for these data in this way:

B1: SUPERMARKET PRICE COMPARISON

A3: ITEM

B3: DIERBERG'S

C3: SCHNUCK'S

D3: SHOP'n SAVE

A4: 1

B4: 1.85

2.8.1 Using Excel to Perform a One-way Analysis of Variance (ANOVA)

Enter the other information into your spreadsheet table. When you have finished entering these data, the last cell on the left should have 28 in cell A31, and the last cell on the right should have 1.04 in cell D31. Center the numbers in each of the columns. Use number format (2 decimals) for all numbers.

Important note: Be sure to double-check all of your figures in the table to make sure that they are exactly correct or you will not be able to obtain the correct answer for this problem!

Save this file as: SUPERMARKET5

Objective: To use Excel to perform a one-way ANOVA test

You are now ready to perform an ANOVA test on these data by using the following steps:

Data (at top of screen)

Data Analysis (far right at top of screen)

ANOVA: Single Factor (scroll up to this formula and highlight it; see Fig. 2.8.2)

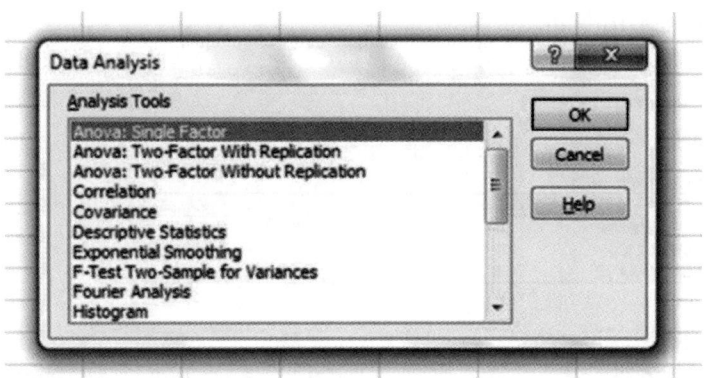

Fig. 2.8.2 Dialog Box for Data Analysis: ANOVA Single Factor

OK

Input range: B3: D31 (note that you have included in this range the column titles that are in row 3)

Important note: Whenever the data set has a different sample size in the groups being compared, the INPUT RANGE that you define must start at the column title of the first group on the left and go to the last column on the right and go down to the lowest row that has a figure in it in the entire data matrix so that the INPUT RANGE has the "shape" of a rectangle when you highlight it.

Grouped by: Columns

Put a check mark in: Labels in First Row

Output range (click on the button to its left): A36 (see Fig. 2.8.3)

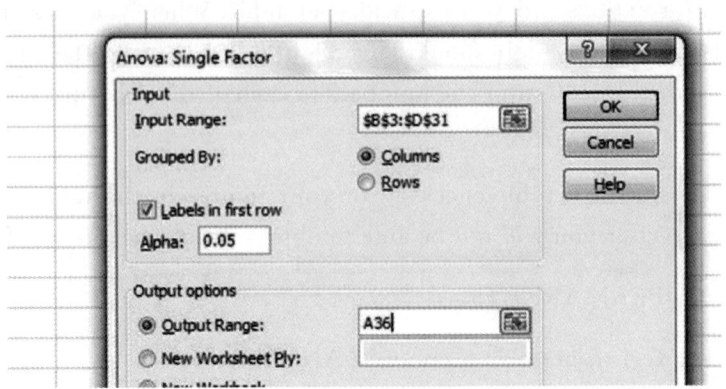

Fig. 2.8.3 Dialog Box for ANOVA: Single Factor Input/Output Range

OK

Save this file as: SUPER6

You should have generated the table given in Fig. 2.8.4. If you round off all figures that are in decimal format to two decimal places and center all numbers in their cells, this will make your table much easier to read.

	A	B	C	D	E	F	G
35							
36	Anova: Single Factor						
37							
38	SUMMARY						
39	Groups	Count	Sum	Average	Variance		
40	DIERBERG'S	28	68.40	2.44	1.32		
41	SCHNUCK'S	28	53.61	1.91	1.22		
42	SHOP 'n SAVE	28	47.36	1.69	1.13		
43							
44							
45	ANOVA						
46	Source of Variation	SS	df	MS	F	P-value	F crit
47	Between Groups	8.34	2	4.17	3.40	0.04	3.11
48	Within Groups	99.23	81	1.23			
49							
50	Total	107.57	83				

Fig. 2.8.4 ANOVA Results for Supermarket Price Comparisons

Print out both the data table and the ANOVA summary table so that all of this information fits onto one page. (Hint: Set the Page Layout/Fit to Scale to 85% size).

As a check on your analysis, you should have the following in these cells:

A36: ANOVA: Single Factor

D40: 2.44

D47: 4.17

E47: 3.40

G47: 3.11

Now, let's discuss how you should interpret this table.

2.8.2 How to Interpret the ANOVA Table Correctly?

Objective: To interpret the ANOVA table correctly

ANOVA allows you to test the differences between means when you have three or more groups of data. This ANOVA test is called the F-test statistic, and is typically identified with the letter: F.

The formula for the F-test is this:

F = Mean Square between groups (MS_b) divided by Mean Square within groups (MS_w)

$$F = MS_b / MS_w$$

The derivation and explanation of this formula is beyond the scope of this Excel Guide. In this Excel Guide, we are attempting to teach you how to use Excel, and we are not attempting to teach you the statistical theory that is behind the ANOVA formulas. For a detailed explanation of ANOVA, see Weiers (2011).

Note that cell D47 contains $MS_b = 4.17$, while cell D48 contains $MS_w = 1.23$. When you divide these two figures by using their cell references in Excel, you get the answer to the F-test of 3.40 which is in cell E47. Let's discuss now the meaning of the figure: $F = 3.40$.

In order to determine whether this figure for F of 3.40 indicates a significant difference between the means of the three groups, the first step is to write the null hypothesis and the alternative hypothesis for the three groups of prices.

In our supermarket price comparisons, the null hypothesis states that the population means of the three groups are equal, while the alternative hypothesis states that the population means of the three groups are not equal and that there is, therefore, a significant difference between the population means of the three groups. Which of these two hypotheses should you accept based on the ANOVA results?

2.8.3 Using the Decision Rule for the ANOVA F-test

To state the hypotheses, let's call Dierberg's as Group 1, Schnuck's as Group 2, and Shop'n Save as Group 3. The hypotheses would then be:

$$H_0 : \mu_1 = \mu_2 = \mu_3$$

$$H_1 : \mu_1 \neq \mu_2 \neq \mu_3$$

The answer to this question is analogous to the decision rule used in this book for both the one-group t-test and the two-group t-test. You will recall that this rule (see Section 2.4.1.6 and Section 2.5.1.8) was:

If the absolute value of t is less than the critical t, you accept the null hypothesis. If the absolute value of t is greater than the critical t, you reject the null hypothesis, and accept the alternative hypothesis.

Now, here is the decision rule for ANOVA:

Objective: To learn the decision rule for the ANOVA F-test

The decision rule for the ANOVA F-test is the following:

If the value for F is less than the critical F-value, accept the null hypothesis. If the value of F is greater than the critical F-value, reject the null hypothesis, and accept the alternative hypothesis.

Note that Excel tell you the critical F-value in cell G47: 3.11

Therefore, our decision rule for the supermarket ANOVA test is this:

Since the value of F of 3.40 is greater than the critical F-value of 3.11, we reject the null hypothesis and accept the alternative hypothesis.

Therefore, our conclusion, in plain English, is:

There is a significant difference between the population means of the three supermarket prices.

Note that it is not necessary to take the absolute value of F of 3.40. The F-value can never be less than one, and so it can never be a negative value which requires us to take its absolute value in order to treat it as a positive value.

It is important to note that ANOVA tells us that there was a significant difference between the population means of the three groups, but it does not tell us which pairs of groups were significantly different from each other.

2.8.4 Testing the Difference Between Two Groups by Using the ANOVA t-test

To answer that question, we need to do a different test called the ANOVA t-test.

Objective: To test the difference between the means of two groups using an ANOVA t-test when the ANOVA results indicate a significant difference between the population means

Since we have three groups of data (one group for each of the three supermarkets), we would have to perform three separate ANOVA t-tests to determine which pairs of groups were significantly different. This means that we would have to perform a separate ANOVA t-test for the following pairs of groups:

① Dierberg's vs. Schnuck's

② Dierberg's vs. Shop'n Save

③ Schnuck's vs. Shop'n Save

We will do just one of these pairs of tests, Dierberg's vs. Shop'n Save, to illustrate the way to perform an ANOVA t-test comparing these two supermarkets. The ANOVA t-test for the other two pairs of groups would be done in the same way.

Comparing Dierberg's vs. Shop'n Save in their prices by using the ANOVA t-test

Objective: To compare Dierberg's vs. Shop'n Save in their prices for the 28 items in the shopping basket by using the ANOVA t-test

The first step is to write the null hypothesis and the alternative hypothesis for these two supermarkets.

For the ANOVA t-test, the null hypothesis is that the population means of the two groups are equal, while the alternative hypothesis is that the population means of the two groups are not equal (i.e., there is a significant difference between these two means). Since we are comparing Dierberg's (Group 1) vs. Shop'n Save (Group 3), these hypotheses would be:

$$H_0 : \mu_1 = \mu_3$$

$$H_1 : \mu_1 \neq \mu_3$$

For Group 1 vs. Group 3, the formula for the ANOVA t-test is:

$$\text{ANOVA } t = \frac{\overline{X}_1 - \overline{X}_2}{se_{\text{ANOVA}}}$$

$$\text{where } se_{\text{ANOVA}} = \sqrt{MS_w \left(\frac{1}{n_1} + \frac{1}{n_2}\right)}$$

The steps involved in computing this ANOVA t-test are:

① Find the difference of the sample means for the two groups (2.44−1.69=0.75).

② Find $1/n_1 + 1/n_3$ (since both groups have 28 supermarket items in them, this becomes: 1/28+1/28=0.0357+0.0357=0.0714)

③ Multiply MS_w times the answer for step 2 (1.23×0.0714=0.0878)

④ Take the square root of step 3 [SQRT (0.0878)=0.30]

⑤ Divide Step 1 by Step 4 to find ANOVA t (0.75/0.30=2.50)

Note: Since Excel computes all calculations to 16 decimal places, when you use Excel for the above computations, your answer will be 2.54 instead of 2.50 that you will obtain if you use your calculator.

Now, what do we do with this ANOVA t-test result of 2.50? In order to interpret this value of 2.50 correctly, we need to determine the critical value of t for the ANOVA t-test. To do that, we need to find the degrees of freedom for the ANOVA t-test as follows:

(1) Finding the degrees of freedom for the ANOVA t-test

Objective: To find the degrees of freedom for the ANOVA t-test.

The degrees of freedom (df) for the ANOVA t-test is found as follows.

df = take the total sample size of all of the groups and subtract the number of groups in your study ($n_{TOTAL} - k$, where k = the number of groups)

In our example, the total sample size of the three groups is 84 since there are 28 prices for each of the three supermarkets, and since there are three groups.

84 − 3 gives degrees of freedom for the ANOVA t-test of 81.

If you look up df = 81 in the t-table in Appendix in the degrees of freedom column (df), which is the second column on the left of this table, you will find that the critical t-value is 1.96.

Important note: Be sure to use the degrees of freedom column (df) in Appendix for the ANOVA t-test critical t value.

(2) Stating the decision rule for the ANOVA t-test

Objective: To learn the decision rule for the ANOVA t-test

Interpreting the result of the ANOVA t-test follows the same decision rule that we used for both the one-group t-test (see Section 2.4.1.6) and the two-group t-test (see Section 2.5.1.8):

If the absolute value of t is less than the critical value of t, we accept the null hypothesis. If the absolute value of t is greater than the critical value of t, we reject the null hypothesis and accept the alternative hypothesis.

Since we are using a type of t-test, we need to take the absolute value of t. Since the absolute value of 2.50 is greater than the critical t-value of 1.96, we reject the null hypothesis (that the population means of the two groups are equal) and accept the alternative hypothesis (that the population means of the two groups are significantly different from one another).

This means that our conclusion, in plain English, is as follows:

The average prices of our market basket of items at Dierberg's were significantly higher than those at Shop'n Save ($2.44 vs. $1.69).

Note that this difference in average prices of $0.75 might not seem like much, but in practical terms, this means that the average prices at Dierberg's are 44% higher than those at Shop'n Save. This, clearly, is an important difference in prices from these two supermarkets based on our hypothetical data.

(3) Performing an ANOVA t-test by using Excel commands

Now, let's do these calculations for the ANOVA t-test by using Excel with the file you created earlier in this chapter: SUPER6

A52: Dierberg's vs. Shop'n Save

A54: $1/n$ of Dierberg's+$1/n$ of Shop'n Save

A56: se of Dierberg's vs. Shop'n Save

A58: ANOVA t-test

D54: =(1/28+1/28)

D56: =SQRT(D48×D54) D58: =(D40−D42)/D56

You should now have the following results in these cells when you round off all these figures in the ANOVA t-test to two decimal points:

D54: 0.07

D56: 0.30

D58: 2.54

Save this final result under the file name: SUPER7. Print out the resulting spreadsheet so that it fits onto one page like Fig. 2.8.5 (Hint: Reduce the Page Layout/Scale to Fit to 75%).

For a more detailed explanation of the ANOVA t-test, see Black (2010).

Important note: You are only allowed to perform an ANOVA t-test comparing the population means of two groups when the F-test produces a significant difference between the population means of all of the groups in your study.

It is improper to do any ANOVA t-test when the value of F is less than the critical value of F. Whenever F is less than the critical F, this means that there was no difference between the population means of the groups, and, therefore, that you cannot test to see if there is a difference between the means of any two groups since this would capitalize on chance differences between these two groups.

SUPERMARKET PRICE COMPARISONS			
ITEM	DIERBERG'S	SCHNUCK'S	SHOP 'n SAVE
1	1.85	1.45	1.25
2	3.95	3.35	3.04
3	2.25	1.75	1.45
4	2.85	2.35	2.25
5	1.65	1.10	0.85
6	3.65	2.95	2.45
7	2.45	1.85	1.45
8	1.95	1.56	1.44
9	1.83	1.25	1.15
10	2.64	2.14	2.04
11	2.84	2.25	2.15
12	1.84	1.20	0.55
13	1.65	1.25	1.15
14	2.75	2.10	2.04
15	2.71	1.86	1.75
16	1.55	0.94	0.85
17	1.85	1.30	1.01
18	0.95	0.55	0.45
19	1.55	1.28	1.06
20	1.44	0.85	0.74
21	1.65	1.25	1.15
22	1.64	1.28	1.04
23	4.21	3.75	3.36
24	1.20	0.71	0.61
25	4.55	3.90	3.25
26	3.45	2.84	2.65
27	5.85	5.30	5.14
28	1.65	1.25	1.04

Anova: Single Factor

SUMMARY

Groups	Count	Sum	Average	Variance
DIERBERG'S	28	68.40	2.44	1.32
SCHNUCK'S	28	53.61	1.91	1.22
SHOP 'n SAVE	28	47.36	1.69	1.13

ANOVA

Source of Variation	SS	df	MS	F	P-value	F crit
Between Groups	8.34	2	4.17	3.40	0.04	3.11
Within Groups	99.23	81	1.23			
Total	107.57	83				

Dierberg's vs. Shop 'n Save

1/n of Dierberg's + 1/n of Shop 'n Save		0.07
se of Dierberg's vs. Shop 'n Save		0.30
ANOVA t-test		2.54

Fig. 2.8.5 Final Spreadsheet of Supermarket Price Comparisons for Dierberg's vs. Shop'n Save

2.8.5 End-of-chapter Practice Problems

(1) Suppose that you wanted to compare your company's premium brand of tire (Brand A) against two major competitors' brands (B and C). You have set up a laboratory test of the three types of tires, and you have measured the number of simulated miles driven before the tread length reached a pre-determined amount.

The hypothetical results are given in Fig. 2.8.6. Note that the data are in thousands of miles driven (1000), so, for example, 63 is really 63000 miles driven.

(a) Enter these data on an Excel spreadsheet.

(b) Perform a one-way ANOVA test on these data, and show the resulting ANOVA table underneath the input data for the three brands of tires.

(c) If the F-value in the ANOVA table is significant, create an Excel formula to compute the ANOVA t-test comparing the average for Brand A against Brand C and show the results below the ANOVA table on the spreadsheet (put the standard error and the ANOVA t-test value on separate lines of your spreadsheet, and use two decimal places for each value).

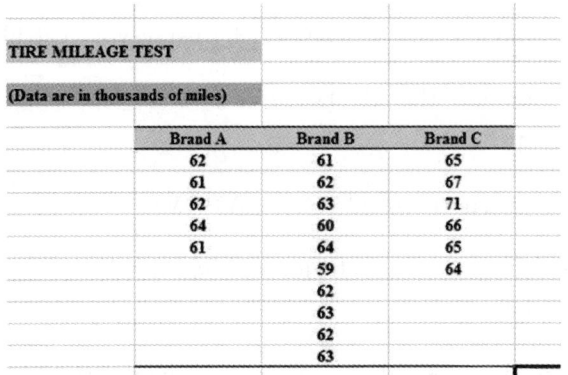

Fig. 2.8.6 Worksheet Data for TIRE MILEAGE TEST: Practice Problem #1

(d) Print out the resulting spreadsheet so that all of the information fits onto one page.

(e) Save the spreadsheet as: TIRE.

Now, write the answers to the following questions by using your Excel printout:

① What are the null hypothesis and the research hypothesis for the ANOVA F-test?

② What is MS_b on your Excel printout?

③ What is MS_w on your Excel printout?

④ Compute $F = MS_b / MS_w$ by using your calculator.

⑤ What is the critical value of F on your Excel printout?

⑥ What is the result of the ANOVA F-test?

⑦ What is the conclusion of the ANOVA F-test in plain English?

⑧ If the ANOVA F-test produced a significant difference between the three brands in miles driven, what is the null hypothesis and the alternative hypothesis for the ANOVA t-test comparing Brand A versus Brand C?

⑨ What is the mean (average) for Brand A on your Excel printout?

⑩ What is the mean (average) for Brand C on your Excel printout?

⑪ What are the degrees of freedom (df) for the ANOVA t-test comparing Brand A vs. Brand C?

⑫ What is the critical t value for this ANOVA t-test in Appendix for these degrees of freedom?

⑬ Compute the se ANOVA by using your calculator.

⑭ Compute the ANOVA t-test value comparing Brand A vs. Brand C by using your calculator.

⑮ What is the result of the ANOVA t-test comparing Brand A vs. Brand C?

⑯ What is the conclusion of the ANOVA t-test comparing Brand A vs. Brand C in plain English?

Note that since there are three brands of tires, you need to do three ANOVA t-tests to determine what the significant differences are between the tires. Since you have just completed the ANOVA t-test by comparing Brand A versus Brand C, let's do the ANOVA t-test next comparing Brand A versus Brand B.

⑰ State the null hypothesis and the alternative hypothesis comparing Brand A vs. Brand B.

⑱ What is the mean (average) for Brand A on your Excel printout?

⑲ What is the mean (average) for Brand B on your Excel printout?

⑳ What are the degrees of freedom (df) for the ANOVA t-test comparing Brand A vs. Brand B?

㉑ What is the critical t value for this ANOVA t-test in Appendix for these degrees of freedom?

㉒ Compute the se ANOVA for Brand A vs. Brand B by using your calculator.

㉓ Compute the ANOVA t-test value comparing Brand A vs. Brand B.

㉔ What is the result of the ANOVA t-test comparing Brand A vs. Brand B?

㉕ What is the conclusion of the ANOVA t-test comparing Brand A vs. Brand B in plain English?

The last ANOVA t-test compares Brand B vs. Brand C. Let's do that test below:

㉖ State the null hypothesis and the alternative hypothesis comparing Brand B vs. Brand C.

㉗ What is the mean (average) for Brand B on your Excel printout?

㉘ What is the mean (average) for Brand C on your Excel printout?

㉙ What are the degrees of freedom (df) for the ANOVA t-test comparing Brand B vs. Brand C?

㉚ What is the critical t value for this ANOVA t-test in Appendix for these degrees of freedom?

㉛ Compute the se ANOVA comparing Brand B vs. Brand C by using your calculator.

㉜ Compute the ANOVA t-test value comparing Brand B vs. Brand C with your calculator.

㉝ What is the result of the ANOVA t-test comparing Brand B vs. Brand C?

㉞ What is the conclusion of the ANOVA t-test comparing Brand B vs. Brand C in plain English?

㉟ What is the summary of the three ANOVA t-tests in plain English?

㊱ What recommendation would you make to your company about these three brands of tires based on the results of your analysis? Why would you make that recommendation?

(2) McDonald's rolled out the "100% Angus Beef Third Pounders Burgers" to compete with the supersize hamburgers sold by Hardee's. Suppose that you had been hired as a consultant by McDonald's to analyze the data from a test market study involving four test market cities matched for population size, average household income, average family size, and number of McDonald's restaurants in each city. Suppose, further, that the market test ran for 12 weeks, and that each city used only one type of advertisement for these burgers:

①Radio, ②Local TV, ③Billboards, and ④Local newspaper. The cities were randomly assigned to one type of ad, and each city spent the same advertising dollars each week on their one type of ad. The hypothetical data for the number of units sold each week of the Angus Burger are given in Fig. 2.8.7.

(a) Enter these data on an Excel spreadsheet.

(b) Perform a one-way ANOVA test on these data, and show the resulting ANOVA table underneath the input data for the four types of ads.

(c) If the F-value in the ANOVA table is significant, create an Excel formula to compute the ANOVA t-test comparing the average number of units sold for Billboard ads against the average for Radio ads, and show the results below the ANOVA table on the spreadsheet

ANGUS BURGER TEST MARKET STUDY			
1	2	3	4
Radio	Local TV	Billboards	Local newspaper
300	310	340	280
320	315	330	285
310	320	345	290
290	326	342	275
280	324	341	282
315	318	351	284
326	330	339	291
295	327	337	284
278	328	329	279
289	319	328	274
287	326	332	283
305	328	335	285

Fig. 2.8.7 Worksheet Data for Chapter 2.8: Practice Problem #2

(put the standard error and the ANOVA t-test value on separate lines of your spreadsheet, and use two decimal places for each value).

(d) Print out the resulting spreadsheet so that all of the information fits onto one page.

(e) Save the spreadsheet as: McD4.

Let's call the Radio ads Group 1, the Local TV ads Group 2, the Billboards ads Group 3, and the Local Newspaper ads Group 4. Now, write the answers to the following questions by using your Excel printout:

① What are the null hypothesis and the research hypothesis for the ANOVA F-test?

② What is MS_b on your Excel printout?

③ What is MS_w on your Excel printout?

④ Compute $F = MS_b / MS_w$ by using your calculator.

⑤ What is the critical value of F on your Excel printout?

⑥ What is the result of the ANOVA F-test?

⑦ What is the conclusion of the ANOVA F-test in plain English?

⑧ If the ANOVA F-test produced a significant difference between the four types of ads in the number of Angus Burgers sold per week, what is the null hypothesis and the alternative hypothesis for the ANOVA t-test comparing Billboards ads (Group 3) versus Radio ads (Group 1)?

⑨ What is the mean (average) for Billboards ads on your Excel printout?

⑩ What is the mean (average) for Radio ads on your Excel printout?

⑪ What are the degrees of freedom (df) for the ANOVA t-test comparing Billboards ads vs. Radio ads?

⑫ What is the critical t value for this ANOVA t-test in Appendix for these degrees of freedom?

⑬ Compute the se ANOVA by using your calculator for Billboards ads versus Radio ads.

⑭ Compute the ANOVA t-test value comparing Billboard ads versus Radio ads using your calculator.

⑮ What is the result of the ANOVA t-test comparing Billboards ads vs. Radio ads?

⑯ What is the conclusion of the ANOVA t-test comparing Billboards ads versus Radio ads in plain English?

(3) Suppose that you have been hired as a consultant by Procter & Gamble to analyze the data from a pilot study involving three recent focus groups who were shown four different television commercials for a new type of Crest toothpaste that have not yet been shown on television. The participants were given a 10-item survey to complete after seeing the commercials, and the hypothetical data from question #8 is given in Fig. 2.8.8 for the four TV commercials.

ITEM #8:	"How believable is this commercial to you?"							
1	2	3	4	5	6	7	8	9
not very believable								very believable

Rating for Focus Groups 1, 2, 3 combined

Television commercial			
A	B	C	D
2	3	5	6
3	4	6	7
5	5	7	4
4	2	5	5
5	6	8	3
3	1	6	8
6	4	7	2
4	3	5	6
3	7	4	7
7	6	6	5
2	5	3	8
1	3	6	9
3	4	8	5
5	2	9	6
6	3	5	7

Fig. 2.8.8 Worksheet Data for Different Commercials' Effect on the New Type Grest Toothpaste: Practice Problem #3

(a) Enter these data on an Excel spreadsheet.

(b) Perform a one-way ANOVA test on these data, and show the resulting ANOVA table underneath the input data for the four types of commercials.

(c) If the F-value in the ANOVA table is significant, create an Excel formula to compute the ANOVA t-test comparing the average for Commercial B against the average for Commercial D, and show the results below the ANOVA table on the spreadsheet (put the standard error and the ANOVA t-test value on separate lines of your spreadsheet, and use two decimal places for each value).

(d) Print out the resulting spreadsheet so that all of the information fits onto one page.

(e) Save the spreadsheet as: TV6.

Now, write the answers to the following questions by using your Excel printout:

① What are the null hypothesis and the research hypothesis for the ANOVA F-test?

② What is MS_b on your Excel printout?

③ What is MS_w on your Excel printout?

④ Compute $F = MS_b / MS_w$ by using your calculator.

⑤ What is the critical value of F on your Excel printout?

⑥ What is the result of the ANOVA F-test?

⑦ What is the conclusion of the ANOVA F-test in plain English?

⑧ If the ANOVA F-test produced a significant difference between the four types of TV commercials in their believeablity, what is the null hypothesis and the alternative hypothesis for the ANOVA t-test comparing Commercial B vs. Commercial D?

⑨ What is the mean (average) for Commercial B on your Excel printout?

⑩ What is the mean (average) for Commercial D on your Excel printout?

⑪ What are the degrees of freedom (df) for the ANOVA t-test comparing Commercial B vs. Commercial D?

⑫ What is the critical t value for this ANOVA t-test in Appendix for these degrees of freedom?

⑬ Compute the se ANOVA by using your calculator for Commercial B vs. Commercial D.

⑭ Compute the ANOVA t-test value comparing Commercial B vs. Commercial D by using your calculator.

⑮ What is the result of the ANOVA t-test comparing Commercial B vs. Commercial D?

⑯ What is the conclusion of the ANOVA t-test comparing Commercial B vs. Commercial D in plain English?

Appendix

TABLE 1 Table of Random Numbers

Row	Column							
	00000 12345	00001 67890	11111 12345	11112 67890	22222 12345	22223 67890	33333 12345	33334 67890
01	49280	88924	35779	00283	81163	07275	89863	02348
02	61870	41657	07468	08612	98083	97349	20775	45091
03	43898	65923	25078	86129	78496	97653	91550	08078
04	62993	93912	30454	84598	56095	20664	12872	64647
05	33850	58555	51438	85507	71865	79488	76783	31708
06	97340	03364	88472	04334	63919	36394	11095	92470
07	70543	29776	10087	10072	55980	64688	68239	20461
08	89382	93809	00796	95945	34101	81277	66090	88872
09	37818	72142	67140	50785	22380	16703	53362	44940
10	60430	22834	14130	96593	23298	56203	92671	15925
11	82975	66158	84731	19436	55790	69229	28661	13675
12	30987	71938	40355	54324	08401	26299	49420	59208
13	55700	24586	93247	32596	11865	63397	44251	43189
14	14756	23997	78643	75912	83832	32768	18928	57070
15	32166	53251	70654	92827	63491	04233	33825	69662
16	23236	73751	31888	81718	06546	83246	47651	04877
17	45794	26926	15130	82455	78305	55058	52551	47182
18	09893	20505	14225	68514	47427	56788	96297	78822
19	54382	74598	91499	14523	68479	27686	46162	83554
20	94750	89923	37089	20048	80336	94598	26940	36858
21	70297	34135	53140	33340	42050	82341	44104	82949
22	85157	47954	32979	26575	57600	40881	12250	73742
23	11100	02340	12860	74697	96644	89439	28707	25815
24	36871	50775	30592	57143	17381	68856	25853	35041
25	23913	48357	63308	16090	51690	54607	72407	55538
26	79348	36085	27973	65157	07456	22255	25626	57054
27	92074	54641	53673	54421	18130	60103	69593	49464
28	06873	21440	75593	41373	49502	17972	82578	16364

Continued

Row	Column							
	00000	00001	11111	11112	22222	22223	33333	33334
	12345	67890	12345	67890	12345	67890	12345	67890
29	12478	37622	99659	31065	83613	69889	58869	29571
30	57175	55564	65411	42547	70457	03426	72937	83792
31	91616	11075	80103	07831	59309	13276	26710	73000
32	78025	73539	14621	39044	47450	03197	12787	47709
33	27587	67228	80145	10175	12822	86687	65530	49325
34	16690	20427	04251	64477	73709	73945	92396	68263
35	70183	58065	65489	31833	82093	16747	10386	59293
36	90730	35385	15679	99742	50866	78028	75573	67257
37	10934	93242	13431	24590	02770	48582	00906	58595
38	82462	30166	79613	47416	13389	80268	05085	96666
39	27463	10433	07606	16285	93699	60912	94532	95632
40	02979	52997	09079	92709	90110	47506	53693	49892
41	46888	69929	75233	52507	32097	37594	10067	67327
42	53638	83161	08289	12639	08141	12640	28437	09268
43	82433	61427	17239	89160	19666	08814	37841	12847
44	35766	31672	50082	22795	66948	65581	84393	15890
45	10853	42581	08792	13257	61973	24450	52351	16602
46	20341	27398	72906	63955	17276	10646	74692	48438
47	54458	90542	77563	51839	52901	53355	83281	19177
48	26337	66530	16687	35179	46560	00123	44546	79896
49	34314	23729	85264	05575	96855	23820	11091	79821
50	28603	10708	68933	34189	92166	15181	66628	58599
51	66194	28926	99547	16625	45515	67953	12108	57846
52	78240	43195	24837	32511	70880	22070	52622	61881
53	00833	88000	67299	68215	11274	55624	32991	17436
54	12111	86683	61270	58036	64192	90611	15145	01748
55	47189	99951	05755	03834	43782	90599	40282	51417
56	76396	72486	62423	27618	84184	78922	73561	52818
57	46409	17469	32483	09083	76175	19985	26309	91536
58	74626	22111	87286	46772	42243	68046	44250	42439
59	34450	81974	93723	49023	58432	67083	36876	93391
60	36327	72135	33005	28701	34710	49359	50693	89311
61	74185	77536	84825	09934	99103	09325	67389	45869
62	12296	41623	62873	37943	25584	09609	63360	47270
63	90822	60280	88925	99610	42772	60561	76873	04117
64	72121	79152	96591	90305	10189	79778	68016	13747
65	95268	41377	25684	08151	61816	58555	54305	86189

Continued

Row	Column							
	00000 12345	00001 67890	11111 12345	11112 67890	22222 12345	22223 67890	33333 12345	33334 67890
66	92603	09091	75884	93424	72586	88903	30061	14457
67	18813	90291	05275	01223	79607	95426	34900	09778
68	38840	26903	28624	67157	51986	42865	14508	49315
69	05959	33836	53758	16562	41081	38012	41230	20528
70	85141	21155	99212	32685	51403	31926	69813	58781
71	75047	59643	31074	38172	03718	32119	69506	67143
72	30752	95260	68032	62871	58781	34143	68790	69766
73	22986	82575	42187	62295	84295	30634	66562	31442
74	99439	86692	90348	66036	48399	73451	26698	39437
75	20389	93029	11881	71685	65452	89047	63669	02656
76	39249	05173	68256	36359	20250	68686	05947	09335
77	96777	33605	29481	20063	09398	01843	35139	61344
78	04860	32918	10798	50492	52655	33359	94713	28393
79	41613	42375	00403	03656	77580	87772	86877	57085
80	17930	00794	53836	53692	67135	98102	61912	11246
81	24649	31845	25736	75231	83808	98917	93829	99430
82	79899	34061	54308	59358	56462	58166	97302	86828
83	76801	49594	81002	30397	52728	15101	72070	33706
84	36239	63636	38140	65731	39788	06872	38971	53363
85	07392	64449	17886	63632	53995	17574	22247	62607
86	67133	04181	33874	98835	67453	59734	76381	63455
87	77759	31504	32832	70861	15152	29733	75371	39174
88	85992	72268	42920	20810	29361	51423	90306	73574
89	79553	75952	54116	65553	47139	60579	09165	85490
90	41101	17336	48951	53674	17880	45260	08575	49321
91	36191	17095	32123	91576	84221	78902	82010	30847
92	62329	63898	23268	74283	26091	68409	69704	82267
93	14751	13151	93115	01437	56945	89661	67680	79790
94	48462	59278	44185	29616	76537	19589	83139	28454
95	29435	88105	59651	44391	74588	55114	80834	85686
96	28340	29285	12965	14821	80425	16602	44653	70467
97	02167	58940	27149	80242	10587	79786	34959	75339
98	17864	00991	39557	54981	23588	81914	37609	13128
99	79675	80605	60059	35862	00254	36546	21545	78179
100	72335	82037	92003	34100	29879	46613	89720	13274

TABLE 2 The Cumulative Standardized Normal Distribution

Entry represents area under the cumulative standardized normal distribution from $-\infty$ to Z

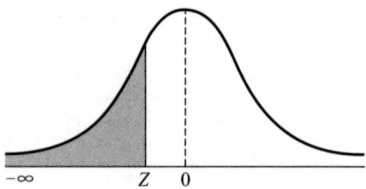

Z	0.00	0.01	0.02	0.03	0.04	0.05	0.06	0.07	0.08	0.09
+6.0	0.000000001									
+5.5	0.000000019									
+5.0	0.000000287									
+4.5	0.000003398									
+4.0	0.000031671									
+3.9	0.00005	0.00005	0.00004	0.00004	0.00004	0.00004	0.00004	0.00004	0.00003	0.00003
+3.8	0.00007	0.00007	0.00007	0.00006	0.00006	0.00006	0.00006	0.00005	0.00005	0.00005
+3.7	0.00011	0.00010	0.00010	0.00010	0.00009	0.00009	0.00008	0.00008	0.00008	0.00008
+3.6	0.00016	0.00015	0.00015	0.00014	0.00014	0.00013	0.00013	0.00012	0.00012	0.00011
+3.5	0.00023	0.00022	0.00022	0.00021	0.00020	0.00019	0.00019	0.00018	0.00017	0.00017
+3.4	0.00034	0.00032	0.00031	0.00030	0.00029	0.00028	0.00027	0.00026	0.00025	0.00024
+3.3	0.00048	0.00047	0.00045	0.00043	0.00042	0.00040	0.00039	0.00038	0.00036	0.00035
+3.2	0.00069	0.00066	0.00064	0.00062	0.00060	0.00058	0.00056	0.00054	0.00052	0.00050
+3.1	0.00097	0.00094	0.00090	0.00087	0.00084	0.00082	0.00079	0.00076	0.00074	0.00071
+3.0	0.00135	0.00131	0.00126	0.00122	0.00118	0.00114	0.00111	0.00107	0.00103	0.00100
+2.9	0.0019	0.0018	0.0018	0.0017	0.0016	0.0016	0.0015	0.0015	0.0014	0.0014
+2.8	0.0026	0.0025	0.0024	0.0023	0.0023	0.0022	0.0021	0.0021	0.0020	0.0019
+2.7	0.0035	0.0034	0.0033	0.0032	0.0031	0.0030	0.0029	0.0028	0.0027	0.0026
+2.6	0.0047	0.0045	0.0044	0.0043	0.0041	0.0040	0.0039	0.0038	0.0037	0.0036
+2.5	0.0062	0.0060	0.0059	0.0057	0.0055	0.0054	0.0052	0.0051	0.0049	0.0048
+2.4	0.0082	0.0080	0.0078	0.0075	0.0073	0.0071	0.0069	0.0068	0.0066	0.0064
+2.3	0.0107	0.0104	0.0102	0.0099	0.0096	0.0094	0.0091	0.0089	0.0087	0.0084
+2.2	0.0139	0.0136	0.0132	0.0129	0.0125	0.0122	0.0119	0.0116	0.0113	0.0110
+2.1	0.0179	0.0174	0.0170	0.0166	0.0162	0.0158	0.0154	0.0150	0.0146	0.0143
+2.0	0.0228	0.0222	0.0217	0.0212	0.0207	0.0202	0.0197	0.0192	0.0188	0.0183
+1.9	0.0287	0.0281	0.0274	0.0268	0.0262	0.0256	0.0250	0.0244	0.0239	0.0233
+1.8	0.0359	0.0351	0.0344	0.0336	0.0329	0.0322	0.0314	0.0307	0.0301	0.0294
+1.7	0.0446	0.0436	0.0427	0.0418	0.0409	0.0401	0.0392	0.0384	0.0375	0.0367
+1.6	0.0548	0.0537	0.0526	0.0516	0.0505	0.0495	0.0485	0.0475	0.0465	0.0455
+1.5	0.0668	0.0655	0.0643	0.0630	0.0618	0.0606	0.0594	0.0582	0.0571	0.0559
+1.4	0.0808	0.0793	0.0778	0.0764	0.0749	0.0735	0.0721	0.0708	0.0694	0.0681

Continued

Z	0.00	0.01	0.02	0.03	0.04	0.05	0.06	0.07	0.08	0.09
+1.3	0.0968	0.0951	0.0934	0.0918	0.0901	0.0885	0.0869	0.0853	0.0838	0.0823
+1.2	0.1151	0.1131	0.1112	0.1093	0.1075	0.1056	0.1038	0.1020	0.1003	0.0985
+1.1	0.1357	0.1335	0.1314	0.1292	0.1271	0.1251	0.1230	0.1210	0.1190	0.1170
+1.0	0.1587	0.1562	0.1539	0.1515	0.1492	0.1469	0.1446	0.1423	0.1401	0.1379
+0.9	0.1841	0.1814	0.1788	0.1762	0.1736	0.1711	0.1685	0.1660	0.1635	0.1611
+0.8	0.2119	0.2090	0.2061	0.2033	0.2005	0.1977	0.1949	0.1922	0.1894	0.1867
+0.7	0.2420	0.2388	0.2358	0.2327	0.2296	0.2266	0.2236	0.2206	0.2177	0.2148
+0.6	0.2743	0.2709	0.2676	0.2643	0.2611	0.2578	0.2546	0.2514	0.2482	0.2451
+0.5	0.3085	0.3050	0.3015	0.2981	0.2946	0.2912	0.2877	0.2843	0.2810	0.2776
+0.4	0.3446	0.3409	0.3372	0.3336	0.3300	0.3264	0.3228	0.3192	0.3156	0.3121
+0.3	0.3821	0.3783	0.3745	0.3707	0.3669	0.3632	0.3594	0.3557	0.3520	0.3483
+0.2	0.4207	0.4168	0.4129	0.4090	0.4052	0.4013	0.3974	0.3936	0.3897	0.3859
+0.1	0.4602	0.4562	0.4522	0.4483	0.4443	0.4404	0.4364	0.4325	0.4286	0.4247
+0.0	0.5000	0.4960	0.4920	0.4880	0.4840	0.4801	0.4761	0.4721	0.4681	0.4641

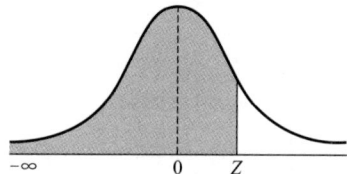

Z	0.00	0.01	0.02	0.03	0.04	0.05	0.06	0.07	0.08	0.09
0.0	0.5000	0.5040	0.5080	0.5120	0.5160	0.5199	0.5239	0.5279	0.5319	0.5359
0.1	0.5398	0.5438	0.5478	0.5517	0.5557	0.5596	0.5636	0.5675	0.5714	0.5753
0.2	0.5793	0.5832	0.5871	0.5910	0.5948	0.5987	0.6026	0.6064	0.6103	0.6141
0.3	0.6179	0.6217	0.6255	0.6293	0.6331	0.6368	0.6406	0.6443	0.6480	0.6517
0.4	0.6554	0.6591	0.6628	0.6664	0.6700	0.6736	0.6772	0.6808	0.6844	0.6879
0.5	0.6915	0.6950	0.6985	0.7019	0.7054	0.7088	0.7123	0.7157	0.7190	0.7224
0.6	0.7257	0.7291	0.7324	0.7357	0.7389	0.7422	0.7454	0.7486	0.7518	0.7549
0.7	0.7580	0.7612	0.7642	0.7673	0.7704	0.7734	0.7764	0.7794	0.7823	0.7852
0.8	0.7881	0.7910	0.7939	0.7967	0.7995	0.8023	0.8051	0.8078	0.8106	0.8133
0.9	0.8159	0.8186	0.8212	0.8238	0.8264	0.8289	0.8315	0.8340	0.8365	0.8389
1.0	0.8413	0.8438	0.8461	0.8485	0.8508	0.8531	0.8554	0.8577	0.8599	0.8621
1.1	0.8643	0.8665	0.8686	0.8708	0.8729	0.8749	0.8770	0.8790	0.8810	0.8830
1.2	0.8849	0.8869	0.8888	0.8907	0.8925	0.8944	0.8962	0.8980	0.8997	0.9015

Continued

Z	0.00	0.01	0.02	0.03	0.04	0.05	0.06	0.07	0.08	0.09
1.3	0.9032	0.9049	0.9066	0.9082	0.9099	0.9115	0.9131	0.9147	0.9162	0.9177
1.4	0.9192	0.9207	0.9222	0.9236	0.9251	0.9265	0.9279	0.9292	0.9306	0.9319
1.5	0.9332	0.9345	0.9357	0.9370	0.9382	0.9394	0.9406	0.9418	0.9429	0.9441
1.6	0.9452	0.9463	0.9474	0.9484	0.9495	0.9505	0.9515	0.9525	0.9535	0.9545
1.7	0.9554	0.9564	0.9573	0.9582	0.9591	0.9599	0.9608	0.9616	0.9625	0.9633
1.8	0.9641	0.9649	0.9656	0.9664	0.9671	0.9678	0.9686	0.9693	0.9699	0.9706
1.9	0.9713	0.9719	0.9726	0.9732	0.9738	0.9744	0.9750	0.9756	0.9761	0.9767
2.0	0.9772	0.9778	0.9783	0.9788	0.9793	0.9798	0.9803	0.9808	0.9812	0.9817
2.1	0.9821	0.9826	0.9830	0.9834	0.9838	0.9842	0.9846	0.9850	0.9854	0.9857
2.2	0.9861	0.9864	0.9868	0.9871	0.9875	0.9878	0.9881	0.9884	0.9887	0.9890
2.3	0.9893	0.9896	0.9898	0.9901	0.9904	0.9906	0.9909	0.9911	0.9913	0.9916
2.4	0.9918	0.9920	0.9922	0.9925	0.9927	0.9929	0.9931	0.9932	0.9934	0.9936
2.5	0.9938	0.9940	0.9941	0.9943	0.9945	0.9946	0.9948	0.9949	0.9951	0.9952
2.6	0.9953	0.9955	0.9956	0.9957	0.9959	0.9960	0.9961	0.9962	0.9963	0.9964
2.7	0.9965	0.9966	0.9967	0.9968	0.9969	0.9970	0.9971	0.9972	0.9973	0.9974
2.8	0.9974	0.9975	0.9976	0.9977	0.9977	0.9978	0.9979	0.9979	0.9980	0.9981
2.9	0.9981	0.9982	0.9982	0.9983	0.9984	0.9984	0.9985	0.9985	0.9986	0.9986
3.0	0.99865	0.99869	0.99874	0.99878	0.99882	0.99886	0.99889	0.99893	0.99897	0.99900
3.1	0.99903	0.99906	0.99910	0.99913	0.99916	0.99918	0.99921	0.99924	0.99926	0.99929
3.2	0.99931	0.99934	0.99936	0.99938	0.99940	0.99942	0.99944	0.99946	0.99948	0.99950
3.3	0.99952	0.99953	0.99955	0.99957	0.99958	0.99960	0.99961	0.99962	0.99964	0.99965
3.4	0.99966	0.99968	0.99969	0.99970	0.99971	0.99972	0.99973	0.99974	0.99975	0.99976
3.5	0.99977	0.99978	0.99978	0.99979	0.99980	0.99981	0.99981	0.99982	0.99983	0.99983
3.6	0.99984	0.99985	0.99985	0.99986	0.99986	0.99987	0.99987	0.99988	0.99988	0.99989
3.7	0.99989	0.99990	0.99990	0.99990	0.99991	0.99991	0.99992	0.99992	0.99992	0.99992
3.8	0.99993	0.99993	0.99993	0.99994	0.99994	0.99994	0.99994	0.99995	0.99995	0.99995
3.9	0.99995	0.99995	0.99996	0.99996	0.99996	0.99996	0.99996	0.99996	0.99997	0.99997
4.0	0.999968329									
4.5	0.999996602									
5.0	0.999999713									
5.5	0.999999981									
6.0	0.999999999									

TABLE 3 Critical Values of t

For a particular number of degrees of freedom, entry represents the critical value of t corresponding to a specified upper-tail area (α)

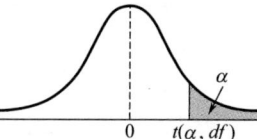

Degrees of Freedom	Upper-tail area(α)					
	0.25	0.10	0.05	0.025	0.01	0.005
1	1.0000	3.0777	6.3138	12.7062	31.8207	63.6574
2	0.8165	1.8856	2.9200	4.3027	6.9646	9.9248
3	0.7649	1.6377	2.3534	3.1824	4.5407	5.8409
4	0.7407	1.5332	2.1318	2.7764	3.7469	4.6041
5	0.7267	1.4759	2.0150	2.5706	3.3649	4.0322
6	0.7176	1.4398	1.9432	2.4469	3.1427	3.7074
7	0.7111	1.4149	1.8946	2.3646	2.9980	3.4995
8	0.7064	1.3968	1.8595	2.2060	2.8965	3.3554
9	0.7027	1.3830	1.8331	2.2622	2.8214	3.2498
10	0.6998	1.3722	1.8125	2.2281	2.7638	3.1693
11	0.6974	1.3634	1.7959	2.2010	2.7181	3.1058
12	0.6955	1.3562	1.7823	2.1788	2.6810	3.0545
13	0.6938	1.3502	1.7709	2.1604	2.6503	3.0123
14	0.6924	1.3450	1.7613	2.1448	2.6245	2.9768
15	0.6912	1.3406	1.7531	2.1315	2.6025	2.9467
16	0.6901	1.3368	1.7459	2.1199	2.5835	2.9208
17	0.6892	1.3334	1.7396	2.1098	2.5669	2.8982
18	0.6884	1.3304	1.7341	2.1009	2.5524	2.8784
19	0.6876	1.3277	1.7291	2.0930	2.5395	2.8609
20	0.6870	1.3253	1.7247	2.0860	2.5280	2.8453
21	0.6864	1.3232	1.7207	2.0796	2.5177	2.8314
22	0.6858	1.3212	1.7171	2.0739	2.5083	2.8188
23	0.6853	1.3195	1.7139	2.0687	2.4999	2.8073
24	0.6848	1.3178	1.7109	2.0639	2.4922	2.7969
25	0.6844	1.3163	1.7081	2.0595	2.4851	2.7874
26	0.6840	1.3150	1.7056	2.0555	2.4786	2.7787
27	0.6837	1.3137	1.7033	2.0518	2.4727	2.7707
28	0.6834	1.3125	1.7011	2.0484	2.4671	2.7633
29	0.6830	1.3114	1.6991	2.0452	2.4620	2.7564
30	0.6828	1.3104	1.6973	2.0423	2.4573	2.7500

Continued

Degrees of Freedom	Upper-tail area(α)					
	0.25	0.10	0.05	0.025	0.01	0.005
31	0.6825	1.3095	1.6955	2.0395	2.4528	2.7440
32	0.6822	1.3086	1.6939	2.0369	2.4487	2.7385
33	0.6820	1.3077	1.6924	2.0345	2.4448	2.7333
34	0.6818	1.3070	1.6909	2.0322	2.4411	2.7284
35	0.6816	1.3062	1.6896	2.0301	2.4377	2.7238
36	0.6814	1.3055	1.6883	2.0281	2.4345	2.7195
37	0.6812	1.3049	1.6871	2.0262	2.4314	2.7154
38	0.6810	1.3042	1.6860	2.0244	2.4286	2.7116
39	0.6808	1.3036	1.6849	2.0227	2.4258	2.7079
40	0.6807	1.3031	1.6839	2.0211	2.4233	2.7045
41	0.6805	1.3025	1.6829	2.0195	2.4208	2.7012
42	0.6804	1.3020	1.6820	2.0181	2.4185	2.6981
43	0.6802	1.3016	1.6811	2.0167	2.4163	2.6951
44	0.6801	1.3011	1.6802	2.0154	2.4141	2.6923
45	0.6800	1.3006	1.6794	2.0141	2.4121	2.6896
46	0.6799	1.3022	1.6787	2.0129	2.4102	2.6870
47	0.6797	1.2998	1.6779	2.0117	2.4083	2.6846
48	0.6796	1.2994	1.6772	2.0106	2.4066	2.6822
49	0.6795	1.2991	1.6766	2.0096	2.4049	2.6800
50	0.6794	1.2987	1.6759	2.0086	2.4033	2.6778
51	0.6793	1.2984	1.6753	2.0076	2.4017	2.6757
52	0.6792	1.2980	1.6747	2.0066	2.4002	2.6737
53	0.6791	1.2977	1.6741	2.0057	2.3988	2.6718
54	0.6791	1.2974	1.6736	2.0049	2.3974	2.6700
55	0.6790	1.2971	1.6730	2.0040	2.3961	2.6682
56	0.6789	1.2969	1.6725	2.0032	2.3948	2.6665
57	0.6788	1.2966	1.6720	2.0025	2.3936	2.6649
58	0.6787	1.2963	1.6716	2.0017	2.3924	2.6633
59	0.6787	1.2961	1.6711	2.0010	2.3912	2.6618
60	0.6786	1.2958	1.6706	2.0003	2.3901	2.6603
61	0.6785	1.2956	1.6702	1.9996	2.3890	2.6589
62	0.6785	1.2954	1.6698	1.9990	2.3880	2.6575
63	0.6784	1.2951	1.6694	1.9983	2.3870	2.6561
64	0.6783	1.2949	1.6690	1.9977	2.3860	2.6549
65	0.6783	1.2947	1.6686	1.9971	2.3851	2.6536
66	0.6782	1.2945	1.6683	1.9966	2.3842	2.6524

Continued

Degrees of Freedom	Upper-tail area(α)					
	0.25	0.10	0.05	0.025	0.01	0.005
67	0.6782	1.2943	1.6679	1.9960	2.3833	2.6512
68	0.6781	1.2941	1.6676	1.9955	2.3824	2.6501
69	0.6781	1.2939	1.6672	1.9949	2.3816	2.6490
70	0.6780	1.2938	1.6669	1.9944	2.3808	2.6479
71	0.6780	1.2936	1.6666	1.9939	2.3800	2.6469
72	0.6779	1.2934	1.6663	1.9935	2.3793	2.6459
73	0.6779	1.2933	1.6660	1.9930	2.3785	2.6449
74	0.6778	1.2931	1.6657	1.9925	2.3778	2.6439
75	0.6778	1.2929	1.6654	1.9921	2.3771	2.6430
76	0.6777	1.2928	1.6652	1.9917	2.3764	2.6421
77	0.6777	1.2926	1.6649	1.9913	2.3758	2.6412
78	0.6776	1.2925	1.6646	1.9908	2.3751	2.6403
79	0.6776	1.2924	1.6644	1.9905	2.3745	2.6395
80	0.6776	1.2922	1.6641	1.9901	2.3739	2.6387
81	0.6775	1.2921	1.6639	1.9897	2.3733	2.6379
82	0.6775	1.2920	1.6636	1.9893	2.3727	2.6371
83	0.6775	1.2918	1.6634	1.9890	2.3721	2.6364
84	0.6774	1.2917	1.6632	1.9886	2.3716	2.6356
85	0.6774	1.2916	1.6630	1.9883	2.3710	2.6349
86	0.6774	1.2915	1.6628	1.9879	2.3705	2.6342
87	0.6773	1.2914	1.6626	1.9876	2.3700	2.6335
88	0.6773	1.2912	1.6624	1.9873	2.3695	2.6329
89	0.6773	1.2911	1.6622	1.9870	2.3690	2.6322
90	0.6772	1.2910	1.6620	1.9867	2.3685	2.6316
91	0.6772	1.2909	1.6618	1.9864	2.3680	2.6309
92	0.6772	1.2908	1.6616	1.9861	2.3676	2.6303
93	0.6771	1.2907	1.6614	1.9858	2.3671	2.6297
94	0.6771	1.2906	1.6612	1.9855	2.3667	2.6291
95	0.6771	1.2905	1.6611	1.9853	2.3662	2.6286
96	0.6771	1.2904	1.6609	1.9850	2.3658	2.6280
97	0.6770	1.2903	1.6607	1.9847	2.3654	2.6275
98	0.6770	1.2902	1.6606	1.9845	2.3650	2.6269
99	0.6770	1.2902	1.6604	1.9842	2.3646	2.6264
100	0.6770	1.2901	1.6602	1.9840	2.3642	2.6259
110	0.6767	1.2893	1.6588	1.9818	2.3607	2.6213
120	0.6765	1.2886	1.6577	1.9799	2.3578	2.6174
∗	0.6745	1.2816	1.6449	1.9600	2.3263	2.5758

TABLE 4 Critical Values of χ^2

For a particular number of degrees of freedom, entry represents the critical value of χ^2 corresponding to a specified upper-tail area (α).

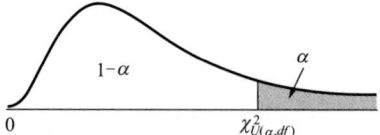

Degrees of Freedom	Upper-Tail Areas(α)											
	0.995	0.99	0.975	0.95	0.90	0.75	0.25	0.10	0.05	0.025	0.01	0.005
1			0.001	0.004	0.016	0.102	1.323	2.706	3.841	5.024	6.635	7.879
2	0.010	0.020	0.051	0.103	0.211	0.575	2.773	4.605	5.991	7.378	9.210	10.597
3	0.072	0.115	0.216	0.352	0.584	1.213	4.108	6.251	7.815	9.348	11.345	12.838
4	0.207	0.297	0.484	0.711	1.064	1.923	5.385	7.779	9.488	11.143	13.277	14.860
5	0.412	0.554	0.831	1.145	1.610	2.675	6.626	9.236	11.071	12.833	15.086	16.750
6	0.676	0.872	1.237	1.635	2.204	3.455	7.841	10.645	12.592	14.449	16.812	18.458
7	0.989	1.239	1.690	2.167	2.833	4.255	9.037	12.017	14.067	16.013	18.475	20.278
8	1.344	1.646	2.180	2.733	3.490	5.071	10.219	13.362	15.507	17.535	20.090	21.955
9	1.735	2.088	2.700	3.325	4.168	5.899	11.389	14.684	16.919	19.023	21.666	23.589
10	2.156	2.558	3.247	3.940	4.865	6.737	12.549	15.987	18.307	20.483	23.209	25.188
11	2.603	3.053	3.816	4.575	5.578	7.584	13.701	17.275	19.675	21.920	24.725	26.757
12	3.074	3.571	4.404	5.226	6.304	8.438	14.845	18.549	21.026	23.337	26.217	28.299
13	3.565	4.107	5.009	5.892	7.042	9.299	15.984	19.812	22.362	24.736	27.688	29.819
14	4.075	4.660	5.629	6.571	7.790	10.165	17.117	21.064	23.685	26.119	29.141	31.319
15	4.601	5.229	6.262	7.261	8.547	11.037	18.245	22.307	24.996	27.488	30.578	32.801
16	5.142	5.812	6.908	7.962	9.312	11.912	19.369	23.542	26.296	28.845	32.000	34.267
17	5.697	6.408	7.564	8.672	10.085	12.792	20.489	24.769	27.587	30.191	33.409	35.718
18	6.265	7.015	8.231	9.390	10.865	13.675	21.605	25.989	28.869	31.526	34.805	37.156
19	6.844	7.633	8.907	10.117	11.651	14.562	22.718	27.204	30.144	32.852	36.191	38.582
20	7.434	8.260	9.591	10.851	12.443	15.452	23.828	28.412	31.410	34.170	37.566	39.997
21	8.034	8.897	10.283	11.591	13.240	16.344	24.935	29.615	32.671	35.479	38.932	41.401
22	8.643	9.542	10.982	12.338	14.042	17.240	26.039	30.813	33.924	36.781	40.289	42.796
23	9.260	10.196	11.689	13.091	14.848	18.137	27.141	32.007	35.172	38.076	41.638	44.181
24	9.886	10.856	12.401	13.848	15.659	19.037	28.241	33.196	36.415	39.364	42.980	45.559
25	10.520	11.524	13.120	14.611	16.473	19.939	29.339	34.382	37.652	40.646	44.314	46.928
26	11.160	12.198	13.844	15.379	17.292	20.843	30.435	35.563	38.885	41.923	45.642	48.290
27	11.808	12.879	14.573	16.151	18.114	21.749	31.528	36.741	40.113	43.194	46.963	49.645
28	12.461	13.565	15.308	16.928	18.939	22.657	32.620	37.916	41.337	44.461	48.278	50.993
29	13.121	14.257	16.047	17.708	19.768	23.567	33.711	39.087	42.557	45.722	49.588	52.336
30	13.787	14.954	16.791	18.493	20.599	24.478	34.800	40.256	43.773	46.979	50.892	53.672

TABLE 5 Critical Values of F

For a particular combination of numerator and denominator degrees of freedom, entry represents the critical values of F corresponding to a specified upper-tail area (α).

$\alpha = 0.05$

$F_{U(\alpha, df_1, df_2)}$

Denominator, df_2	Numerator, df_1																	
	1	2	3	4	5	6	7	8	9	10	12	15	20	24	30	40	60	120	∞
1	161.40	199.50	215.70	224.60	230.20	234.00	236.80	238.90	240.50	241.90	243.90	245.90	248.00	249.10	250.10	251.10	252.20	253.30	254.30
2	18.51	19.00	19.16	19.25	19.30	19.33	19.35	19.37	19.38	19.40	19.41	19.43	19.45	19.45	19.46	19.47	19.48	19.49	19.50
3	10.13	9.55	9.28	9.12	9.01	8.94	8.89	8.85	8.81	8.79	8.74	8.70	8.66	8.64	8.62	8.59	8.57	8.55	8.53
4	7.71	6.94	6.59	6.39	6.26	6.16	6.09	6.04	6.00	5.96	5.91	5.86	5.80	5.77	5.75	5.72	5.69	5.66	5.63
5	6.61	5.79	5.41	5.19	5.05	4.95	4.88	4.82	4.77	4.74	4.68	4.62	4.56	4.53	4.50	4.46	4.43	4.40	4.36
6	5.99	5.14	4.76	4.53	4.39	4.28	4.21	4.15	4.10	4.06	4.00	3.94	3.87	3.84	3.81	3.77	3.74	3.70	3.67
7	5.59	4.74	4.35	4.12	3.97	3.87	3.79	3.73	3.68	3.64	3.57	3.51	3.44	3.41	3.38	3.34	3.30	3.27	3.23
8	5.32	4.46	4.07	3.84	3.69	3.58	3.50	3.44	3.39	3.35	3.28	3.22	3.15	3.12	3.08	3.04	3.01	2.97	2.93
9	5.12	4.26	3.86	3.63	3.48	3.37	3.29	3.23	3.18	3.14	3.07	3.01	2.94	2.90	2.86	2.83	2.79	2.75	2.71
10	4.96	4.10	3.71	3.48	3.33	3.22	3.14	3.07	3.02	2.98	2.91	2.85	2.77	2.74	2.70	2.66	2.62	2.58	2.54
11	4.84	3.98	3.59	3.36	3.20	3.09	3.01	2.95	2.90	2.85	2.79	2.72	2.65	2.61	2.57	2.53	2.49	2.45	2.40
12	4.75	3.89	3.49	3.26	3.11	3.00	2.91	2.85	2.80	2.75	2.69	2.62	2.54	2.51	2.47	2.43	2.38	2.34	2.30
13	4.67	3.81	3.41	3.18	3.03	2.92	2.83	2.77	2.71	2.67	2.60	2.53	2.46	2.42	2.38	2.34	2.30	2.25	2.21
14	4.60	3.74	3.34	3.11	2.96	2.85	2.76	2.70	2.65	2.60	2.53	2.46	2.39	2.35	2.31	2.27	2.22	2.18	2.13

Continued

Denominator, df_2	Numerator, df_1																	
	1	2	3	4	5	6	7	8	9	10	12	15	20	24	30	40	60	120	∞
15	4.54	3.68	3.29	3.06	2.90	2.79	2.71	2.64	2.59	2.54	2.48	2.40	2.33	2.29	2.25	2.20	2.16	2.11	2.07
16	4.49	3.63	3.24	3.01	2.85	2.74	2.66	2.59	2.54	2.49	2.42	2.35	2.28	2.24	2.19	2.15	2.11	2.06	2.01
17	4.45	3.59	3.20	2.96	2.81	2.70	2.61	2.55	2.49	2.45	2.38	2.31	2.23	2.19	2.15	2.10	2.06	2.01	1.96
18	4.41	3.55	3.16	2.93	2.77	2.66	2.58	2.51	2.46	2.41	2.34	2.27	2.19	2.15	2.11	2.06	2.02	1.97	1.92
19	4.38	3.52	3.13	2.90	2.74	2.63	2.54	2.48	2.42	2.38	2.31	2.23	2.16	2.11	2.07	2.03	1.98	1.93	1.88
20	4.35	3.49	3.10	2.87	2.71	2.60	2.51	2.45	2.39	2.35	2.28	2.20	2.12	2.08	2.04	1.99	1.95	1.90	1.84
21	4.32	3.47	3.07	2.84	2.68	2.57	2.49	2.42	2.37	2.32	2.25	2.18	2.10	2.05	2.01	1.96	1.92	1.87	1.81
22	4.30	3.44	3.05	2.82	2.66	2.55	2.46	2.40	2.34	2.30	2.23	2.15	2.07	2.03	1.98	1.94	1.89	1.84	1.78
23	4.28	3.42	3.03	2.80	2.64	2.53	2.44	2.37	2.32	2.27	2.20	2.13	2.05	2.01	1.96	1.91	1.86	1.81	1.76
24	4.26	3.40	3.01	2.78	2.62	2.51	2.42	2.36	2.30	2.25	2.18	2.11	2.03	1.98	1.94	1.89	1.84	1.79	1.73
25	4.24	3.39	2.99	2.76	2.60	2.49	2.40	2.34	2.28	2.24	2.16	2.09	2.01	1.96	1.92	1.87	1.82	1.77	1.71
26	4.23	3.37	2.98	2.74	2.59	2.47	2.39	2.32	2.27	2.22	2.15	2.07	1.99	1.95	1.90	1.85	1.80	1.75	1.69
27	4.21	3.35	2.96	2.73	2.57	2.46	2.37	2.31	2.25	2.20	2.13	2.06	1.97	1.93	1.88	1.84	1.79	1.73	1.67
28	4.20	3.34	2.95	2.71	2.56	2.45	2.36	2.29	2.24	2.19	2.12	2.04	1.96	1.91	1.87	1.82	1.77	1.71	1.65
29	4.18	3.33	2.93	2.70	2.55	2.43	2.35	2.28	2.22	2.18	2.10	2.03	1.94	1.90	1.85	1.81	1.75	1.70	1.64
30	4.17	3.32	2.92	2.69	2.53	2.42	2.33	2.27	2.21	2.16	2.09	2.01	1.93	1.89	1.84	1.79	1.74	1.68	1.62
40	4.08	3.23	2.84	2.61	2.45	2.34	2.25	2.18	2.12	2.08	2.00	1.92	1.84	1.79	1.74	1.69	1.64	1.58	1.51
60	4.00	3.15	2.76	2.53	2.37	2.25	2.17	2.10	2.04	1.99	1.92	1.84	1.75	1.70	1.65	1.59	1.53	1.47	1.39
120	3.92	3.07	2.68	2.45	2.29	2.17	2.09	2.02	1.96	1.91	1.83	1.75	1.66	1.61	1.55	1.50	1.43	1.35	1.25
∞	3.84	3.00	2.60	2.37	2.21	2.10	2.01	1.94	1.88	1.83	1.75	1.67	1.57	1.52	1.46	1.39	1.32	1.22	1.00

$\alpha = 0.025$

$F_{U(\alpha, df_1, df_2)}$

Denominator, df_2	Numerator, df_1																	
	1	2	3	4	5	6	7	8	9	10	12	15	20	24	30	40	60	120	∞
1	647.80	799.50	864.20	899.60	921.80	937.10	948.20	956.70	963.30	968.60	976.70	984.90	993.10	997.20	1,001.00	1,006.00	1,010.00	1,014.00	1,018.00
2	38.51	39.00	39.17	39.25	39.30	39.33	39.36	39.39	39.39	39.40	39.41	39.43	39.45	39.46	39.46	39.47	39.48	39.49	39.50
3	17.44	16.04	15.44	15.10	14.88	14.73	14.62	14.54	14.47	14.42	14.34	14.25	14.17	14.12	14.08	14.04	13.99	13.95	13.90
4	12.22	10.65	9.98	9.60	9.36	9.20	9.07	8.98	8.90	8.84	8.75	8.66	8.56	8.51	8.46	8.41	8.36	8.31	8.26
5	10.01	8.43	7.76	7.39	7.15	6.98	6.85	6.76	6.68	6.62	6.52	6.43	6.33	6.28	6.23	6.18	6.12	6.07	6.02
6	8.81	7.26	6.60	6.23	5.99	5.82	5.70	5.60	5.52	5.46	5.37	5.27	5.17	5.12	5.07	5.01	4.96	4.90	4.85
7	8.07	6.54	5.89	5.52	5.29	5.12	4.99	4.90	4.82	4.76	4.67	4.57	4.47	4.42	4.36	4.31	4.25	4.20	4.14
8	7.57	6.06	5.42	5.05	4.82	4.65	4.53	4.43	4.36	4.30	4.20	4.10	4.00	3.95	3.89	3.84	3.78	3.73	3.67
9	7.21	5.71	5.08	4.72	4.48	4.32	4.20	4.10	4.03	3.96	3.87	3.77	3.67	3.61	3.56	3.51	3.45	3.39	3.33
10	6.94	5.46	4.83	4.47	4.24	4.07	3.95	3.85	3.78	3.72	3.62	3.52	3.42	3.37	3.31	3.26	3.20	3.14	3.08
11	6.72	5.26	4.63	4.28	4.04	3.88	3.76	3.66	3.59	3.53	3.43	3.33	3.23	3.17	3.12	3.06	3.00	2.94	2.88
12	6.55	5.10	4.47	4.12	3.89	3.73	3.61	3.51	3.44	3.37	3.28	3.18	3.07	3.02	2.96	2.91	2.85	2.79	2.72
13	6.41	4.97	4.35	4.00	3.77	3.60	3.48	3.39	3.31	3.25	3.15	3.05	2.95	2.89	2.84	2.78	2.72	2.66	2.60
14	6.30	4.86	4.24	3.89	3.66	3.50	3.38	3.29	3.21	3.15	3.05	2.95	2.84	2.79	2.73	2.67	2.61	2.55	2.49
15	6.20	4.77	4.15	3.80	3.58	3.41	3.29	3.20	3.12	3.06	2.96	2.86	2.76	2.70	2.64	2.59	2.52	2.46	2.40

Continued

Continued

Denominator, df_2	Numerator, df_1																	
	1	2	3	4	5	6	7	8	9	10	12	15	20	24	30	40	60	120	∞
16	6.12	4.69	4.08	3.73	3.50	3.34	3.22	3.12	3.05	2.99	2.89	2.79	2.68	2.63	2.57	2.51	2.45	2.38	2.32
17	6.04	4.62	4.01	3.66	3.44	3.28	3.16	3.06	2.98	2.92	2.82	2.72	2.62	2.56	2.50	2.44	2.38	2.32	2.25
18	5.98	4.56	3.95	3.61	3.38	3.22	3.10	3.01	2.93	2.87	2.77	2.67	2.56	2.50	2.44	2.38	2.32	2.26	2.19
19	5.92	4.51	3.90	3.56	3.33	3.17	3.05	2.96	2.88	2.82	2.72	2.62	2.51	2.45	2.39	2.33	2.27	2.20	2.13
20	5.87	4.46	3.86	3.51	3.29	3.13	3.01	2.91	2.84	2.77	2.68	2.57	2.46	2.41	2.35	2.29	2.22	2.16	2.09
21	5.83	4.42	3.82	3.48	3.25	3.09	2.97	2.87	2.80	2.73	2.64	2.53	2.42	2.37	2.31	2.25	2.18	2.11	2.04
22	5.79	4.38	3.78	3.44	3.22	3.05	2.93	2.84	2.76	2.70	2.60	2.50	2.39	2.33	2.27	2.21	2.14	2.08	2.00
23	5.75	4.35	3.75	3.41	3.18	3.02	2.90	2.81	2.73	2.67	2.57	2.47	2.36	2.30	2.24	2.18	2.11	2.04	1.97
24	5.72	4.32	3.72	3.38	3.15	2.99	2.87	2.78	2.70	2.64	2.54	2.44	2.33	2.27	2.21	2.15	2.08	2.01	1.94
25	5.69	4.29	3.69	3.35	3.13	2.97	2.85	2.75	2.68	2.61	2.51	2.41	2.30	2.24	2.18	2.12	2.05	1.98	1.91
26	5.66	4.27	3.67	3.33	3.10	2.94	2.82	2.73	2.65	2.59	2.49	2.39	2.28	2.22	2.16	2.09	2.03	1.95	1.88
27	5.63	4.24	3.65	3.31	3.08	2.92	2.80	2.71	2.63	2.57	2.47	2.36	2.25	2.19	2.13	2.07	2.00	1.93	1.85
28	5.61	4.22	3.63	3.29	3.06	2.90	2.78	2.69	2.61	2.55	2.45	2.34	2.23	2.17	2.11	2.05	1.98	1.91	1.83
29	5.59	4.20	3.61	3.27	3.04	2.88	2.76	2.67	2.59	2.53	2.43	2.32	2.21	2.15	2.09	2.03	1.96	1.89	1.81
30	5.57	4.18	3.59	3.25	3.03	2.87	2.75	2.65	2.57	2.51	2.41	2.31	2.20	2.14	2.07	2.01	1.94	1.87	1.79
40	5.42	4.05	3.46	3.13	2.90	2.74	2.62	2.53	2.45	2.39	2.29	2.18	2.07	2.01	1.94	1.88	1.80	1.72	1.64
60	5.29	3.93	3.34	3.01	2.79	2.63	2.51	2.41	2.33	2.27	2.17	2.06	1.94	1.88	1.82	1.74	1.67	1.58	1.48
120	5.15	3.80	3.23	2.89	2.67	2.52	2.39	2.30	2.22	2.16	2.05	1.94	1.82	1.76	1.69	1.61	1.53	1.43	1.31
∞	5.02	3.69	3.12	2.79	2.57	2.41	2.29	2.19	2.11	2.05	1.94	1.83	1.71	1.64	1.57	1.48	1.39	1.27	1.00

Continued

$\alpha = 0.01$

$F_{U(\alpha, df_1, df_2)}$

Denominator, df_2	Numerator, df_1																	
	1	2	3	4	5	6	7	8	9	10	12	15	20	24	30	40	60	120	∞
1	4,052.00	4,999.50	5,403.00	5,625.00	5,764.00	5,859.00	5,928.00	5,982.00	6,022.00	6,056.00	6,106.00	6,157.00	6,209.00	6,235.00	6,261.00	6,287.00	6,313.00	6,339.00	6,366.00
2	98.50	99.00	99.17	99.25	99.30	99.33	99.36	99.37	99.39	99.40	99.42	99.43	44.45	99.46	99.47	99.47	99.48	99.49	99.50
3	34.12	30.82	29.46	28.71	28.24	27.91	27.67	27.49	27.35	27.23	27.05	26.87	26.69	26.60	26.50	26.41	26.32	26.22	26.13
4	21.20	18.00	16.69	15.98	15.52	15.21	14.98	14.80	14.66	14.55	14.37	14.20	14.02	13.93	13.84	13.75	13.65	13.56	13.46
5	16.26	13.27	12.06	11.39	10.97	10.67	10.46	10.29	10.16	10.05	9.89	9.72	9.55	9.47	9.38	9.29	9.20	9.11	9.02
6	13.75	10.92	9.78	9.15	8.75	8.47	8.26	8.10	7.98	7.87	7.72	7.56	7.40	7.31	7.23	7.14	7.06	6.97	6.88
7	12.25	9.55	8.45	7.85	7.46	7.19	6.99	6.84	6.72	6.62	6.47	6.31	6.16	6.07	5.99	5.91	5.82	5.74	5.65
8	11.26	8.65	7.59	7.01	6.63	6.37	6.18	6.03	5.91	5.81	5.67	5.52	5.36	5.28	5.20	5.12	5.03	4.95	4.86
9	10.56	8.02	6.99	6.42	6.06	5.80	5.61	5.47	5.35	5.26	5.11	4.96	4.81	4.73	4.65	4.57	4.48	4.40	4.31
10	10.04	7.56	6.55	5.99	5.64	5.39	5.20	5.06	4.94	4.85	4.71	4.56	4.41	4.33	4.25	4.17	4.08	4.00	3.91
11	9.65	7.21	6.22	5.67	5.32	5.07	4.89	4.74	4.63	4.54	4.40	4.25	4.10	4.02	3.94	3.86	3.78	3.69	3.60
12	9.33	6.93	5.95	5.41	5.06	4.82	4.64	4.50	4.39	4.30	4.16	4.01	3.86	3.78	3.70	3.62	3.54	3.45	3.36
13	9.07	6.70	5.74	5.21	4.86	4.62	4.44	4.30	4.19	4.10	3.96	3.82	3.66	3.59	3.51	3.43	3.34	3.25	3.17
14	8.86	6.51	5.56	5.04	4.69	4.46	4.28	4.14	4.03	3.94	3.80	3.66	3.51	3.43	3.35	3.27	3.18	3.09	3.00
15	8.68	6.36	5.42	4.89	4.56	4.32	4.14	4.00	3.89	3.80	3.67	3.52	3.37	3.29	3.21	3.13	3.05	2.96	2.87

Continued

Denominator, df_2	Numerator, df_1																	
	1	2	3	4	5	6	7	8	9	10	12	15	20	24	30	40	60	120	∞
16	8.53	6.23	5.29	4.77	4.44	4.20	4.03	3.89	3.78	3.69	3.55	3.41	3.26	3.18	3.10	3.02	2.93	2.81	2.75
17	8.40	6.11	5.18	4.67	4.34	4.10	3.93	3.79	3.68	3.59	3.46	3.31	3.16	3.08	3.00	2.92	2.83	2.75	2.65
18	8.29	6.01	5.09	4.58	4.25	4.01	3.84	3.71	3.60	3.51	3.37	3.23	3.08	3.00	2.92	2.84	2.75	2.66	2.57
19	8.18	5.93	5.01	4.50	4.17	3.94	3.77	3.63	3.52	3.43	3.30	3.15	3.00	2.92	2.84	2.76	2.67	2.58	2.49
20	8.10	5.85	4.94	4.43	4.10	3.87	3.70	3.56	3.46	3.37	3.23	3.09	2.94	2.86	2.78	2.69	2.61	2.52	2.42
21	8.02	5.78	4.87	4.37	4.04	3.81	3.64	3.51	3.40	3.31	3.17	3.03	2.88	2.80	2.72	2.64	2.55	2.46	2.36
22	7.95	5.72	4.82	4.31	3.99	3.76	3.59	3.45	3.35	3.26	3.12	2.98	2.83	2.75	2.67	2.58	2.50	2.40	2.31
23	7.88	5.66	4.76	4.26	3.94	3.71	3.54	3.41	3.30	3.21	3.07	2.93	2.78	2.70	2.62	2.54	2.45	2.35	2.26
24	7.82	5.61	4.72	4.22	3.90	3.67	3.50	3.36	3.26	3.17	3.03	2.89	2.74	2.66	2.58	2.49	2.40	2.31	2.21
25	7.77	5.57	4.68	4.18	3.85	3.63	3.46	3.32	3.22	3.13	2.99	2.85	2.70	2.62	2.54	2.45	2.36	2.27	2.17
26	7.72	5.53	4.64	4.14	3.82	3.59	3.42	3.29	3.18	3.09	2.96	2.81	2.66	2.58	2.50	2.42	2.33	2.23	2.13
27	7.68	5.49	4.60	4.11	3.78	3.56	3.39	3.26	3.15	3.06	2.93	2.78	2.63	2.55	2.47	2.38	2.29	2.20	2.10
28	7.64	5.45	4.57	4.07	3.75	3.53	3.36	3.23	3.12	3.03	2.90	2.75	2.60	2.52	2.44	2.35	2.26	2.17	2.06
29	7.60	5.42	4.54	4.04	3.73	3.50	3.33	3.20	3.09	3.00	2.87	2.73	2.57	2.49	2.41	2.33	2.23	2.14	2.03
30	7.56	5.39	4.51	4.02	3.70	3.47	3.30	3.17	3.07	2.98	2.84	2.70	2.55	2.47	2.39	2.30	2.21	2.11	2.01
40	7.31	5.18	4.31	3.83	3.51	3.29	3.12	2.99	2.89	2.80	2.66	2.52	2.37	2.29	2.20	2.11	2.02	1.92	1.80
60	7.08	4.98	4.13	3.65	3.34	3.12	2.95	2.82	2.72	2.63	2.50	2.35	2.20	2.12	2.03	1.94	1.84	1.73	1.60
120	6.85	4.79	3.95	3.48	3.17	2.96	2.79	2.66	2.56	2.47	2.34	2.19	2.03	1.95	1.86	1.76	1.66	1.53	1.38
∞	6.63	4.61	3.78	3.32	3.02	2.80	2.64	2.51	2.41	2.32	2.18	2.04	1.88	1.79	1.70	1.59	1.47	1.32	1.00

Continued

$\alpha = 0.005$

$F_{U(\alpha, df_1, df_2)}$

Denominator, df_2	Numerator, df_1																	
	1	2	3	4	5	6	7	8	9	10	12	15	20	24	30	40	60	120	∞
1	16,211.00	20,000.00	21,615.00	22,500.00	23,056.00	23,437.00	23,715.00	23,925.00	24,091.00	24,224.00	24,426.00	24,630.00	24,836.00	24,910.00	25,044.00	25,148.00	25,253.00	25,359.00	25,465.00
2	198.50	199.00	199.20	199.20	199.30	199.30	199.40	199.40	199.40	199.40	199.40	199.40	199.40	199.50	199.50	199.50	199.50	199.50	199.50
3	55.55	49.80	47.47	46.19	45.39	44.84	44.43	44.13	43.88	43.69	43.39	43.08	42.78	42.62	42.47	42.31	42.15	41.99	41.83
4	31.33	26.28	24.26	23.15	22.46	21.97	21.62	21.35	21.14	20.97	20.70	20.44	20.17	20.03	19.89	19.75	19.61	19.47	19.32
5	22.78	18.31	16.53	15.56	14.94	14.51	14.20	13.96	13.77	13.62	13.38	13.15	12.90	12.78	12.66	12.53	12.40	12.27	12.11
6	18.63	14.54	12.92	12.03	11.46	11.07	10.79	10.57	10.39	10.25	10.03	9.81	9.59	9.47	9.36	9.24	9.12	9.00	8.88
7	16.24	12.40	10.88	10.05	9.52	9.16	8.89	8.68	8.51	8.38	8.18	7.97	7.75	7.65	7.53	7.42	7.31	7.19	7.08
8	14.69	11.04	9.60	8.81	8.30	7.95	7.69	7.50	7.34	7.21	7.01	6.81	6.61	6.50	6.40	6.29	6.18	6.06	5.95
9	13.61	10.11	8.72	7.96	7.47	7.13	6.88	6.69	6.54	6.42	6.23	6.03	5.83	5.73	5.62	5.52	5.41	5.30	5.19
10	12.83	9.43	8.08	7.34	6.87	6.54	6.30	6.12	5.97	5.85	5.66	5.47	5.27	5.17	5.07	4.97	4.86	4.75	4.61
11	12.23	8.91	7.60	6.88	6.42	6.10	5.86	5.68	5.54	5.42	5.24	5.05	4.86	4.75	4.65	4.55	4.44	4.34	4.23
12	11.75	8.51	7.23	6.52	6.07	5.76	5.52	5.35	5.20	5.09	4.91	4.72	4.53	4.43	4.33	4.23	4.12	4.01	3.90
13	11.37	8.19	6.93	6.23	5.79	5.48	5.25	5.08	4.94	4.82	4.64	4.46	4.27	4.17	4.07	3.97	3.87	3.76	3.65
14	11.06	7.92	6.68	6.00	5.56	5.26	5.03	4.86	4.72	4.60	4.43	4.25	4.06	3.96	3.86	3.76	3.66	3.55	3.41
15	10.80	7.70	6.48	5.80	5.37	5.07	4.85	4.67	4.54	4.42	4.25	4.07	3.88	3.79	3.69	3.58	3.48	3.37	3.26
16	10.58	7.51	6.30	5.64	5.21	4.91	4.69	4.52	4.38	4.27	4.10	3.92	3.73	3.64	3.54	3.44	3.33	3.22	3.11

Continued

Denominator, df_2	Numerator, df_1																		
	1	2	3	4	5	6	7	8	9	10	12	15	20	24	30	40	60	120	∞
17	10.38	7.35	6.16	5.50	5.07	4.78	4.56	4.39	4.25	4.14	3.97	3.79	3.61	3.51	3.41	3.31	3.21	3.10	2.98
18	10.22	7.21	6.03	5.37	4.96	4.66	4.44	4.28	4.14	4.03	3.86	3.68	3.50	3.40	3.30	3.20	3.10	2.99	2.87
19	10.07	7.09	5.92	5.27	4.85	4.56	4.34	4.18	4.04	3.93	3.76	3.59	3.40	3.31	3.21	3.11	3.00	2.80	2.78
20	9.94	6.99	5.82	5.17	4.76	4.47	4.26	4.09	3.96	3.85	3.68	3.50	3.32	3.22	3.12	3.02	2.92	2.81	2.69
21	9.83	6.89	5.73	5.09	4.68	4.39	4.18	4.02	3.88	3.77	3.60	3.43	3.24	3.15	3.05	2.95	2.84	2.73	2.61
22	9.73	6.81	5.65	5.02	4.61	4.32	4.11	3.94	3.81	3.70	3.54	3.36	3.18	3.08	2.98	2.88	2.77	2.66	2.55
23	9.63	6.73	5.58	4.95	4.54	4.26	4.05	3.88	3.75	3.64	3.47	3.30	3.12	3.02	2.92	2.82	2.71	2.60	2.48
24	9.55	6.66	5.52	4.89	4.49	4.20	3.99	3.83	3.69	3.59	3.42	3.25	3.06	2.97	2.87	2.77	2.66	2.55	2.43
25	9.48	6.60	5.46	4.84	4.43	4.15	3.94	3.78	3.64	3.54	3.37	3.20	3.01	2.92	2.82	2.72	2.61	2.50	2.38
26	9.41	6.54	5.41	4.79	4.38	4.10	3.89	3.73	3.60	3.49	3.33	3.15	2.97	2.87	2.77	2.67	2.56	2.45	2.33
27	9.34	6.49	5.36	4.74	4.34	4.06	3.85	3.69	3.56	3.45	3.28	3.11	2.93	2.83	2.73	2.63	2.52	2.41	2.29
28	9.28	6.44	5.32	4.70	4.30	4.02	3.81	3.65	3.52	3.41	3.25	3.07	2.89	2.79	2.69	2.59	2.48	2.37	2.25
29	9.23	6.40	5.28	4.66	4.26	3.98	3.77	3.61	3.48	3.38	3.21	3.04	2.86	2.76	2.66	2.56	2.45	2.33	2.21
30	9.18	6.35	5.24	4.62	4.23	3.95	3.74	3.58	3.45	3.34	3.18	3.01	2.82	2.73	2.63	2.52	2.42	2.30	2.18
40	8.83	6.07	4.98	4.37	3.99	3.71	3.51	3.35	3.22	3.12	2.95	2.78	2.60	2.50	2.40	2.30	2.18	2.06	1.93
60	8.49	5.79	4.73	4.14	3.76	3.49	3.29	3.13	3.01	2.90	2.74	2.57	2.39	2.29	2.19	2.08	1.96	1.83	1.69
120	8.18	5.54	4.50	3.92	3.55	3.28	3.09	2.93	2.81	2.71	2.54	2.37	2.19	2.09	1.98	1.87	1.75	1.61	1.43
∞	7.88	5.30	4.28	3.72	3.35	3.09	2.90	2.74	2.62	2.52	2.36	2.19	2.00	1.90	1.79	1.67	1.53	1.36	1.00

References

These lecture notes have been used at basics of statistics course held in Hubei University of Technology, China. These notes are heavily based on the following books.

Agresti A, Finlay B. Statistical Methods for the Social Sciences [M]. 3th Edition. Englewood [liffs, N]: Prentice Hall, 1997.

Anderson T W, Sclove S L. Introductory Statistical Analysis [M]. Houghton: Mifflin Company, 1974.

Black K. Business Statistics: For Contemporary Decision Making. 6th ed. Hoboken, [N]: Wiley, 2010.

Clarke G M, Cooke D. A Basic Course in Statistics. Arnold, 1998. Electronic Statistics Textbook. http://www.statsoftinc.com/textbook/stathome.html.

Freund J E. Modern Elementary Statistics [M]. Englewood [liffs, N]: Prentice Hall, 2001.

Johnson R A, Bhattacharyya G K. Statistics: Principles and Methods [M], 2nd Edition. Hoboken, [N]: Wiley, 1992.

Keller G. Statistics for Management and Economics. 8th ed. Mason: South-Western Cengage learning, 2009.

Leppälä, R., Ohjeita tilastollisen tutkimuksen toteuttamiseksi EXCEL for Windows-ohjelmiston avulla, Tampereen yliopisto, Matematiikan, tilastotieteen ja filosofian laitos, B53, 2000.

Levine D M. Statistics for Managers Using Microsoft Excel [M]. 6th ed. Boston: Prentice Hall/Pearson, 2011.

McDaniel C, Gates R. Marketing Research [M]. 8th ed. Hoboken, [N]: Wiley, 2010.

Moore D. McCabe G. Introduction to the Practice of Statistics [M]. 3th Edition. Freeman, 1998.

Moore D. The Basic Practice of Statistics Freeman, 1997.

Newbold P., Statistics for Business and Econometrics. Englewood [liffs, N]: Prentice Hall, 1995.

Quirk T J. Excel 2013 for Business Statistics, Excel for Statistics, Springer International Publishing, 2015.

Salkind N J. Statistics for People Who (Think They) Hate Statistics [M]. 2nd Excel 2007 ed.

U. S. Census Bureau Census 2000 PHC-T-4. Ranking Tables for Counties 1990 and 2000. Retrieved form http://www.census.gov/population/www/cen2000/briefs/phc-t4/tables/tab01.pdf

Weiers R M. Introduction to Business Statistics [M]. 7th ed. Mason: South-Western Cengage Learnihg, 2011.

Weiss N A. Introductory Statistics. Addison Wesley, 1999.

Zikmund W G, Babin B J. Exploring Marketing Research [M]. 10th ed. Mason: South-Western Cengage learning, 2010.

Zikmund W G, Babin B J. Exploring Marketing Research [M]. 10th ed. Mason: South-Western Cengage learning, 2010.